Sleep Well

peaceful nights for your child and you

DR MARC WEISSBLUTH

UNWIN PAPERBACKS
London   Sydney

First published in Great Britain by Unwin® Paperbacks, an imprint of
Unwin Hyman Limited, in 1987

UNWIN HYMAN LIMITED
Denmark House, 37–39 Queen Elizabeth Street,
London SE1 2QB
and
40 Museum Street, London WC1A 1LU

Allen & Unwin Australia Pty Ltd
8 Napier Street, North Sydney, NSW 2060, Australia

Allen & Unwin with the Port Nicholson Press
60 Cambridge Terrace, Wellington, New Zealand

British Library Cataloguing in Publication Data

Weissbluth, Marc
    Sleep well : peaceful nights for your
    child and you.
1. Sleep disorders in children
I. Title
618.92'849   RJ506.S55
ISBN 0-04-649055-8

Set in 10 on 11 point Palatino by Pentacor Limited, High Wycombe
and printed in Great Britain by
The Guernsey Press Co. Ltd., Guernsey, Channel Islands

Encouraging healthy sleep habits is the aim of all parents for their babies and children, but this area so often becomes a battle of wills reducing all concerned to a state of chronic fatigue.

Dr Marc Weissbluth, the director of a children's sleep disorder centre in America, believes that this needn't be the case and *Sleep Well* offers *practical* advice on how to change poor sleep patterns in children.

Starting with *How children sleep*, the author describes healthy sleep, sleep problems and common myths about sleeping. *What happens when children don't sleep well* covers the effect of poor sleep on the baby or child – and on the rest of the family. Finally, *How parents can help their child sleep well* will give hope to every bleary-eyed parent that something really can be done – and now.

Contents

Introduction

All children are occasionally firecrackers when things are not going their way. But why do some have much shorter fuses than others?

This book will explain how fatigue caused by poor quality sleep makes some children irritable, fussy and always cranky. It also will explain how chronic fatigue can reduce your child's ability to succeed in school. I will then teach you how you can nurture, enhance, and maintain calm and alert behaviour in your child by focusing on good sleep habits.

I will lead you on a tour through the shadows of your child's night and shine my flashlight on the most frustrating nocturnal problems that can disrupt sleep. As with any other tour, please start at the first signpost – Chapter 1. Each chapter builds upon the next; if you start in the middle, you may miss a signpost and get lost.

The first leg of our journey covers terrain that may not be familiar to even experienced parents – 'How children sleep' describes healthy sleep, disturbed sleep, sleep problems, and common myths about sleeping. The second part covers some sad territory that has not been previously explored: 'What happens when our children don't sleep well' – everyone in the family suffers from fatigue. Finally, in the third part of our journey, we learn 'How parents can help their child sleep well'.

When we finish our tour, you will be able to direct your own child towards healthy sleep habits.

What do I mean by healthy sleep?

Do you know how to get a good night's sleep and feel rested? I think I do. But sometimes I go to bed too early, sometimes too late. And I'm supposed to know a lot about sleeping! The truth is no one really knows exactly how to programme good sleep to always feel rested. In fact, we're really in the Dark Ages when it comes to understanding how sleep works. Interestingly enough, deep, dark caves were the homes for adult volunteers in early sleep studies. This was done to eliminate day/night time cues, so that researchers could study how sleep affects our body and our feelings. Of course, sleep researchers now use specially designed laboratories to look into how our biological rhythms or internal clocks work when external time cues are removed. Scientists sometimes also use trick clocks that run faster or slower than 'real' time. Studies also have been performed on shift workers and Air Force pilots who often cross time zones and suffer from jet-lag syndrome.

But children's sleep habits have not been studied previously in such detail. Obviously it's a bigger problem if a bomber crew carrying nuclear weapons is inattentive or if their vigilance is impaired from jet-lag syndrome, than if a child has fatigue-driven temper tantrums. If it's your child, however, you might disagree!

I have studied both healthy and disturbed sleep in thousands of children as Director of the Sleep Disorders Center at the Children's Memorial Hospital in Chicago. Based on this research, my general paediatric practice spanning more than thirteen years, and life with my own four sons, I have discovered that there is hope for bleary-eyed parents! The following chapters will explain everything sleep researchers currently know about what constitutes healthy sleep. I will examine in detail all the typical problems and help you modify your child's sleep habits, so that all of you can enjoy those wonderful peaceful nights.

Part I How Children Sleep

In this part, I will explain what is meant by healthy sleep. The four basic elements of healthy sleep are long sleep durations, naps, sleep consolidation, and appropriate sleep schedules. These four components are discussed in detail, so that you can decide whether your child has a healthy sleep habit. Also, I will discuss specific sleep problems, what is meant by disturbed sleep, and how it affects our children. Finally, I will explode common myths that have bothered and confused previous generations of parents.

1 Healthy Sleep

Are your child's sleep patterns healthy? There are four elements of healthy sleep for children:

1. Sleep duration
2. Naps
3. Sleep consolidation
4. Sleep schedule

When these four items are in proper balance, then children get the rest they need.

1. SLEEP DURATION

If you don't sleep long enough, you feel tired. This sounds very simple and obvious, but how much sleep really is 'enough'?

During their first few days, newborns sleep about 16 to 17 hours total, although their longest single sleep period is only 4 to 5 hours. It makes no difference whether your baby is breastfed or bottle fed or whether it's a boy or a girl.

Practical Point
New mothers often misinterpret these first several days of sweet infant slumber as weakness, and worry unnecessarily that long sleep periods deprive their baby of adequate breast milk. Weight checks with your doctor will reassure you that all is well.

Between 1 week and 4 months, the total daily sleep duration drifts down from 16.5 to 15 hours, while the longest single sleep period – usually the night – increases from 4 to 9 hours. We know from several studies that this development reflects neurological maturation and is *not* related to the start of feeding solid foods.

Some newborns and infants under the age of 4 months sleep much longer and others much shorter. During the first few months, trust nature that your baby is getting sufficient sleep. But if your baby cries too much or has colic, you might assist Mother Nature by trying the helpful hints described in Chapter 4 on crybabies.

Practical Point

When they are 1 or 2 weeks old, many infants have several-hour periods of increasingly alert, wakeful, fussy behaviour until about 6 weeks of age after which they start to calm down. This increasingly irritable and wakeful state is often misinterpreted as resulting from maternal anxiety, or insufficient or 'bad' breast milk. Nonsense! The culprit is a temporarily uninhibited nervous system which causes excessive arousal. Relax, this developmental phase will pass as the baby's brain matures. It's not your fault.

Figures 1, 2 and 3 describe how much total sleep, daytime sleep, and night sleep occur at different ages for older children. The first point, marked '0', on the horizontal scale labelled 'Age of child' is for children between 4 and 11 months of age. The bottom curve on each graph means that only 10 per cent of children sleep less than shown, while the top curve means that 90 per cent of children sleep less than shown for each age. These curves were generated by my own research using data collected from 2,019 children who were mostly white, middle-class residents of northern Illinois and northern Indiana in 1980. These graphs have never before been published in this fashion, and for the first time you can tell whether your child's sleep is above the 90th percentile or below the 10th percentile. Other studies have used only the 50th percentile – or average values – and do not tell you whether your child's brief sleep duration is slightly below average or extremely below average. Other studies of similar social classes in 1911 in California and in 1927 in Minnesota, also involving thousands of children, showed results identical to my average values for sleep duration. Studies in England in 1910 and Japan in 1925, again using thousands of

Figure 1

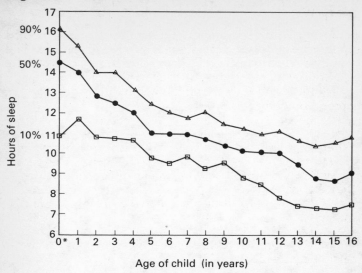

Hours of sleep

Age of child (in years)

* Note: '0' represents babies between 4 and 11 months of age.

Figure 2

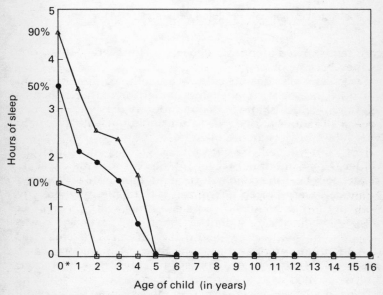

Hours of sleep

Age of child (in years)

* Note: '0' represents babies between 4 and 11 months of age.

Figure 3

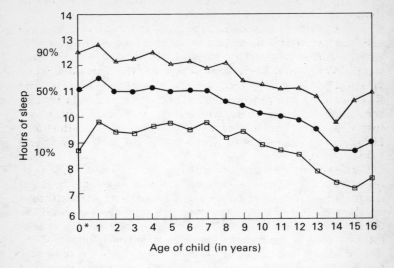

Age of child (in years)

*Note: '0' represents children between 4 and 11 months of age.

children, showed identical sleep curves for average durations as they became older.

So it seems that despite cultural and ethnic differences and given all the social changes and modern inventions such as television, which shape our contemporary lifestyles, the age-specific durations of sleep are firmly and universally rooted in our children's developing biology.

How can you tell if *your* child is getting enough sleep? Under 3 or 4 months of age, infants' sleep patterns seem mostly to reflect the child's developing brain. These younger infants are very portable. You can take them anywhere you want and when they want to sleep, they will. I remember when, as a medical student at Stanford University, I was playing tennis with my wife one day and my first child was sleeping in an infant seat near the fence. A huge lorry came crashing down this narrow street making an awful racket, and we rushed over to our son only to be surprised that he remained sweetly asleep. After about 4 months of age, he –

like all children – became interested in barking dogs, wind in the trees, clouds, and many other low intensity and curious things, all of which could and did disturb his sleep.

Under about 3 or 4 months of age, most infants, like my son, are not much disturbed by things in the environment when it comes to sleeping. When their body says sleep, they sleep. When their body says wake up, they awaken, even when it's not convenient for their parents! This is true whether they are fed on demand or according to a regular schedule. It also is true when they are continuously fed intravenously, because of birth defects of the intestines. Hunger, in fact, seems to have little to do with how young babies sleep.

Furthermore, infants brought up in constant light conditions evolve normal sleep patterns just as babies brought up in homes where lights are turned on and off routinely. Another bit of evidence to suggest that environment has little effect on sleep patterns under 3 to 4 months of age is that infants born prematurely tend to mature in their sleep development just as babies born on time. This means that biological sleep–wake development in our brain does not speed up in those premature babies who are exposed to more social stimulation.

What we can conclude, therefore, is that you should try to flow with your child's need to sleep and not try to rigidly enforce or expect predictable sleep schedules, under 3 or 4 months. However, some babies do develop regular sleep–wake rhythms quite early, say at about 6 to 8 weeks. These babies tend to be very mild, cry very little, and sleep for long periods of time. Consider yourself blessed, if you are one of these lucky parents.

After about 4 months, I think that parents can influence sleep durations, and as you will see, sleep durations for these older infants and toddlers are especially important.

I recently studied sixty healthy children in my paediatric practice at 5 months of age and then again at 36 months. At 5 months of age, the infants who were cooing, smiling, adaptable, regular, and who approached curiously towards unfamiliar things or people slept longer than infants with opposite characteristics. These easy and calm infants slept about 3.5 hours during the day and 12.0 hours at night or 15.5

hours total. Infants who were fussy, crying, irritable, hard to handle, irregular, and more withdrawn slept almost three hours less overall, almost a 20 per cent difference (3.0 hours during the day and 9.5 hours at night or 12.5 hours total).

In addition, for all the 5-month-olds studied, persistence or attention span was the trait most highly associated with day-time sleep or nap duration. *In other words, children who slept longer during the day had longer attention spans.*

As I will discuss in a later chapter, infants who sleep more during the day are more able to learn from their environment, because they have a better developed ability to maintain focused or sustained attention. Like a sponge in water, they soak up information about their surroundings. They learn simply from looking at the clouds and trees, touching, feeling, smelling, hearing, and watching their mother's and father's faces. Infants who sleep less in the daytime appear more fitful and socially demanding, and they are less able to entertain or amuse themselves. Toys and objects are less interesting to these more tired children.

By 3 years of age, the easier-to-manage children in my study who were mild, positive in mood, adaptable, and approaching towards unfamiliar people slept 12.5 hours total as shown in Table A. The difficult-to-manage children who were intense, more negative, slow to adapt and withdrawing slept about 1.5 hours less – almost the equivalent of a daytime nap.

An important conclusion is that the 3-year-olds who nap are more adaptable than those who do not. But, napping did not affect the length of sleep at night. Comparing nappers and non-nappers, night sleep duration was 10.5 hours in

Table A Sleep durations of 3-year-old children

	Sleep durations (hours)		
	Day	*Night*	*Total*
Easy to manage	1.9	10.6	12.5
Difficult to manage	0.9	10.4	11.2
Children who do not nap	–	10.5	10.5
Children who nap	2.0	10.5	12.5

both groups. Those who napped, however, slept about 2.0 hours during the day, so their total sleep was 12.5 hours. Therefore, it simply is not true that children who miss naps will tend to 'make up' for it by sleeping more at night. In fact, the sleep they miss is gone forever.

Warning
Missing a nap here and there probably will cause no harm. But if this becomes a routine, you can expect your child to sink further and further behind in his sleep – and become increasingly difficult to handle in this overfatigued state.

All in all, at age 3, the children who slept more were more fun to have around, more engageable, and more sociable, easier to handle children. The children who slept less not only tended to be more socially demanding, bratty, and fussy, but they also behaved somewhat like hyperactive children. Later, I will explain how these fatigued, fussy children are also more likely to become overweight (see pp. 91–2).

Looking at our original sleep curves again, we see that throughout early and middle childhood, the duration of sleep declines until adolescence when the curve shown in Figure 1 (p.5) levels off and then slightly increases. This increase has been noted in other studies and suggests that teenagers actually need more sleep than pre-teens. Yet, academic demands, social events, and school sports combine during adolescence to pressure teenagers to stay up later and later. This is the time when chronic and cumulative sleep losses begin to take their toll, and can make a normally rough period in life unbearably rocky.

Conclusion

It is my belief that infant behaviour and sleep duration are mostly influenced by biological factors under about 3 or 4 months of age. But after that, parenting practices can influence sleep duration and, consequently, behaviour. In fact, as I will discuss later in more detail, I think that parents can promote more charming, calm, alert behaviours, by becoming sensitive to their growing child's need to sleep and by maintaining healthy sleep habits for them.

2 NAPS

Having grown up in a highly achievement-orientated society, most Western adults tend to think of naps as a waste of time. We tend to view other adults who nap as either lazy, undermotivated, ill, or elderly. In turn, we do not attach much positive benefit to daytime sleep in our infants and young children.

Let me explain why naps are indeed very important for learning or cognitive development in our children.

Naps are not little bits of night sleep randomly intruding upon our children's awake hours. Actually, night sleep, daytime sleep, and daytime wakefulness have rhythms that are partially independent of each other. During the first 3 to 4 months of life, these rhythms develop at different rates, so they may be out of synchrony with each other. Only later do these sleep–wake rhythms become linked with fluctuations in temperature and activity levels.

For example, most of us have experienced drowsiness in the early or mid-afternoon. This sensation is partially related to how long you have been up and how long you slept the night before. It's also partially independent of those times. That's because our mental state also fluctuates during the day between 'alert' and 'drowsy', just as fluctuations occur during the night between 'light' and 'deep' sleep stages.

Understanding that these rhythms of night sleep, daytime sleep, and daytime wakefulness are somewhat independent leads to two important ideas.

First, under 3 to 4 months of age, when these rhythms are out of synchrony with each other, the baby may be getting opposing messages from different parts of the brain. The sleep rhythm says 'deep sleep', but the wake rhythm says 'alert' instead of 'drowsy'. Wakeful but tired, the confused child cries fitfully – we might call this behviour colic.

Second, if these rhythms are somewhat independent, they might have different functions. I think that mothers are right when they say there must be a separate nap god. I believe that healthy naps lead to optimal daytime alertness for learning. That is, naps adjust the 'alert-drowsy' control to just the right setting for optimal daytime arousal. Without naps, the child is too drowsy to learn well. Also, when chronically sleep-deprived, the fatigued child becomes fitfully fussy or hyperalert in order to fight sleep and, therefore, cannot learn from his environment.

My recent studies show that most children take two or three naps at 4 months of age. By 6 months, the vast majority of children (90 per cent) are taking only two naps and by 9 months virtually all children are taking one or two naps. About 15 per cent of babies have dropped to a single nap by their first birthday and this increases to 50 per cent by 15 months.

The time in the day that the nap is taken is also significant. Some studies have suggested that the first nap, occurring in the mid-morning hours, is different in quality from the second nap that occurs early in the afternoon. There is more active or rapid eye movement (REM) sleep than quiet sleep in the first nap; this pattern is reversed in the second nap. So naps occurring at different times are different! Even for adults, when you nap earlier in the day the sleep is lighter and less restorative than an afternoon nap which is comprised of more deep sleep. *Long naps occurring at the right times make the child feel rested.* Brief naps or naps occurring out of synchrony with other biological rhythms are less restful, less restorative.

Children can be taught how to take naps! A nap does not begin and end like an electric light turned on and off, even though some parents say their child goes down as if somebody had pulled out her plug. In fact, a nap or night sleep involves three periods of time: the time required for the process called 'falling asleep'; the sleep period itself; and the time required to 'wake up'. I will help you teach your children how to 'fall asleep' in later chapters.

Practical Point and Warning

Do not expect your baby to nap well outside his cot after 4 months of age. You can protect your baby's nap schedules or you can produce nap deprivation. It's your choice.

When children do not nap well, they pay a price. Infants at 4 to 8 months who do not nap well have shorter attention spans or appear less persistent when engaged in activities. By 3 years of age, children who do not nap or who nap very little are described as non-adaptable or even hyperactive. Adaptability is thought to be a very important trait for school success.

One mother of a non-adaptable child said that every morning she prayed to the nap god to give her a break. In contrast, another mother described her son as a very easy child as long as she had a bed around. Sometimes, it appears that the older toddler needs exactly '1½' naps: one nap is insufficient, but two are impossible to achieve. These children are rough around the edges in the late afternoon or early evening, but parents can temporarily and partially compensate by putting the child to bed earlier on some nights.

No naps means lost sleep. It cannot be completely compensated for by sleeping later the next morning. Spending hours holding your child in your arms or in a rocking chair while he is in a light, twilight sleep also is lost sleep. It's also a waste of your time. Brief sleep during the day, catnaps, 'motion' sleep in cars, swing-sleep, light sleep in the pushchair, and naps at the wrong time are poor quality sleep.

Here is an example of how one family learned to appreciate napping:

How Charlie's parents became nap enthusiasts

'I am aware that the practice of toting your baby along with you on every occasion is the new social trend. No doubt it stems from the "Me" generation's philosophy that a baby should not be allowed to interfere with your lifestyle. So parents everywhere are seen with their infants: in grocery shops, restaurants, the homes of friends . . . and for the unflappable, at cocktail parties, dinners out, even cross-country trips. Whereas some of these examples may appear to be extreme, be advised, new mothers, that the pressure is on to be a "nouvelle" mum.

'As with anything vogue, you have to have the appropriate raw material to make it work. (You can buy the latest in string bikinis, but if you don't have the body, forget it!) And the fact is, my husband, Tom, and I simply do not have the baby to make this new "porta-kid" trend work for us. Oh, we tried. But it was, and continues to be, completely futile. So we gave it up when Charlie was 3 months old.

'Charlie is now 7 months into his life. From the beginning, there has been only one of life's necessities that he required as much as milk, as much as oxygen – and that is sleep. We, in fact, used to shake him when we first brought him home, to make certain that he was alive. The baby slept . . . serious sleep.

'In the beginning he would sleep anywhere. After his second month, he would only sleep in his crib. And that's another subject . . . I maintain that the person(s) who decreed that a child's bed should be "stimulating" and full of coloured linens, mobiles, etc., did not have a child of his/her own! After Charlie's second month, he would spend hours on end trying to pick the red, white, and blue flowers off the sheets. This is no lie. And he would scream unmercifully for us to remove this distraction that was preventing him from needed slumber!

'Since his second month, Charlie has slept through the night and half of the day. If we disallowed him this necessity, he became a different baby. "Crabby" did not do justice to his fatigued condition. Without this sleep, our peaceful, alert, sweet, and cuddly baby turned into a raging beast. We did this to him, when we denied him sleep . . . not according to our expectations, but according to his own internal requirements.

'Charlie gives us his cues, simply and clearly. He doesn't cry at first. He mumbles, then grumbles, and finally, if his unaware parents or sitters persist, then he wails.

'At first we couldn't believe he was tired so often. We changed his nappies a thousand times and force-fed bottles. We took him on endless trips in the buggy, and walked him incessantly in the Snugli, trying to calm our "miserable" baby with the rhythm of our heartbeats. Nothing worked. Nothing, that is, until we finally, out of sheer nervous exhaustion, lay him in his bed to sleep.

'Charlie still naps four to five times during the course of a day. He's also a very happy child. When Tom and I go anywhere, we go alone, leaving our contented, sleeping son in the hands of a competent babysitter. Our friends, especially our childless friends, think we're overprotective. Well, thank god Charlie is not their baby. We are no longer concerned about our parental image; uneducated criticism doesn't count. If we cannot find a babysitter, we don't go. We simply would have a better time watching television; anything, even doing the washing, beats the hell out of making your baby and yourselves crazy. And our family is now harmonious, having discovered the secret of sleep.'

Practical Point

When you maintain a healthy nap schedule and your child sleeps well during the day, jealous friends will accuse you of being overprotective. They'll say, 'It's not real life,' 'Bring her along so she'll learn to play with other children,' or 'You're really spoiling her.'

Suggestion: Change friends or keep your baby's long naps a family secret.

SLEEP CONSOLIDATION

Consolidated sleep means uninterrupted sleep, sleep that is continuous and not disrupted by awakenings. When awakenings or complete arousals break our slumber, we call it disrupted sleep or sleep fragmentation. Abnormal shifts of sleep rhythms towards lighter sleep, even if we do not awaken completely, also cause sleep fragmentation. Ten hours of consolidated sleep are not the same as ten hours of fragmented sleep. Doctors, firemen, and mothers of newborns or sick children, who have their sleep interrupted frequently, know this very well.

The effects of sleep fragmentation are similar to the effects of reduced total sleep: daytime sleepiness increases and performance measurably decreases. Adults with fragmented sleep often fight the ill-effects of fragmented sleep with extra caffeine. Alcohol unmasks or uncovers their hidden fatigue and makes them 'feel tired'. Well-rested pre-teens given the same amount of alcohol do not 'feel tired'.

Major Point
Let sleeping babies lie! Never awaken a sleeping baby.
Destroying sleep continuity is unhealthy.

Protective arousals

Sometimes our brain causes us to awaken to protect us from asphyxiating in our sleep. These awakenings, or protective arousals, occur when we have difficulty breathing during sleep, which can be caused by large tonsils or adenoids obstructing our airway. I will discuss this problem in detail in a later chapter.

Another example where arousals may provide protection is to prevent cot death or Sudden Infant Death Syndrome, which kills young infants. This tragedy is thought to be caused by a failure to maintain breathing during sleep or a failure to awaken when breathing quality starts to become dangerous.

Sleep fragmentation

After several months of age – beyond the age of cot death – frequent arousals are usually harmful, because they destroy sleep continuity. Arousals can be either a complete awakening from light sleep, deep sleep, or Rapid Eye Movement (REM) sleep. Arousals can also be thought of as a quick shift from deep sleep to light sleep without complete awakening.

Figure 4 is a simplified illustration of the cycling from deep sleep to light sleep that normally occurs after about 4 months of age. During partial arousals, we stay in a light sleep state

Figure 4 Arousals during sleep

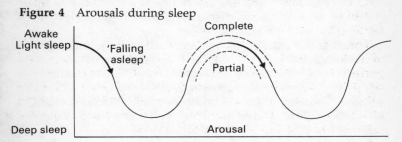

and do not awaken. But during complete arousals, or awakenings, we might become aware that we are looking at the clock, rolling over, changing arm positions, or scratching an arm. This awareness is dim and brief, and we return to sleep promptly.

So we see that arousals come in several forms, and depending on which types occur, how many times they happen, and how long they last, we pay a price: increased daytime sleepiness and decreased performance. But some arousals always occur naturally during healthy sleep.

Major Point
Some arousals from sleep are normal.

It's not just night sleep that can be fragmented. I think that even naps also might be fragmented when parents rely on swing-sleep and motion sleep, or when they allow cat-naps in the car or pushchair. Holding your dozing child in your arms in a rocking chair during the day also probably prevents good quality day sleep. These naps are too brief or too light to be restorative.

Helpful Hint
Naps much less than an hour cannot count as real naps.

By 4 to 8 months of age, infants should have a mid-morning and an early afternoon·nap, and the total nap duration should be 2 to 4 hours. Night sleep is 10 to 12 hours, with only one or no interruptions for feeding. When children do not get healthy, consolidated sleep, we call the problem 'night waking'. As I will discuss later, the night waking itself is usually due to normally occurring arousals. The real problem is the child's inability to or difficulty in returning to sleep *unassisted*.

Reminder
Some arousals from sleep are normal. Problems occur when children have difficulty returning to sleep by themselves.

4 SLEEP SCHEDULE

Figures 5 and 6 show the times when most children awaken or go to sleep. These graphs are based on my same study of 2,019 children mentioned previously. Remember, the '0' point on the graph represents 4 to 11 months of age. Under 4 months of age, no regular clock pattern exists because biological sleep/wake rhythms during these early months are not well established. But after 4 months, for example, 90 per cent of pre-school children, under age 6 years, fall asleep before 9 pm and 10 per cent of children between 2 and 6 years fall asleep before 7 pm.

When sleep/wake schedules are out of synchrony with other biological rhythms, attentiveness, vigilance, and task performance often are measurably decreased and moods are altered. Jet-lag syndrome is one example of this, while another is the poor sleep quality some shift workers suffer due to their abnormal sleep schedules.

Night sleep organization

Before 6 weeks of age, the longest single sleep period – unfortunately for parents – is randomly distributed around the clock. In some babies, this longest sleep may actually be only 2 to 3 hours! But by 6 weeks of age, the longest single sleep period will predictably occur in the evening hours and last 3 to 5 hours.

A Practical Point
During these early weeks, you may find breastfeeding too demanding or too frequent, and think that you might want to quit so that you can get some rest. But on the other hand, you also may want to continue nursing for your baby's health. Stay with it, and wait until your baby is past 6 weeks of age. Then you, too, will get more night sleep.

After 6 weeks of age, babies sleep longer at night. So do mums! Also, babies start smiling at their parents, and they

Figure 5

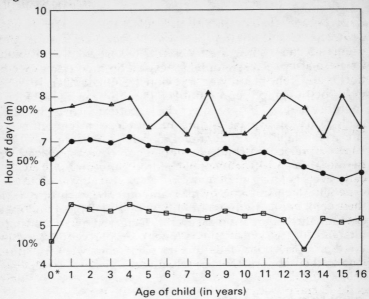

*Note: '0' represents children between 4 and 11 months of age.

Figure 6

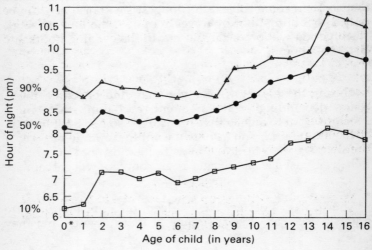

*Note: '0' represents children between 4 and 11 months of age.

then become less fussy or irritable. Life in the family definitely changes after 6 weeks. One exception is the premature baby whose parents might have to wait until about 6 weeks after the expected date of delivery. Another exception is the colicky baby whose parents might have to wait until their baby is 3 or 4 months old.

Daytime sleep organization

At about 3 to 4 months of age, daytime sleep is organized into two long naps (sometimes with a third, shorter one in the early evening) instead of many brief, irregular ones. Mothers, especially breastfeeding mothers, should learn to nap when their baby naps. You never know what the night will bring, and you might be up a lot then holding, walking or nursing.

Abnormal sleep schedules usually evolve in infants and young children when parents keep them up too late at night. Parents do this because they: (a) enjoy playing with their baby; (b) cannot put their child to sleep, but wait for their child to crash from total exhaustion; or (c) both.

The time when your own child *needs* to go to sleep at night depends on his age, how long his previous nap lasted, and how long his wakeful period was just before the bedtime hour. The time when he *wants* to go to sleep may be altogether different! Obviously, the bedtime hour is not fixed or unchanging. If your child is unusually active in the afternoon or she misses a good afternoon nap, then she should be put to sleep earlier. This is true even if a parent returning home late from work that night does not see her. Keeping a tired child up to play with a tired parent coming home late from work does no one any good!

Allowing brief naps in the early evening or long late afternoon naps in order to keep a child up late at night will ruin healthy sleep schedules.

Helpful Hint
To establish healthy sleep schedules at 4 to 8 months of age, become your infant's timekeeper. Set his clock on healthy time.

Biological rhythms

To better understand the importance of maintaining sleep schedules, let's look at how three distinctive biological rhythms develop. Immediately after birth, babies are wakeful, then fall asleep, awaken, and then fall asleep a second time over a 10-hour period. These periods of wakefulness are predictable and are not due to hunger, although what causes them is unknown. Thus, a partial sleep–wake pattern emerges immediately after birth.

After one month of life, body temperature rhythms appear, and thereafter also influence sleep–wake cycles. Body temperature typically rises during the daytime and drops to lower levels at night. A third pattern is added by 6 months of age when an important hormone, called cortisol, also shows a similar characteristic rhythm, with peak concentrations in the early morning and lowest levels around midnight. This hormone is also related to both mood and performance, and will be discussed later in the chapter on disturbed sleep. Interestingly, a part of the cortisol secretion rhythm is related to the sleep–wake rhythm and another part is coupled to the body temperature rhythm. (I wish Mother Nature were more simple!)

So even at only a few months of age, interrelated, internal rhythms already are well developed: sleep–wake pattern, body temperature, and the cortisol hormone level. In adults, it appears that a long night's sleep is most highly dependent on going to sleep at or just after the peak of the temperature cycle. Bedtimes occurring near the lower portion of the temperature cycle result in shorter sleep durations.

Shift work or jet travel in adults, or parental mismanagement in children might cause disorganized sleep.

What does disorganized sleep mean?

1. Internal desynchronization.

2. Uncoupling of rhythms normally closely linked.

3. Shifting rhythms out of phase

Possible consequences of abnormal sleep schedules include fatigue, stress, and elevated cortisol levels. This sets in motion other disturbances of sleep.

Reminder Again
Never wake a sleeping baby.

I often tell parents to become sensitive to the child's personal sleep signals. This means that you should capture that magic moment when the child is tired, ready to sleep, and easily falls asleep. The magic moment is a slight quieting, a lull in being busy, a slight staring off, a hint of calmness develops. If you miss this magic moment of tiredness and the child becomes overtired, it is much harder for the child to fall asleep, because he is trying to fall asleep out of phase with other biological rhythms. Careful timing is essential.

25-hour cycles

Although harmonious biological rhythms promote healthy sleep, random bad days are bound to occur. One explanation of 'off' days, when the child's sleep is irregular for no apparent reason, is that our basic biological clocks have about 25 hours in their cycles, not 24! In other words, without time cues, our free-running sleep–wake rhythms appear to cycle on a 25-hour schedule. As long as we train our children to match sleep–wake rhythms to night and day shifts, problems usually are avoided. Other babies appear to get off schedule every few weeks, and parents then must work to keep them well rested. I suspect that babies, like adults, differ in their individual abilities to adjust their 25-hour biological rhythms to society's 24-hour clocks. Most parents, however, find that the effort to reset baby's clock is worth it, because otherwise the child becomes increasingly tired, fatigued, and crabby.

When parents put forth the effort to help the child get needed sleep, the better rested the child becomes, the easier it becomes for the child to accept sleep, expect to sleep, take long naps, and go to sleep by herself. Some parents have to always endure days of disruption following trips, illnesses, or immunizations because irregularity of schedules due to travelling or pain upsets sleep rhythms.

Here is one family's account:

'Susan's sleep problem is one we'll have to live with'

'Last summer, Susan's night waking had become so frequent that she was basically awake more than she was asleep. We had been instructed at the parenting class we attend, given by a paediatrician, to "meet our child's needs". So, we were getting up as frequently as she asked and rocking her back to sleep. This happened three and four times a night and often took between 30 to 60 minutes to do so. A part of me wanted to do this. Women are trained to serve from very young and, even though I see myself as being liberated, serving came naturally. Needless to say, however, after months of this night-time routine, my husband and I became quite exhausted and began to resent our child. I knew I was in trouble when I would get up and go into the baby's room and yell at her, and then begin crying myself because of the conflict of meeting her needs and meeting my own sleep needs. The point I'm trying to make is simply that when a problem like a child's sleep habits gets so out of hand, the parents are partially responsible too. Finally, on our own, we decided to let her cry it out. By the way, my husband had a much easier time psychologically with letting her cry. He knew it was in her best interest and was able to remain unemotional about it. It took about a week and she cried for about two hours for quite a few of those nights. Finally, it seemed that she had got the idea.

'Unfortunately, the next week we were scheduled to go away for our summer holiday. We didn't want to cancel our trip, but we knew we were taking a chance on destroying the results of our hard work. We stayed at an inn, and there were no cots, so we made a sleeping area for her in the corner of the room. She'd wake up in the middle of the night and think it was playtime.

'When we got back from the trip we tried to get back into the routine of letting her cry it out, but by that time we didn't have the energy to go through a week of crying baby again only two weeks after we had just done it. So, we fell back into a poor night-time routine again. By the way, Susan was only 11 months at this time. Another month went by and we knew we could not go on. We discussed it with the teacher at our parenting class, and she finally recommended the process of letting her cry it out again.

'This time it took about five days and she was back to sleeping through the night. This lasted about a month.

'She received a vaccination shortly after that. I went into her room for only a moment to check up on her one night and then she began waking each night and we were into our old routine. We repeated the process yet one more time. I think it took about five nights to get her to sleep through the night. After that, Susan slept through the night regularly for months. She eventually asked to be put down before she was asleep at night rather than being rocked to sleep. She began taking very long naps this spring which seemed slightly strange.

'This summer we went on holiday for a week and Susan slept in a cot in our room. She'd wake and again think it was play time. It didn't take long for her to get back into her old bad habits. We had hoped we were beyond that, since she had been sleeping through the night for so many months, but since our trip she's been up at night practising long dialogues and it looks like we'll have to go through this one more time. She's also feeling very needy and clingy. I'm sure it's all interrelated, having to do with separation.

'In conclusion, raising a child is not always easy. I expect Susan's sleep problem is one we'll have to live with and may come up from time to time and we'll have to keep working on it.'

Conclusion

The four elements of healthy sleep are: (1) sleep duration (daytime sleep, night sleep, total sleep); (2) naps; (3) sleep consolidation, and (4) sleep schedule. Parents can start to structure, programme or coordinate these elements in a deliberate way when a baby reaches about 4 months of age, and his internal rhythms are well developed. When children do not sleep well, we can say that they have disturbed sleep or sleep problems.

Helpful Hint
A well-rested baby with a healthy sleep habit wakes up with a cheerful, happy attitude. A tired baby wakes up grumpy.

2 Disturbed Sleep and Sleep Problems

We really do not know how our young children feel when they cannot talk to us; all we can do is observe them and guess at their feelings. When they do not sleep well, their behaviour changes and presumably they feel differently. I think we should consider carefully how we feel and behave when our sleep is disturbed, so that we can better understand and sympathize with our sleepy children.

Daytime sleepiness resulting from disturbed sleep typically causes us to feel a mild itching or burning of the eyes and heavy eyelids. Our limbs feel heavy, too, and we tend to be lethargic. We are less motivated, lose interest easily, and have difficulty concentrating. Our speech slows down, we yawn and rub our eyes. As we get sleepier, our eyes begin to close and we may even catch our head nodding. Sometimes we feel chilly.

But this familiar picture of adult sleepiness is not usually seen in infants and young children who suffer from disturbed sleep. While it is true that well-rested infants yawn when occasionally overtired, it seems that chronically tired infants do not yawn much, semi-sleep, or nod off. Instead, when most very tired, young kids get sleepy, they get grumpy and excitable. My first son at age 3 coined the perfect word to describe this turned-on state: 'upcited' from 'upset' and 'excited'. As in 'Don't make me upcited!', when we admonished him for behaving like a monster.

Remember
When your infant or young child appears particularly excited and over the top, he may well be tired.

MOOD AND PERFORMANCE

Before we look at common sleep problems, let's review how disturbed sleep affects mood and performance.

Two very interesting Australian studies on adults have helped to shed light on childhood 'upcited' behaviour. A 1971 study showed that the level of activation of the nervous system was associated with personality traits, sleep habits, and activity of the adrenal gland. Poor sleepers were more anxious and had higher levels of those hormones, such as cortisol, which typically rise during stressful situations.

A second study published in 1984 was complex, but I think its results will better help you to read your child's behaviours. Adult volunteers reported their moods on four scales:

1. Tired to rested
2. Sluggish to alert
   Sluggish: Having little motion, to feel lazy or lethargic
   Alert: A watchful promptness for action
3. Irritable to calm
   Irritable: Peevishness, impatience, fretfulness, excitability
   Calm: Undisturbed, unruffled, still
4. Tense to relaxed
   Tense: To feel under mental or nervous strain
   Relaxed: To feel relieved from strain or effort

The first two scales reflect degrees of *arousal* while the third and fourth scales reflect degrees of *stress*.

The researchers measured four different chemicals (cortisol, noradrenaline, adrenaline, and dopamine) that our bodies make naturally. These powerful chemicals affect our brain and how we feel, and are related to the four scales in different ways.

For example, fatigue produces an increase in adrenaline concentrations. That is, when we are tired, our body chemically responds with a burst of adrenaline to give us more drive or energy. We become more aroused, alert, and excitable. Cortisol concentrations also increase with increasing alertness. Increasing irritability and tenseness – the stress factors – are both associated with increasing concentrations of adrenaline, noradrenaline, and dopamine. Yet, the specific chemical patterns or biochemical fingerprints for irritability (the third scale) and tenseness (the fourth scale) are not the same.

Different chemicals, different feelings.

These studies support the notion that when our overtired child appears wild, 'on the edge', excitable, and unable to fall asleep easily or stay asleep, he is precisely this way because of his body's instinctive response to being overtired. It's a vicious cycle: sleep begets sleep but sleeplessness also begets sleeplessness. When our babies miss the sleep that they *need*, the fatigue causes a physical or chemical change in their bodies. These chemical changes directly affect their behaviour and interferes with maintaining the calm–alert wakeful state or blissful sleep. They are fractious because they are overtired. Have you ever had too much caffeine while studying and then tried to sleep or relax before a test? That's very much how your child feels when overtired.

Other studies have proved also that adults who sleep for brief durations are more anxious. When we study adults who are irritable, tense, poor sleepers and have high concentrations of these hormones, it's the old chicken–egg dilemma. Which came first?

I think an experience familiar to all of us helps solve the dilemma. If we work hard to get an important job done, we can push our bodies with lots of caffeine-laden coffee and very little sleep. At the end of the work project, though, if we suddenly stop to take a holiday, it takes a few days to 'unwind' and get rid of our accumulated 'nervous energy'. We really cannot enjoy low-intensity pleasures, like walking on the grass barefoot or playing quietly with the children, because we are 'all keyed up'. After a few days, we eventually calm down and relax, and can enjoy recreational reading and quiet activities. This tells me that our lifestyle and sleep habits can affect our internal chemical machinery, which in turn causes us to feel certain ways. In one study at Dartmouth College, coronary-prone 'Type A' students had more night wakings than 'Type B' students. A vicious reinforcing cycle could develop whereby the fragmented sleep causes increased arousal, the student feels more energized, and sensing this greater level of energy he works even harder late into the night to achieve more, but at the same time he loses more sleep.

Babies only 2 to 3 days old also have elevations of their cortisol levels during the period of behavioural distress following circumcision. Infants over 4 months of age and children can push themselves hard fighting sleep to enjoy the pleasure of their parents' company and play. The resulting sleep disturbances might produce fatigue, and the body would naturally respond by turning up those chemicals, such as cortisol, responsible for maintaining alertness and arousal. Perhaps researchers may some day find that different patterns of sleep deprivation (total sleep loss, abnormal schedules, nap deprivation, or sleep fragmentation) produce different patterns of chemical imbalances.

Here are some terms used by professionals to describe hyperalert children:

Physiological activation
Neurological arousal
Excessive wakefulness
Emotional reactivity
Heightened sensitivity

Obviously, we all get slightly irritable, short-tempered, and grumpy when we do not get the sleep we need; jokes and cartoons never seem very funny when you are tired. But children might be even more sensitive to mild sleep loss, and yet simply appear to be more wild or unmanageable. Or, antisocial behaviours in our children may be due to sleep loss that is severe, chronic, and prolonged, but not recognized as such by the parents.

How often have I heard, 'She's so tired, she's running around in circles.' A classic paper called 'Sleeplessness in Infants', published in 1922, described this 'increased reflex-irritability of a sleepy child'.

In dramatic contrast, over and over again, I have seen well-rested children in my practice who spend enormous amounts of time in a state of alert/calmness. They take in everything with wide open eyes, never missing a thing. They find simple little toys amusing or curious. They never appear bored, although the toy they pick up is a familiar toy they have played with many times previously. Parents of children 4 to 12 months of age can dramatically change their children's behaviours from alert/calm to drowsy/active depending on how much sleep they allow their children to get.

Remember, Again
A sign of sleeping well is a calm and alert state. Upon awakening, these children are in good cheer and are able to play by themselves.

Warning
A constant small deficit in sleep produces a cumulative reduction in daytime wakefulness.

In infants and young children I think a cause-and-effect relationship exists between disturbed sleep and fitful, fussy behaviours. This means that there will be a *progressive* worsening in a child's mood and performance even when the amount of lost sleep each day or night is *constant*. So the baby becomes *increasingly* crabby, even if the nightly sleep is *constantly* just a little too brief.

As the child develops, the relationship between disturbed sleep and problems of mood and performance becomes less clear, because of the increasing complexity of psychological and intellectual function. It is even possible that chronic, disturbed sleep causes children to grow up experiencing excessive daytime sleepiness, low self-esteem or mild depression. In one study, about 13 per cent of teenagers with disturbed sleep were reported to be like this. They usually took longer than 45 minutes to fall asleep or awoke frequently at night. Some of these teenagers simply may never have learned self-soothing skills to fall asleep easily when they were much younger. As adults, they are described as insomniacs.

One theory of adult insomnia is that it is characterized by an internalization of emotions associated with a heightened or constant state of emotional arousal plus physiological activation that causes disturbed sleep. But, distinct differences exist between adult insomniacs whose insomnia started in childhood compared with those whose insomnia started in adult life. The childhood-onset insomniacs took longer to fall asleep and slept less than the adult-onset insomniacs. I think this kind of data tends to support the notion that the failure to establish good sleeping habits in infancy or early childhood may have long-term harmful effects, such as adult insomnia. And, among psychologically unhealthy adults, the more severe the sleep difficulty, the more severe is the degree of mental illness.

Let's now review some of the most common sleep problems which can disrupt our children's sleep.

EARLY BLOOMERS . . . WHO FADE FAST

The easiest sleep problem to deal with is the baby about 3 months of age who had been sleeping well, but now wakes up crying at night and during the day. The parents also may note heightened activity with these wild screaming spells. These are regular, adaptable, mild infants who matured early, but, at 3 months, began to decide they would rather play with their parents than be placed in a dark, quiet, and boring room. Parents who have not had enough experience believe this new night waking represents hunger due to a 'growth spurt' or insufficient breast milk.

When these parents begin to focus on establishing a regular daytime nap schedule, when they put these babies in their cradles when they need to sleep, and when they avoid overstimulation, the frequent night waking stops. If the children had developed irritability or fussiness, this disappears, too.

Overstimulation
Think of overstimulation not as excessive intensity with which you play with your child, but rather too long a *duration* of baby's normal period of wakefulness. It's not too much of a good thing, it's just being up too long.

Remember
The more rested a child is, the more she accepts sleep and expects to sleep.

NIGHT WAKING

When children wake up frequently at night, we call this a night waking problem. The truth is that awakenings at night or complete arousals are normally occurring events as discussed in Chapter 1. Problems arise when the child has difficulty or is unable or unwilling to return to sleep unassisted. The more often these events occur, the longer each separate awakening lasts.

Infants

Brief awakenings in young infants under 4 months of age are acceptable to most parents, because these usually are thought to be caused by hunger. For the older child, especially if he had been sleeping overnight previously, night wakings are often thought of as a behavioural problem.

Older infants

Two separate groups of infants between 4 and 8 months of age seem especially prone to night waking.

The first and larger group – about 20 per cent of infants – are those infants who had colic when they were younger. These infants not only wake more often, but their total sleep time is less. Although boys and girls in this group awaken the same number of times, parents are more likely to state that it is their sons who have a night waking problem. In fact, boys are handled in a more irregular way than girls when they wake at night. This was shown in studies using videotapes in dim light in the children's own bedrooms at home. Even when the colic had been successfully treated with a drug during the first few months, by 4 months of age the children still were reported as frequently awakening at night.

My conclusion is that some biological disturbances in infants can cause an overaroused, hyperalert, irregular state, full of crying, especially in the late afternoon or early evening, and this is called colic. In the past, the crying part of colic has been thought to be the major problem. But while this evening crying diminishes at about 3 to 4 months, the wakeful, not sleeping, state may continue and thus be more serious and harmful in the long run.

This is because the parents have the correct impression that regular and consistent parenting does not much affect the colic, and unfortunately they give up the effort permanently. They do not know that after 4 months, regular and consistent attention to bedtimes and naptimes really does help the older infant sleep better. The parents' failure to develop and maintain healthy sleep patterns in these older post-colic babies then leads to prolonged fussiness driven by chronic fatigue. I will return to this issue of parental control in a later chapter on parental management.

The second group of frequent night wakers in the 4- to 8-month-old age group are the 10 per cent of infants who snore or breathe through their mouths when asleep. Difficulty breathing during sleep might be due to allergies, and allergies will be discussed more in a later chapter. These infants wake as frequently as those with post-colic night waking, but their parents do not label this night waking as a problem. Probably they had not worried about problems in these children when they were younger, because they had not suffered from colic. Those infants who snored also had shorter sleep durations compared to other infants. As in many sleep disturbances, when one element of healthy sleep is disrupted, other elements are disturbed. I will discuss why snoring is more than an acoustical annoyance in a later chapter.

A third frequent cause of night waking in this age group is sometimes associated with abnormal sleep schedules. Going to bed too late and getting up too late seem to set the stage for frequent night waking. One child I cared for took 2 to 2½ hours of soothing, rocking, or holding before she would go to sleep, and then would usually waken three to four times each night and sometimes as often as ten times. This prolonged period to put her to sleep is called increased latency to sleep. It can also be called a waste of parents' time, because the off/ on twilight sleep for the child during the rocking, walking, and hugging represents lost, good quality sleep.

Remember

Fatigue causes increased physiological or biological arousal. Therefore, the more tired your child is, the harder it is for him to fall asleep, stay asleep, or both.

One consequence of increased arousal, which is discussed in more detail later, is that disturbed sleep produces more wakeful, irritable and *active* behaviours in children. Also, they often have *increased physical activity* when asleep. Although all babies may have gross movements involving limbs and the entire body, localized movements or twitches involving only one limb, these are brief motions lasting only a second or less. But chronically fatigued babies who are overly aroused move around more in a restless, squirmy, crawly fashion when sleeping. It seems that their motor is always running at a higher speed, awake and asleep. Later, I will explain how you can reduce your child's idle speed by making sure that they get the sleep they need.

What Is Disturbed Sleep?

Any combination of one or more of the following:

Abnormal sleep schedules (going to bed too late/sleeping too late in the morning, napping at wrong times);
Brief sleep durations (not enough sleep overall);
Sleep fragmentation (waking up too often);
Nap deprivation (no naps or brief naps);
Prolonged latency to sleep (taking a long time to fall asleep);
Active sleep (lots of tossing and turning).

Night Waking Is Not Caused By:

Too much sugar in the diet
Hypoglycaemia at night
Zinc deficiencies
Teething
Pinworms

Night Waking May Often Be Caused By:

Fever
Painful ear infections

Older children

In one study of children between 1 and 2 years old, about 20 per cent woke up five or more times a week, while in another study of 3-year-old children, 26 per cent woke up at least three times a week. Unfortunately, you cannot assume that difficulties in returning to sleep unassisted will magically go away. Returning to sleep unassisted is a learned skill. You should expect problems to persist in your child until she learns how to soothe herself back to sleep without your help.

Also, in the study of 1- and 2-year-old children, those who woke up frequently were much more likely to have an injury, such as a broken bone or a cut, requiring medical attention than those who slept through – while only 17 per cent of good sleepers had injuries, 40 per cent of the night wakers were injured!

The majority of children between ages 1 and 5 have a bedtime routine less than 30 minutes long, go to sleep with the lights off, and fall asleep about 30 minutes or less after lights out. Night waking occurs in the older children in this group once per week; only a few awaken once per night. If your child's pattern is substantially different, consider the possibility that your child is among the 20 per cent of children in this age range with disturbed sleep. If so, then you might notice the excessive daytime sleepiness that has been observed in about 5 to 10 per cent of children between ages 5 and 14 years.

EXCESSIVE DAYTIME SLEEPINESS

Superficially, we tend to think of being either awake or asleep. But just as there are gradations between light sleep and deep sleep, there are gradations of wakefulness. Task performance, attentiveness, vigilance, and mood may be influenced by the degree of daytime wakefulness. When we do not feel very awake during the day, we say that we feel 'sleepy'. Excessive daytime sleepiness or impaired daytime alertness is a result of disturbed sleep.

The Stanford Sleepiness Scale is a self-rating instrument developed at Stanford University in the United States to describe the different stages or levels of daytime sleepiness. Obviously older children who are down in the dumps due to sleep deprivation will have high numerical ratings.

Level 1 Feeling active and vital; alert; wide awake.

Level 2 Functioning at a high level, but not at peak; able to
         concentrate.
Level 3 Relaxed; awake; not at full alertness, responsive.
Level 4 A little foggy; not at peak; let down.
Level 5 Fogginess; beginning to lose interest in remaining
         awake; slowed down
Level 6 Sleepiness; preferring to be lying down; fighting
         sleep; woozy.
Level 7 Almost in reverie; sleep onset soon; lost struggle to
         remain awake.

Young children and infants, of course, cannot tell us how
they feel, but watch their behaviours. Does your child behave
as though he is active, alert, vital, wide awake or fighting
sleep, woozy?

Remember
Fatigue is the main enemy.

SLEEP WALKING

Between 6 and 16 years old, sleep walking occurs about 3 to
12 times per year among 5 per cent of children. An additional
5 to 10 per cent of children walk in their sleep once or twice a
year. When it starts under age 10 and ends by age 15, sleep
walking is not associated with any emotional stress, negative
personality types or behavioural problems.

Sleep walking episodes usually occur within the first 2 to 3
hours after falling asleep. The sleep walk itself may last up to
30 minutes. Usually, the sleep walker appears to be little
concerned about his environment. His gait is not fluid and his
movement not purposeful. In addition to walking, other
behaviours such as eating, dressing, or opening doors often
occur.

Treatment consists only of safety measures to prevent sleep
walkers from falling down stairs or out of open windows. Try
to remove toys or furniture from your child's path, but don't
expect to be able to waken him. Trying to waken him won't
hurt, but usually the child spontaneously wakens without
any memory of the walk.

SLEEP TALKING

Sleep talkers do not make good conversationalists! They seem to talk to themselves and respond to questions with single syllable answers. Adults appear annoyed or preoccupied. Infants often repeat simple phrases like 'get down' or 'no more' as if they were remembering important stressful events which had occurred that day.

Between ages 3 to 10 years, about half of all children will talk in their sleep once a year. Older studies had suggested that sleep walking and sleep talking tended to occur together and were more common in boys; however, newer studies do not support this association.

NIGHT TERRORS

Your child has a piercing scream or cry and you rush to see him; he appears wild-eyed, anxious, frightened. The pupils are dilated, sweat is covering his forehead, and as you pick him up to hug him you notice his heart is pounding and his chest heaving. He is inconsolable. Your heart is full of dread, and you fear this evil spirit which has gripped your child. After 5 to 15 minutes, the agitation/confused state finally subsides. This is a night terror.

Night terrors, sleep walking and sleep talking occur *during* sleep. They do not occur when we dream; they are not 'bad' dreams. In fact, children have no recall or memory of them.

Night terrors usually start between 4 and 12 years of age. When they start before puberty, they are not associated with any emotional or personality problems. Night terrors appear more often with fever or when sleep patterns are disrupted naturally, such as on long trips, during school holidays, or when relatives come to visit. Recurrent night terrors also often are associated with chronically abnormal sleep schedules. Overtired children who have frequent night terrors are best treated by enabling them to get more sleep.

Drug therapy is not warranted for most children with night terrors, sleep walking, or sleep talking. Most children should be allowed to outgrow these problems without complex tests, such as CAT scans, drug treatments, or psychotherapy.

NIGHTMARES

In old English mythology, a nightmare was 'a female spirit or monster supposed to beset people and animals by night, settling upon them when they are asleep and producing a feeling of suffocation by its weight'.

I have nightmares of suffocation, strangulation, breathlessness, choking, being crushed or trapped, drowning, entrapment, asphyxiation, and of being buried alive only when I sleep on my back. And only when my wife wakes me. She says I sound like a diesel truck with a bad motor that can't get started. She pokes me to get me up, the nightmare ends and I breathe normally again. You see, my nightmares occur when my upper airway is partially blocked. This obstruction only occurs when I sleep on my back or drink alcohol before bedtime. Occasionally, my dreams are not so dramatic, but consist only of breathlessness such as running, flying (by myself, without a plane, of course) or being chased. If my wife does not waken me, I wake up to breathe, but I have no dream recall. Maybe some children have similar nightmares when they have bad colds or throat infections which partially obstruct their upper airway.

The child with a nightmare can be woken and consoled in contrast to a night terror, which spontaneously subsides. About 30 per cent of secondary school students have one nightmare a month. Adults who have more frequent nightmares (more than two per week) often have other sleep problems: frequent night wakenings, increased time required to fall asleep, and decreased sleep duration. They appear more anxious and distrustful, and experience fatigue in the morning.

But nightmares in most young children do not seem to be associated with any specific emotional or personality problems. Analysis, really guesswork, of dream content in disturbed children who have been referred to psychologists or psychiatrists should not be generalized to normal populations of children with the assumption that normal anxieties or fears represent a mental or emotional problem. We really do not know the exact value or limitations of dream interpretation. If you think your child is having a nightmare, shower him with hugs and kisses and try to waken him.

HEAD BANGING AND BODY ROCKING

My third son banged his head against the cot every night when we moved into a new house. Actually, he struck his shoulder blades more than his head against the headboard of his cot. My solution was to use clothes-line rope and sofa cushions to pad both ends and both sides completely. Now, when he banged away, there was no racket, no pain, and no parental attention. After a few days, he stopped. Thank goodness, because my wife's back was killing her as we could not lower the side railing! Other parents are not so lucky.

About 5 to 10 per cent of children will bang or roll their heads before falling asleep during their first few years. This usually starts at about 8 months of age. No behavioural or emotional problems are seen in these children as they develop, and they certainly have no neurological problems. Body rocking before falling asleep also occurs in normal children.

All this rhythmic behaviour usually stops before the fourth year, if there are no underlying neurological diseases. Your paediatrician can diagnose these uncommon neurologic conditions, if they are present.

BRUXISM

Teeth grinding during sleep occurs commonly in children. At the Laboratory School at the University of Chicago, about 15 per cent of the students were reported by their parents as having a history of bruxism. In the age range of 3 to 7 years, the percentage of bruxists was about 11 per cent, between 8 to 12 years it was 6 per cent and between 13 to 17 years the percentage dropped to about 2 per cent.

The teeth grinding does not occur during dreams or nightmares. Furthermore, no association has been made between emotional or personality disturbances and teeth grinding.

NARCOLEPSY

The major characteristic of narcolepsy is excessive or abnormal sleepiness. It appears as if the child has a sudden sleep attack while engaged in ordinary activities, such as reading or watching television. In mild form, the child may drift into a state of excessive drowsiness and in more severe form, the child might fall stone asleep in the middle of a conversation.

Narcolepsy is less common under the age of 10. When it begins in older children, it may be mistaken for 'lack of concentration' or inattentiveness.

Other features of narcolepsy seen in older children are: (a) cataplexy, which is muscular weakness triggered by emotional stress; (b) sleep paralysis, which is the passing sensation of being unable to move while drifting off to sleep; and (c) hypnagogic hallucinations, which are visual or auditory experiences occurring as sleep begins.

FAMILY BED

About a third of white urban families frequently sleep together in a family bed for all or part of the night. By itself, this is neither good nor bad. Studies from the United States suggest that the family bed might encourage or lead to a variety of emotional stresses within the child; opposite results were found in studies in Sweden. Probably this reflects differences in social attitudes towards family nudity, family bathing, and sexuality. Think of it as a family style that does not necessarily reflect or cause emotional or psychological problems in parents and children.

But when someone is not getting enough sleep, either parent or child, consider this to be a potential problem. I suspect this often develops in older toddlers, because by age 1 to 2 years sleeping together is often associated with night waking. But now there is a well-established habit, and the child is unwilling to go to or return to his own bed.

So if you want to enjoy a family bed, fine. But understand that your cuddling in bed together will make any future changes in sleep arrangements very difficult to execute. Remember that while it sounds like an easy solution to your baby's sleep problems, you may wind up with a 24-hour child even when he gets older. In contrast, many families use a family bed only during the first few months, and then shift the baby to her own bed for overnight sleep. But at 5 or 6 am, they still might bring their older infant or child into their bed for a limited period of warm cuddling.

3 Common Myths About Sleeping

As we have seen, sleep–wake rhythms in early infancy evolve internally, from the developing nervous system. In older infants, however, changes in the environment, such as noises, lights, and mobiles, have a direct effect on sleeping habits and might well interfere with sleep because they become more interesting and stimulating to the child. Parents often do not recognize that their soothing efforts may be so pleasurable to their baby that she might fight sleep in order to get more soothing comfort! This confusion over what helps or does not help children sleep has led to many myths about sleeping.

Please ignore opinions and theories not based on at least some factual information. Popular ideas, no matter how firmly stated or widely believed, can still be completely wrong. After all, there was once a time when trusted common sense told everybody that the earth was flat! Here are some popular misconceptions about sleep that I would put in the 'flat earth' category.

MYTH NUMBER 1:
SOLID FOODS AND FEEDING
PRACTICES AFFECT SLEEPING

Do you remember how drowsy you felt after eating all that Christmas turkey? Big meals make us sleepy, so shouldn't solids make babies sleep better? Wrong. Feeding rhythms do not alter the pattern of waking and sleeping.

Sleeping for long periods at night is *not related* to the method of feeding whether it be breast, bottle, or continuous intravenous as in infants with certain intestinal birth defects. This is a fact – if you don't believe it, please look at the eleven studies cited at the end of this book. Perhaps the most convincing studies are those which compare the development of sleep/wake rhythms in demand-fed infants with those who are fed intravenously because of birth defects. The babies fed on demand oscillate between being hungry and being full. The babies being fed intravenously have a continuous input of food and are never allowed to become hungry. The objective recordings of sleep patterns in the two groups of babies taken in special sleep laboratories show that there are *no* differences in terms of sleep between these groups of infants. No published research studies, including all those looking at the effect of solid foods on sleeping patterns and comparing methods of feeding (breast versus bottle, scheduled versus demand, etc.), have ever shown opposite results.

Some studies, however, have shown that bottle feeding is more popular among mothers who were more restrictive or less permissive than breastfeeding mothers. Mothers who bottle fed their babies tended to be more interested in controlling their infant's behaviour. Because they could see the number of ounces of formula given at each feed, they were more likely to perceive night waking in a problem/solution framework and consider the social *wants* of the child instead of nutritional *needs*. In contrast, the nursing mother, perhaps more sensitive to the health benefits of breast-feeding, might respond to night waking more often or more rapidly, because she perceived herself primarily responding to her infant's need for nourishment. After a while, of course, the child learns to enjoy this nocturnal social contact. Over time, the baby learns to expect attention when he wakens.

This explains why there is no difference in night waking between breast- and bottle-fed infants at 4 months, but by 6 to 12 months, night waking is more of an issue among breastfed babies.

So the bottom line is that cereal sticking to babies' stomachs does not fill them up more and make them sleep better. Formula may appear thicker than breast milk, but both contain the same 20 calories per ounce. So giving formula or weaning breastfed babies will not directly cause longer sleeping at night, although it is possible that attitudes toward breastfeeding may indirectly foster a habit of night waking.

Here is one family's account of how breastfeeding until the child falls asleep led to the habit of waking at night:

'Jane was born on 18 July 1984, after an uneventful pregnancy and an easy Lamaze delivery, three days past term. We were committed to breastfeeding, with no preconceived expectations for its duration. Jane behaved as a normal infant for about 2 weeks, at which point persistent crying episodes began to occur daily. Though we were assured that real colic was worse, we came to refer to these spells as Jane's colic. We tried to endure inconsolable crying without too much complaint. Although most crying bouts lasted 1 to 2 hours, the worst individual days would include unabated crying spells for 8 to 10 hours. We tried various experiments to ease the colic suffering, including having Jane sleep with us, having her sleep on a hot-water bottle, etc. Predictably, none worked. At 2 months, the colic ended relatively abruptly.

'From 2 months on, a very happy, trusting relationship between me and the baby developed. For about 7 months, Jane was fed virtually exclusively on breast milk, but from 7 to 10 months, we introduced increasing amounts of solid food at breakfast and lunch. Jane has always been a very happy, bubbly, joyful child, and the breastfeeding seemed to contribute to this sunny disposition. Jane's nap patterns were completely normal. Generally, I would catch up on my sleep with her in the morning as part of the feeding ritual for these 10 months included twice nightly breastfeeding, interrupting my sleep.

'Massive campaigns were mounted by both sets of grandparents to convince me that breastfeeding needed to end. These began at 2 months and reached fever pitch around 7 months. We just listened politely. Except for a brief experiment at around 8 months, I made no attempt to express milk so I could get extra sleep; this was a conscious decision, because direct feeding was easier and more satisfying for both of us.

'Breastfeeding, in addition to the satisfaction it provided, was an indispensable part of the sleeping ritual. From birth to 11 months, Jane expected me to hold, feed, and gently rock or lull her to sleep. However at around 9 months, Jane's rapid growth was taking its toll and after such a long time without a full night's sleep, I was beginning to reach a whole new level of fatigue. Jane was being given more solid food in the daytime now.

'We decided to make new attempts to get Jane to sleep without my direct attention. Sometimes her father would give her a bottle, rock her, sing to her, etc. Or we asked female friends of the family, familiar to Jane, to do the same. Jane was a good sport about these experiments, but much preferred me to put her to bed. When she was 11 months old, we agreed that it was time to wean Jane to a bottle.

'Jane didn't like the plan much. She obviously disliked formula as much as I disliked feeding it to her. For nearly a week she rejected cow's milk. I ended the morning nap breastfeeding ritual first. Juices (orange, apple, pear) in the morning or in car rides helped to improve Jane's familiarity with and affection for bottles. Also Larry would feed her while I rested later in the mornings. Putting cow's milk in a special bottle (formed and painted to look like a dog) allowed this unpleasant white stuff to become gradually more acceptable. After a few days, Jane started to respond more favourably to her "pooch juice" and the games I created and associated with it.

'Jane was fully weaned at 11 months, with the last feeding to change over being the bedtime one. But even if she was fed milk at bedtime, Jane continued to wake up once or twice per evening, crying to be fed. I experienced some depression with the cessation of breastfeeding. As that special link came to an end, my contribution to Jane's development suddenly seemed more mundane, repetitive, and less satisfying. This depression came on and off for 2 months. It was a strange feeling, since it was offset at all times by the joy that comes of having a bright, personable, and developing child.

'We were repeatedly advised that the only way to get her to sleep through the night was to let her cry herself to sleep. The phrase "even for 5 or 6 hours" was used, a reminder of colic days. We considered this proposition, but continued to feed Jane warm milk, sing lullabies, and rock her to sleep, once or twice per night. The big question: what was waking her up?

'We decided it was mostly habit, and that she just wanted the comfort of our company. A new go-to-sleep ritual was introduced: after much playing and affection, Jane was put to bed alone with her favourite doll, not rocked to sleep. If she woke, warm milk was provided, but Jane was purposely not picked up. Jane cried for 10 minutes when left alone the first night, then rested her head on top of her favourite doll and drifted off to sleep. After expecting possibly an hour or more of crying, this was an unbelievable, almost anticlimactic relief to us. After two or three nights of feeding without picking her up, Jane began sleeping through the night.

'At the end of month eleven, the go-to-sleep ritual is routine and Jane rarely cries at all. Key elements: a big dinner, a bath, gentle play, 8 ozs of warm milk, hugs and her favourite doll. Even a babysitter can do it. At one year, Jane had finally learned to sleep 8 hours straight.'

Jane's parents' thoughts: 'First-time parents are like that'

'Jane is our first child; we hope to have one or two more. Except for the period of mild colic for Jane's first two months, we have never considered her to have any "sleep disorders". The rest of the phases we have gone through seemed to be a constant question of balance: how to balance Jane's satisfaction and her nutritional needs with our basic sleep needs. And as always with young parents, there are other nagging questions: are we spoiling her? Is she controlling us? Is the advice of our parents correct or old-fashioned? What is "normal" for other babies?

'We consider our experiences unexceptional compared with other parents we know. Perhaps the biggest differences are that we were committed to breastfeeding more completely and longer than most, with all the sacrifice that such a commitment entails. We gave up going out socially for a year, despite the enjoyment we both derived from going out to dinner, movies or just quiet evenings together. Relationships with our friends, virtually all of whom were childless, waned. We pushed ourselves nearly to exhaustion.

'We did a few things we are sure were right. For us, especially me, it was important that we sensed Jane's needs and delivered them unasked. This created an extraordinary self-assurance in Jane, and led to a happy household. Jane seemed to cry less than other children, and to be a bright, curious quick-learner. Other things we are happy about: lots of new games all the time; plenty of visual stimulation; rough-housing motions and playing; exposure to music, texture, any stimulation we could dream up. It all seemed to add to her alertness, her trust for us, and the regularity of her sleeping.

'There are also some things we may not have done so well. We may have gone too long before we tried to get Jane to sleep alone. Our parents continuously warned us we were being too indulgent. They may have been right . . . but then, first-time parents are like that.'

MYTH NUMBER 2:
TEETHING CAUSES NIGHT WAKING

If you ask parents what happens when teething occurs, the answer is . . . everything! All illnesses, fevers, and ear infections that happen to occur around the time a tooth erupts are blamed on teething. Throughout medical history, doctors used the diagnosis 'teething problems' as a smoke-screen to hide their ignorance. In fact, at the turn of the century, 5 per cent of deaths in children in England were attributed to teething!

A proper study of problems caused by eruption of teeth was performed in Finland in 1969. Based on daily visits and testing of 233 children between 4 and 30 months, it concluded that teething does not cause fevers, elevated white blood cell counts, or inflammation. And most importantly, teething did not cause night waking.

Night waking between 6 and 18 months is more likely due to nap deprivation, overstimulation, or abnormal sleep schedules – not teething.

Warning: Protect Your Child's Teeth
Putting your baby to bed holding a bottle of milk or juice or resting it on a pillow to solve a sleep problem will cause 'baby bottle cavities'. Protect your child's teeth – always hold your baby in your arms when you give a bottle.

MYTH NUMBER 3:
GROWING PAINS CAUSE NIGHT WAKING

One study examined 2,178 children between 6 and 19 years of age and found that 16 per cent complained of severe pain localized deep in the arms or legs. Usually the pain was deep in the thighs, behind the knees, or in the calves. The pain usually occurred late in the afternoon or in the evening.

But when the growth rates of these affected children were compared to children without pain, there was no difference! In other words, growing pains do not occur during periods of rapid growth! Therefore, I think it is reasonable to doubt that growth spurts cause limb pain in normal children.

Blaming night waking on growing pains is a handy excuse. But the rubbing, massaging, hot water bottles, or other forms of parental soothing at night is really serving the emotional needs of the parent or child and not reducing organic pain.

MYTH NUMBER 4:
A LONG NIGHT'S SLEEP
WILL MAKE UP FOR SHORT NAPS

Brief naps or no naps mean lost sleep. Over a long period of time, children do not sleep longer at night when their naps are brief. Of course, once in a while – when there is a holiday visit from relatives or a painful ear infection – a child will make up lost daytime sleep with longer night sleep. But day in and day out, you should not expect to satisfy your child's need to sleep by cutting corners on naps and then trying to compensate by putting your child asleep earlier for the night. What you wind up with is a socially demanding brat in the late afternoon or early evening. Or maybe your otherwise sweet child is just rough around the edges at those hours. Either way, your child pays a price for nap deprivation. And so do you.

MYTH NUMBER 5:
CHILDREN SLEEP BETTER ON
THEIR STOMACHS

A Chinese mother said she knew something was really wrong with her baby, because all Chinese babies slept on their back. She could not understand why her own baby preferred her stomach! She truly worried that stomach sleeping was unhealthy. Also, some non-Chinese babies actually seem to sleep better and fuss or cry less when asleep on their backs. But the truth is that most babies seem not to care at all whether they are looking down or up.

But tradition and social circumstances, however, dictate which sleeping position is selected by most parents. Fortunately, most babies sleep equally well on their side, their back or their stomach.

A variant of this myth is that when the child rolls over away from the less popular or traditional sleeping position selected by the parents, the parent assumes he has to intervene and roll the child back. What a waste of time for parents! Leaving the child alone allows the child to learn to sleep in different positions. On the other hand, going to your child to roll him back can become a game for the infant.

Also, when the older child pulls herself to a standing position in her cot, parents have no business rushing in to 'help their child get down'. A child might fall down in an awkward heap, but she will not hurt herself. Next time she will think twice about standing up and shaking the cot railings or be more careful when letting go.

Parents who rush in to roll the baby over or help a child down run the risk of reinforcing this behaviour or encouraging it to be repeated night after night. Children are very crafty and learn quickly how to get parents to give them extra attention at night.

These next four myths are often held to be true statements among certain mothers who use them as excuses to justify not modifying their own lifestyles to meet their children's sleep needs.

MYTH NUMBER 6:
CHILDREN WILL SLEEP AS MUCH
AS THEY NEED

During the first few weeks of life, **infants** are not much interested in objects, such as toys or mobiles, or environmental stimuli, such as playground noises or barking dogs. Biological needs, such as the need for oxygen, calories, fluid, and perhaps sleep, determine behaviours. Only during these first few weeks is it true that sleep durations equal sleep needs.

After a few weeks of age, overstimulation, excessive handling, or too much noise or light usually interfere with sleeping. By 6 to 8 weeks of age, some socially responsive infants clearly can express a preference for the pleasure of their parents' company by smiling and eye contact, even when they need to sleep. They encourage their parents to play with them, because this is more stimulating and fun than sleeping. They *want* their parents' company even at the times when they *need* to sleep.

Parents who play with their children when they should be sleeping are sabotaging healthy sleep.

Warning
Playing with your child when he needs to sleep robs
him of sleep.

MYTH NUMBER 7:
SLEEPING TOO LONG INTERFERES
WITH LEARNING SOCIALIZATION SKILLS
OR INFANT STIMULATION

When thinking about how a child learns social skills, please do not confuse the quantity of time spent in scheduled/ organized activities such as mother and toddler groups, playgroups and so on with the high quality social awareness that well-rested children exhibit. The truth is that these infant groups, especially in cities, are often not so important for young infants, as for their parents, allowing them to meet other parents and escape from what is often a socially isolated environment for many young families:

MYTH NUMBER 8:
CATERING TO CHILDREN'S REGULAR
SLEEP SCHEDULES PRODUCES INFLEXIBLE
CHILDREN

Adaptability can be thought of as the ease or difficulty with which a child's behaviour can be changed in socially desirable directions. In other words, a flexibility or ability to modify behaviours in new conditions. My studies have shown that when 3-year-old children slept longer during the day, they were *more* adaptable! In fact, the trait of adaptability was more related to naps than mood, attention span, or activity levels. Furthermore, only adaptability was related to the absence of night wakings.

So the truth is that an irregular nap schedule produces briefer naps, which in turn cause children to become fatigued, non-adaptable, inflexible, and ultimately less able to sleep through the night.

MYTH NUMBER 9:
DURING SLEEP-TIMES, EMOTIONAL
PROBLEMS DEVELOP IF PARENTS
IGNORE THEIR CHILD'S CRYING

I have saved the hardest myth for the last. Let me be very clear about this – I am talking only about children over age 4 months and only during normal day and night sleep-times. At these times such older infants do not really feel neglected, abandoned, or resentful when you ignore their cries. They do not *need* your nurturing; they might *want* the pleasure of your soothing company.

How can I be so sure?

Two prominent child psychiatrists followed a group of infants until they were about 20 years old. They were sensitive to irregular sleep patterns in those infants. Many of those infants also had frequent and prolonged bouts of loud crying. When I asked one of them, Dr Alexander Thomas, what advice he had given to the parents of those crying babies who did not sleep at night, he responded, 'Close the door and walk away.' Did this create or produce any problems? His answer, 'No. None at all.'

As I will explain in more detail later, positive emotional benefits can be gained by learning self-soothing skills, learning to accept being alone, learning how to fall asleep unassisted, and encouraging the growth of the child as an individual who is separate from his mother and his father.

Always going to your crying child at night interferes with this natural learning and growth. Always going to your child produces sleep fragmentation, destroys its continuity, and creates insomnia in your child.

Part II What Happens When Children Don't Sleep Well

In the first part, we looked at the four components of healthy sleep (sleep duration, naps, consolidation and schedule), disturbed sleep and other sleep problems, and their effects on mood and performance. We also examined and refuted common myths about sleeping, ranging from teething and eating to emotional problems.

Now we'll look at what happens when otherwise healthy children develop unhealthy sleep habits – and some of the reasons behind them. And we'll examine the risks and dangers when unhealthy sleep habits are allowed to continue, such as poor school performance, hyperactivity, accidents and injuries, and even child abuse.

4 How Crybabies Become Crabby Kids (Or, Once a Crab Always a Crab)

If your child suffered from colic during infancy – and 20 per cent of all babies suffer from this mysterious condition – then you'll be most interested in learning how your crybaby's colicky first months could have set the stage for unhealthy sleep habits as an older baby and child. But this chapter will be of interest to you even if your baby never had 'colic', because *all* babies experience unexplained fussiness and crying in their first weeks of life, no matter what your ethnic group, no matter what birthing method brought her into the world, no matter if your lifestyle is jet-setter or stay-at-home.

What is common among all parents are the *techniques* or strategies successfully used to weather those first few months of life with the baby, whether they were fair sailing for the most part or storm-tossed by colicky waves of crying. Sleep problems arise when some parents don't change their techniques for coping with crying and fussiness *at bedtimes and nap-times* after about 3 or 4 months of age, when their babies have become more settled. That's when unhealthy sleep habits and their resulting problems begin.

Remember
Parenting 'tricks of the trade' effective for infants under 3 or 4 months of age may create bad sleep and nap-time habits when used with older babies.

Let's take a brief look at why parents adopt certain strategies for comforting crying infants, and particularly for colicky babies.

SOME BABIES CRY A LITTLE,
SOME CRY A LOT

All babies cry or fuss at times without 'explanation'. Wet nappies, hunger, vomiting, cramped positions, chilling or overheating, bright lights, loud noises, or equilibrium are *not* the cause. We learned earlier that one out of every five infants experience this unexplained fussiness severely enough to be called 'colicky'. And while all babies can develop poor sleep habits due to parental mismanagement – by not shifting gears after about 3 or 4 months of age – colicky babies are even more at risk of developing unhealthy sleep as older children. I'll explain why just a little later in this chapter.

How can you tell if your baby's fussy, crying spells merit the term 'colic'? If those periods of unexplained crying followed this checklist, then he probably experienced what researchers call colic:

1. Crying spells started at about 2 weeks of age and did *not* dramatically decrease in intensity after about 6 weeks.
2. Spells lasted 3 or more hours per day and occurred more than 3 days per week for more than 3 weeks.
3. Most attacks started between 5 pm and 8 pm and ended by midnight.
4. Crying spells generally tapered off at about 3 to 4 months of age.

It would be helpful to add the 'cause' of colic to this checklist, but unfortunately, no generally accepted reason has been found. In fact, we know a great deal more about what doesn't cause colic. As I discussed at length in *Crybabies*, researchers have ruled out gastrointestinal or allergic causes, as well as maternal anxiety or maternal diet, in the case of breastfed infants. Instead, we now believe it may be set off by one or more physiological disturbances, such as disordered breathing during sleep, sleeping patterns that are out of synchrony with other body rhythms, or abnormal levels or naturally occurring substances (like prostaglandins or progesterone). According to *Crybabies*, it is most likely that colic is related to these physiological factors, as well as a baby's measurable temperament characteristics.

Warning

In many so-called studies of colic published in reputable medical journals, 'colic' is really not defined. Crying only after meals is discussed, or results are based only on parents' hazy memories years after the event. False conclusions from such studies include: colic is caused by parental smoking, colic occurs more commonly among breastfed babies, or colic is more common among higher social classes.

What is important here is the impact that unexplained crying has on the development of healthy or unhealthy sleep habits. Unexplained crying, whether moderate or severe as with colicky babies, can undermine parents' self-confidence and set the stage for future sleep problems. Here is one vivid personal account:

A father remembers colic or is the French Foreign Legion accepting applications?

'Sleep? Hmmm . . . Oh, yes! I remember that! We used to do that frequently before Michelle was born. Two years and another baby later, I still replay Michelle's birth in my mind at least daily. I joked in the delivery room that the newborn was 'ugh-lie', but it was just a ruse to help me hold back the tears. A healthy, normal baby! The demons of the past nine months disappeared in a flash.

'The first few days were spectacular. While my wife and the baby recovered in the hospital from a long, tough, toxaemic labour, I played the role of red-eyed, tired-but-ecstatic new father to the hilt. I went to work the next day, ostensibly to guard against using up any holiday days, but actually to show off the Polaroid pictures that I had carried home with me in the wee hours of that post-partum morning to avoid waiting an ungodly 24 hours for the 35 millimetre prints to be developed.

'Everything was perfect. I was getting the house in shape, making the phone calls, bringing goodies to the hospital. Breastfeeding was going well for my wife, Sharon, and our new baby was peaceful and thriving.

'The false security even lasted through the first few days they were home. Michelle would wake up about every 3 or 4 hours, and with a tiny, delicate cry, let us know that it was time to feed again. We marvelled at the fact that no matter how soft the cry or what room it came from we could always hear it. Isn't parenthood amazing? And as Michelle fed, she would usually doze off again. When the baby had fed, Sharon would put her back in her cradle, and we would just stare down at her, enjoying the peaceful sight of our sleeping baby.

'Just as she crossed the boundary into her second week of life, the scene started to change – same little cry, same feeding routine, but then, when the breastfeeding stopped, a new cry would start. This one was different. Louder. More agitated. More demanding. I rather enjoyed it at first. It gave me a role. I could pick her up, and with a few minutes of rocking and patting, the crying would stop. It was my first fleeting sense of competency as a father.

'But the crying grew worse and worse. Five minutes of rocking were replaced by hour-long midnight jaunts in the pushchair. On rainy nights, I'd carry her around the "kitchen-to-dining-room-to-living-room-to-kitchen" circuit so many times, that I actually started to vary my route in fear of imbedding a path in the carpet. The left shoulder of every T-shirt I owned had spit-up stains on it. I switched to the football carry: holding Michelle face down with my hand on her tummy and my fingers supporting her chin, I would swing from my hips, back-and-forth, back-and-forth, back-and-forth. At 3 am, I would strap on the Snugli and set off for another trek with my frantic daughter.

'Each of these stratagems worked for a short time, but Michelle had become a motion junkie. Take away the motion and she would shriek and scream violently and tirelessly, literally for hours at a time. She would become hoarse, but even that failed to deter her.

'Everyone we knew had a theory, even some people we had only just met in the supermarket check-out! All the advice was offered freely and generously, but never without the subliminal undercurrent that the real problem was our *incompetence as parents*: she was breastfeeding too often; she wasn't getting enough food from the breast, give her formula; mix some cereal in with the formula; wait four hours between feedings; put her on a schedule; relax, she senses your stress – and on and on and on. There was no end to the advice. All of it contradictory, much of it accusatory, and none of it helpful.

'Michelle got worse and worse. And we got more and more tired, more and more frazzled, and more and more irritable. Then we got "The Swing".

'The Swing was one of those wind-up affairs where you place the baby in the seat, turn the crank fifty times, and the seat swings back and forth with a mechanical click as it reaches the apex of each direction. The Swing was the true definition of a mixed blessing. While it was in action, clicking away, Michelle was quiet and often fell asleep. But within two minutes after the final click, Michelle would stir, stretch her arms, fill her lungs, and scream. One good crank would last about 20 minutes, so we organized our lives into neat, 20-minute intervals, always trying to catch the sound of lessening momentum so we could crank *it* up before Michelle got cranked up. And it worked.

'It worked so well that Michelle would accept no substitute. Unless she was hungry, there was no longer any time that we could hold our child without her screaming. All our fears, all the subliminal messages we had received, were coming true. We were rotten parents. A mechanical swing could calm our child, but we could not. We hated the Swing, but we dared not, could not, put it away.

'Our paediatrician gave us a copy of what was then just a manuscript for his forthcoming book, *Crybabies*. Sharon and I each devoured the book in one sitting. One section was particularly important and encouraging to us: it was a bell-shaped curve, along the bottom, horizontal axis were the first twelve weeks of life; along the vertical axis was the amount of what was laughingly called "unexplained fussiness". "Un-explained fussiness" is a medical jargon for unending, sharp, fierce shrieks that push parents to the edge of insanity.

'The point is this: all newborn babies cry a lot, and a portion of that crying is for no good reason, as far as we in the grown-up world can tell. If you normalize the daily variations in the amount of this crying, what you find is that it keeps going up for the first six weeks of life, then gradually falls off over the next six weeks. Then it's gone.

'We weren't sure it was true, but we decided to delay our mutual suicide pact for twelve weeks to see if it was. As Michelle reached her eighth week of life, we started to notice a strange phenomenon: there were brief periods of time when she was awake and not crying! And those periods of calm were starting to increase! *We were believers.*'

While this father's story may sound extreme, it actually is typical of the lengths parents will go to help their babies through their crying spells. Although many remedies have been suggested for colic, including cat-nip or herbal tea, papaya juice, peppermint drops, heart-beat or womb recordings, hot water bottles, or switching formulas, only three manoeuvres have been found that do calm fussiness and crying:

1. Rhythmic motions: rocking chairs, swings, cradles with springs attached to the castors, prams and pushchairs, walking, ceiling tours, using your baby for weight-lifting exercises to strengthen biceps, and rides in the car. Maybe all rhythmic rocking soothes babies by encouraging regular breathing, thus taking away the need for the baby to 'make' colic in order to breathe well.
2. Sucking: at breast, bottle, fist, wrist, thumb, or dummy.
3. Swaddling: wrapping in blankets, snuggling, cuddling, and nestling, like a Chinese egg roll. After a few weeks, this manoeuvre is often less effective.

You should avoid trying gimmick after gimmick, because you will only feel more frustrated or helpless as the crying continues. You may also feel resentment or anger since your child, unlike your friend's child, doesn't seem to respond as well to home remedies.

Remember
Feelings of anger towards your crying child are frightening – and normal. You can love your baby and hate her crying spells. All parents sometimes have contradictory feelings toward their baby.

Please take breaks when your baby is crying. The breaks will better enable you to nurture your baby; it's an intelligent strategy for baby-care, not a selfish idea for parent-care.

You may have the impression that during the first few months you are not influencing your colicky child's behaviour very much. Consider this to be a *rehearsal*. Your hugs, kisses, and loving kindness is expressing the way you feel and a way of *practising* showering affection on your baby, even when he's crying. This loving attention is important for both you and your baby, but . . .

This unceasing attention showered on your crybaby, whether colicky or just occasionally fussy during the first few months, can have complications, if you maintain this strategy of intervention for the older, *post-colic* child *at bedtime and nap-times*. Thus, after the colic passes, the older child is never left alone at sleep times and is deprived of the opportunity to develop self-soothing skills. These children never learn to fall asleep unassisted. The resultant sleep fragmentation/sleep deprivation in the child, driven by intermittent positive parental reinforcement, leads to fatigue-driven fussiness long after the biological factors which had caused colic are resolved.

WHAT HAPPENS WHEN YOUR BABY DOES NOT STOP CRYING

When the excessive crying and fussiness of your baby's first few months have passed and he seems more settled, what next? After about four months of age, most parents have learned to differentiate their child's *need* for consolidated sleep from their child's *preference* for soothing, pleasurable company at night. Most parents can learn to appreciate that prolonged, uninterrupted sleep is a healthy habit that they can influence; they can quickly learn to stop reinforcing night wakings and irregular nap schedules that rob children of much-needed rest. A 'social' weaning process from the pleasure of Mum's or Dad's or caretaker's company at naps and bedtimes is underway.

These parents and children are on the road to healthy sleep and more silent nights! Some of the reinforcement techniques in later chapters will be especially helpful in maintaining this blissful night-and-nap sleep schedule.

But parents of post-colic children still have a few challenges to face. That's because children who have had colic appear more likely to develop difficult temperaments, shorter sleep durations, and more frequent night wakings between 4 and 8 months of age than other babies. My research also has shown that parents of post-colic children are more likely to view frequent, instead of prolonged, night wakings as a problem. Furthermore, boys are more likely than girls to be labelled by their parents as having a night waking problem. Let's see how these patterns could have emerged.

Temperament differences among babies were described by Dr Alexander Thomas and his associates based on both their own careful observations and interviews with parents. Dr Thomas noted interrelations among four temperament characteristics: mood, intensity, adaptability, and approach/withdrawal. Infants who were negative in mood, intense, slowly adaptable, and withdrawing in Dr Thomas's study also were rated as *irregular* in all bodily functions. Thus, they were diagnosed as having 'difficult' temperaments because they were difficult for parents to manage! We don't know why these particular traits cluster together, but we do know that infants with 'easy' temperaments had opposite characteristics. In Dr Thomas's study, four additional temperament characteristics were described: persistence, activity, distractibility, and threshold (eg sensitivity to light, noise). These latter four temperament characteristics were not part of either the easy or difficult temperament clusters.

Infants who have had colic during the first few months are significantly more likely to develop a difficult temperament at age 4 months than are non-colicky babies. This progression occurs even when colic is successfully treated with dicyclomine hydrochloride, a prescribed drug which is no longer used to treat colic. Since careful studies show that maternal emotional or personality factors do not directly lead to the development of colic and because the difficult temperament develops even when the colicky crying is abolished, it seems that congenital factors, that is, factors present at birth, and not parental behaviours lead initally to colic and subsequently to difficult temperaments at age 4 months.

Remember

Babies are 'born' with colic. Parents don't give their infants colic due to poor handling.

Congenital factors may be inherited, such as skin colour, or acquired prenatally, such as birth defects from maternal drugs taken during pregnancy. We know that congenital factors do influence a baby's degree of irritability, sociability, emotionality, breathing control, and even sleep patterns. Much of our knowledge regarding these biological differences comes from comparing fraternal and identical twins.

One congenital factor recently investigated was plasma progesterone concentrations. Progesterone is a hormone that can, along with its byproducts, depress the central nervous system and can even be used as an anaesthetic agent. Progesterone could have calming, sleep-inducing properties by dulling the brain in normal infants. A possible mechanism for the quieting, calming, sleep-inducing and anaesthetic effects of progesterone is the reduction of another potent chemical in the brain, called dopamine. Progesterone is also capable of suppressing or inhibiting rhythmic, jerking movements in experimental animals. In newborn infants progesterone is derived mostly from the placenta, but the levels fall dramatically to insignificant levels by the fifth day of life. Thereafter, it is made by the newborn, probably in the adrenal gland. In fact, these high progesterone concentrations derived from the placenta might account for the delayed onset of unexplained crying or colic until after the first week of life.

If congenital factors indeed are the cause of colic/difficult temperament, perhaps this condition might serve some biologically useful functions. 'Colic' historically has implied inadequate maternal soothing skills, while 'difficult' temperament has a Western middle-class negative implication, suggesting that a child has a problem requiring treatment. Western middle-class mothers tend to view crying as 'difficult' behaviour, because it forces the mother to spend more time with her baby. The crying child is more socially demanding, because he demands more attention and stimulation and he provides less self-entertainment. In a Western setting, the crying child might be quieted by too much feeding, and the result can be overfeeding or obesity.

However, in a study in an East African village where drought conditions were causing starvation of many infants, the temperamentally difficult infants were more likely to be among the survivors. In other words, the squeaky wheel gets oiled.

Similarly, temperamentally more intense infants were observed to have fewer breathing pauses and less irregular breathing during sleep, and thus, they might be at a lower risk from Sudden Infant Death Syndrome (SIDS). It's possible that the pumping breathing, increased muscle tone, and jerky movements occurring during a colic spell occur during a storm of one particular type of REM sleep, called phasic REM sleep, and that this storm really represents the baby's struggle against a deep, dangerous sleep period. We do know that infants who almost die from SIDS tend to have brief night sleep durations and that infants who are temperamentally more active, intense and stimulus-sensitive have better breathing quality during sleep, as shown in Figure 7.

Therefore, colic or difficult temperament might confer some biologically adaptive or protective advantage to some infants in some settings. Usually, however, after 4 months, many of these crying infants in Western, middle-class families proceed to develop sleep disturbances instead of developing healthy sleep habits.

Figure 7

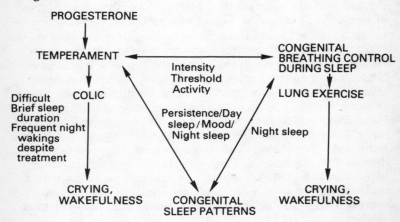

Here's how a child development specialist described a post-colicky baby:

'Susan at 4 months was difficult and unpredictable, with less than average sleep and cuddling and more than average crying. Observations over five weeks revealed an extremely sensitive infant. For a period of time, she could not tolerate touches on her abdomen. Swaddling helps a little, and the rhythmic swing movement gives her some relief. If these things fail, the parents walk her around. Sometimes these efforts quiet her fussiness, but at other times it escalates to panic crying. Susan seems to have no capacity to console herself, and very little capacity to be consoled by usual methods of touch. The dummy has been helpful, but not always successful. Susan does not have good state regulation; she can be in a panic cry state when she seems to be asleep.

'Susan goes from sleep to distress in seconds. She becomes overtired and cannot sleep, which contributes to her irritability. She does not habituate easily to sensory stimulation of light and touch. Susan requires a very protective environment, which puts great stress on her parents, particularly her mother. Her cries are very hard to read, her parents feel that she is unpredictable, and often uncommunicative.'

BRIEF SLEEP DURATIONS AND NIGHT WAKINGS

One of my studies showed that infants at 4 months of age who had had colic slept hours less than infants who had not. Similarly, infants diagnosed as having a difficult temperament slept less than those with an easy temperament. Persistence, or attention span, was the infant temperament characteristic most highly correlated with *day* sleep duration, while mood was the infant temperament characteristic most highly correlated with night and *total* sleep, as shown in Figure 7. Thus, those infants who slept less during the day had shorter attention spans, while those with less total sleep had more negative moods, fussiness, or crying. What this means is that a post-colic baby who is not getting enough sleep overall and is missing naps has a shorter attention span and is going to be more difficult to control.

In another study I performed, I showed that a past history

of colic was associated significantly with the parents' affirmative answer to the question that they considered night waking to be a current problem. Specifically, parents stated that the number of wakings each night was a major problem in 76 per cent of infants, while the duration of each waking was a major problem in 8 per cent. Both the number and the duration were problems in 16 per cent of the infants. Although there were no significant group differences in the number of night wakings based on the infant's sex, parents of boys more often reported night waking as a problem. Overall, infants who had had colic awoke twice as often as those who had not had colic.

But here is a continuation of the story of our girl, Michelle, who has extreme unexplained fussiness or colic . . .

A father remembers colic or is the French Foreign Legion accepting applications? (continued)

'Of course, nothing children do ever conforms entirely to what the books say. Getting Michelle settled down to sleep remained a long-drawn-out ritual well past her twelfth week. And getting her to sleep through the night was still an impossible dream. We were still tired (especially Sharon, who had gone back to work but still breastfed her at night and expressed milk for her during the day!). But we were no longer frantic and frazzled. We had regained a sense of time, a sense of day and night. And we no longer felt like miserable failures at the baby business.

'We let it ride until Michelle reached 5 months. Then, after another series of consultations with our doctor, we decided to manage Michelle's sleep patterns a little more determinedly, so both we and she could get some meaningful rest. The theory was that Michelle was waking up at night at various times just as we all do. But instead of turning over and going back to sleep, she was demanding food and attention from us. She no longer needed the food, and the attention was robbing both her and us of a satisfying night's sleep.

'The first rule was no more middle-of-the-night feedings. And because of that, we decided that Sharon should not go to the baby at all during the night, since the sight and smell of her would be too tempting for Michelle. So when she cried, I would go in and rock, cuddle, sing or swing . . . whatever it took to get her back to sleep.

'After a few nights of this routine, we discovered that she had not lapsed into malnutrition, had not stopped growing, and had not faded away into nothingness. We were ready to move on to the next step. For the next few nights, I did my entire moonlit song and dance number, but I didn't pick Michelle up. And sure enough she continued to survive.

'The next phase was no more talking. Now when I was summoned to her room for a soirée, I would just lean over her cot and pat her on the back until she was fast asleep. In fact, anything short of a full 5 minutes would lead to a revival meeting shortly thereafter.

'A few days later we held our final strategic planning session with our paediatrician. The moment of truth was upon us. He suggested that we make the room as dark as possible, put Michelle in her bed, and not open the door until morning. He recommended that Sharon spend the night with a friend, and promised us that this final step would not take more than three nights of prolonged screaming. Very encouraging!

'Sharon decided to see it out with me. When the designated time approached, we started the bedtime ritual. Then we put Michelle in her cot, turned, marched out of the room, and shut the door. The crying started immediately. But it only lasted 10 minutes; 10 minutes! That was it.

'Neither of us slept well that night. We kept craning our necks and straining our ears to hear the cries. But there were none. And when daylight came, we rushed into Michelle's room – and lo-and-behold – she was fine.

'And that was it – ten tough minutes and the three of us were free from this five-month ordeal. As the days passed, we noticed some very positive side-effects – just like us, Michelle was becoming much more pleasant and fun now that she was well-rested. She was thriving and we were loving it. Life has resumed.

'One more thing – the Swing is gone. One evening, after we had put Michelle to bed for the night, we dismantled the thing, brought it down to the basement, and opened a bottle of champagne. We never used the Swing again, and I'm extremely pleased to say that it is no longer in our possession. It served us well, but I still cringe every time I hear a click.'

ARE POOR SLEEP HABITS CONGENITAL?

The observation that brief and interrupted sleep often follows colic might suggest that some congenital, biological factors led initially to colic, and that they are still affecting the baby. This is supported by the observation at age 4 months that despite successful drug therapy that eliminated or reduced crying, brief sleep periods were still the norm. In addition, some, but not all, post-colic infants continue to behave as if they had *heightened activity levels and excessive sensitivity to environmental stimuli*. For instance, when my first son had colic, I had to keep the cot railing up and locked in place, because the 'clunk' of the spring lock would always waken him. This made it awkward for me to place him in his cot, but fortunately I was limber from college gymnastics. For my wife, it was an impossible situation until we got a sturdy stool for her to stand on – but it still hurt our backs!

These two temperament characteristics (high activity and low threshold) are not part of the diagnostic criteria for the 'difficult' temperament category. Also, some of these post-colic infants were exquisitely sensitive to irregularities of their nap or night sleep schedule. Disruptions of regular routines, due to painful ear infections, holidays or trips, subsequently caused extreme resistance to falling asleep and frequent night wakings lasting up to several days after the disruptive event. These prolonged recovery periods might reflect easily disorganized internal biological rhythms caused by enduring congenital imbalances in arousal/inhibition or sleep/wake control mechanisms.

'CRAB-OLOGY ' AND 'MUM-ITIS'

Some post-colic children have boundless energy. 'She crawls like lightning' was how one mother described her baby. These babies are constantly on the move. They would rather crawl up mum's chest to perch on her shoulder than sit quietly in her lap. But once having reached the shoulder, they immediately want to get down and check out that piece of paper or some equally exciting object off in the corner. They appear easily bored and stimulus sensitive, especially to rough mechanical noises, such as a vacuum cleaner, hair dryer, or coffee-bean grinder. It's as if they have a heightened level of arousal, activity and curiosity. When tired, they are always crabby, socially demanding, needing mummy's presence and wanting to be held all the time. They also are quick to fuss when their mother leaves the room for only a minute. But, when they are well-rested, it's a different story.

When they have plenty of sleep, these same babies appear to have boundless curiosity, actively seeking opportunities to learn to touch or to taste. Maybe these are very intelligent children who are so alert, curious, and bright, they have difficulty in controlling their impulses to explore or investigate the world. No data supports the conclusion that post-colic kids in general are more intelligent, but maybe a small number are so exceptionally bright that they gave birth to this myth. One study of infants published in 1964 connected increased crying induced by snapping a rubber band on the sole of the foot at age 4 to 10 days to increased intelligence at age 3 years. Whether this artificial crying and its link with intelligence can be generalized to colic crying is an open question.

A STRATEGY TO BEAT THE 'CRYBABY SYNDROME'

When you become your child's time-keeper and programme her sleep schedules, she will be able to sleep day and night on a regular clock schedule. For most parents, this is a relatively easy adjustment to make, but for post-colic infants, expect to put forth great effort to be regular and consistent. Your effort to keep your child well-rested will be rewarded by a calmer, happier, more even-tempered child. One family thanked me when they were finally able to permanently 'de-crab' their baby and they responded to their active explorer by saying, 'The "other" baby is back!'

But without your effort to maintain sleep schedules, your child will have a tendency to sleep irregularly and become unmanageably wild, screaming out of control with the slightest frustration, and spending most of the day engaged in crabby, demanding, impatient behaviours. The majority of post-colic infants do not fit this extreme picture, but they do require more parental control to establish healthy sleep schedules compared to non-colicky infants.

Reminder

For all post-colic infants after 4 months of age, my clinical observations are that frequent night wakings may be eliminated and the sleep durations lengthened if, and only if, *parents* establish and maintain regular sleep schedules for their child.

It appears that most post-colic sleep problems are caused less by a primary biological disturbance of sleep–wake regulation, but rather more by a secondary failure of parents to establish regular sleep patterns when the colic dissipates at about 4 months of age. Both obvious and subtle reasons can be cited as to why parents have difficulty in enforcing sleep schedules when colic ends.

Three months of crying sometimes adversely and permanently shape parenting styles. The inconsolable infant behaviour triggers in some parents a perception that their baby is out of their control. They observe no obvious benefit to their colicky child when they try to be regular according to clock times or to be consistent in bedtime routines. Naturally, they then assume that this handling will not help their post-colic child either. Unfortunately, they do not observe the transition at age 4 months from *need-based*, colicky crying to *contingency-based* fatigue-driven crying.

Alternatively, some parents may unintentionally and permanently become inconsistent and irregular in their responses to their infant, simply because of their own fatigue. The constant, complex, and prolonged efforts they used to soothe or calm their colicky baby are continued. But these ultimately lead to an overindulgent, oversolicitous approach to sleep scheduling when the colic has passed. Their nurturing at night, for example, becomes stimulating overattentiveness after 4 months of age. In responding to their child's every cry, the parents inadvertently deprive their child of the opportunity to learn how to fall asleep un-assisted. The child then fails to learn this important, self-soothing skill, which she will need for her entire life.

In addition, my studies have shown that when daytime sleep is interrupted, the same consequences occur. The nap-deprived infant develops a short attention span. Remember, other studies have shown that the difficult child is irregular. It is exactly these two temperament traits, short attention span and irregularity, that have been shown to interfere with a child's ability to learn – unfortunately, beginning right from the start with learning how to fall asleep without their parents' help.

Effective behavioural therapy to establish healthy post-colic sleep patterns by teaching the child how to fall asleep and stay asleep may or may not be acceptable to you depending on your ability to perceive and respond to the sleep needs of your infant. A variety of ways to achieve healthy sleep will be discussed in detail in the last section.

Other parents, usually mothers, despite educational efforts, have extreme difficulty separating from their child, especially at night, as mentioned in Myth Number 9 and discussed in a following chapter by Patricia Della-Selva. They may have some difficulty themselves being alone at night, because their husband's work requires frequent or prolonged absences or nights have always been lonely times. They perceive every cry as a need for nurturing. These are wonderful mothers, but they may be too good. According to this view, the infant is robbed of desire, because his every need is anticipated and met before it is experienced. The infant is left with undischarged aggression. The mother unintentionally thwarts the development of her child's capacity to be alone; she interferes with this developmental process in which the mother's role of soothing and nurturing is taken over by the child. The mother blocks attempts of her infant to provide substitutes (such as thumb sucking or dummies) for her physical presence.

These parents perpetuate brief and fragmented sleep patterns in their children. Their infants become, according to a child psychiatrist, 'addicted to the actual physical presence of the mother and [can]not sleep unless they were being held. These infants were unable to provide themselves an internal environment for sleep.' Although the *child* has disturbed sleep, here the focus of the problem and its solution is within the *parent*.

Colic does not cause the parents to have difficulty in separating from their child, but it is more than a sufficient stimulus to cause them to regress toward the least adaptive level of adjustment. The result is severe, enduring sleep disturbance in the child. In this setting, simplistic suggestions to help the child sleep better often fail to motivate a change in parental behaviours. Thus, while it is the wakeful child who may be brought for professional help, it is often the parent who has the unappreciated problem.

Summary

In this chapter, we learned how parenting techniques effective in dealing with crying and fussiness during a baby's first months of life may create bad sleep habits at night and nap-times after 3 or 4 months of age, unless a process of 'social' weaning is begun. We also reviewed how babies who suffered from colic are even more at risk, because of their 'difficult temperaments'.

5 Sleeping and Learning: Rest for Success

In the previous chapter, I discussed how the rocking, walking and other soothing techniques parents use with their young infants when they cry may later lead to sleeping difficulties, if these practices are not modified as the children grow. We saw how some parents failed to give their children opportunities to learn how to soothe themselves at night or for naps. Children learn to sleep better by practising sleeping. Just like learning other tasks, the more they do it, the better they perform!

In this chapter, we'll focus on the critical relationship between sleeping and learning. And we'll look at special groups of children who have medical problems that interfere with sleeping, and thus, learning. For example, children who can't breathe well during sleep can't sleep well, and the resulting excessive daytime drowsiness in turn causes problems in mood and performance. How do I know that behavioural, developmental, and academic problems result from poor quality sleep? Because when breathing quality is medically improved in these children, they sleep better, and their problems are dramatically and rapidly reduced or even eliminated.

Major Point
Behavioural, developmental, and academic problems caused by poor quality sleep are *reversible*.

SLEEP PATTERNS, INTELLIGENCE, LEARNING AND SCHOOL PERFORMANCE

Let's begin by focusing on perfectly normal, healthy children. Do sleep patterns really affect learning in our children? Yes!

Different studies of children at different ages all agree on this point. Let's consider the data by age groups: infants, preschoolers, and school-age children.

Infants

One recent study at the University of Connecticut showed that there was a strong association between the amount of time infants were in REM sleep and the amount of time they spent when awake in the behavioural state called 'quiet–alert'. In the quiet–alert state, babies have open, 'bright' eyes, they appear alert and their eyes are scanning, their faces are relaxed, and they do not smile or frown. Their bodies are relatively quiet and inactive. One mother described her 4-month-old who was frequently in this quiet–alert state as a 'looker and a thinker'. She's right! These infants don't miss a thing. This and another study from Stanford University of sleep development both agreed that environmental factors, not simply brain maturation, are responsible for the proportion of time infants spend in REM sleep. Unfortunately, the exact environmental factors were not identified, but presumably parental handling could influence all of these items: sleep patterns, the proportion of REM sleep, and the amount of time the child is quiet–alert.

Infants who are notoriously *not* quiet–alert are those with colic/difficult temperament. As previously discussed, their fussy behaviour may be due to imbalances of internal chemicals such as progesterone . . . or even cortisol. High cortisol concentrations in infants have been shown to be associated with decreased duration of quiet or non-REM sleep. So, even in infants, as in adults, there seems to be connections among internal chemicals, sleep patterns, and behaviour when awake. Also, as I discussed in my last chapter, these fussy children tend to be irregular and impersistent or have short attention spans. Among 2- to 3-month-old infants, one study showed that the more irregular and impersistent the child was, the slower the rates of learning. Looking ahead to Figure 9 (p. 86), you can see how the colic/difficult temperament child with brief sleep durations, who is irregular and who has short attention span might not easily learn to fall asleep unassisted when parents remove their soothing efforts. Thus, they quickly could become sleep-deprived, fatigued, and hyperactive older children. This concept of increased alertness, wakefulness, and irritability due to increased neurotransmitters was described previously in Chapter 2.

One reason I think naps are especially important for infants is because my study showed day sleep durations to be most highly associated with persistence or attention span. Infants who took long naps had longer attention spans. They spend more awake time in the quiet–alert state and seem to learn faster.

Major Point
Naps promote optimal alertness for learning. Children
who nap well appear quiet–alert when awake.

Infants who do not nap well are either drowsy or fitfully fussy and, in either case, they do not learn well.

Pre-Schoolers:

Three-year-old children who nap well are more adaptable, and *adaptability is the single most important trait for school success*. The briefer the naps, the less adaptable is the child. In fact, the major temperament feature of 3-year-old children who do not nap at all is non-adaptability. It is exactly these non-napping, non-adaptable children who also have more night wakings!

My research also has shown that when easy infants at age 5 months develop into more crabby, difficult 3-year-old children, they also develop a brief sleep pattern. In contrast, those difficult infants who mellow into easier 3-year-old children develop a long sleep pattern. I think that parents' efforts in helping or hindering regular sleep patterns caused these shifts to occur between 5 months and 3 years of age.

But let's now consider measurable intelligence in older children.

School-age children

In 1925, the father of the Stanford-Binet Intelligence Test, Dr

Lewis M. Terman, published his landmark book, *Genetic Studies of Genius*. In this he compared approximately 600 children with IQ scores over 140 to a group of almost 2,700 children with IQ scores below 140. For every age examined, the gifted children slept longer!

Two years later, about 5,500 Japanese school children were studied, and those with better grades, slept longer!

These two studies were followed by three others in the early 1930s which did not support the notion that bright children sleep longer. But, they did not support the opposite either. In fact, they were worthless studies because the numbers of children tested (34, 166 and 42) were too small for a proper survey-type study.

Even sixty years later, Dr Terman's study stands apart in design, execution, and thoroughness. Furthermore, a 1983 scientific sleep laboratory study from Canada conclusively proved that Dr Terman's research was right. This study provided objective, sleep-laboratory evidence that children of superior IQ had greater total sleep time. The Canadian researchers and Dr Terman even agreed on the sleep duration differences: brighter children slept about 30 to 40 minutes longer each night than average children of similar ages.

Warning

Please don't think that when we routinely keep our child up too late, for our own pleasure after work or because we want to avoid bedtime confrontations, or when we cut corners on naps in order to run errands or visit friends it has no lasting effect, simply because it's only for maybe a half-hour each day. Once in a while, for a special occasion or reason, OK. But day-in, day-out sleep deprivation at night or for naps as a matter of habit could be very damaging to your child. *Cumulative, chronic sleep losses, even of brief durations, may be harmful for learning.*

Another modern study from the University of Louisville School of Medicine examined a group of identical twins who were selected because one twin slept less than his co-twin. At about 10 years old, the twin with the long sleep pattern had higher total reading, vocabulary, and comprehension scores than the co-twin with brief sleep patterns.

Now that we've looked at the connection between sleep and school performance in normal, healthy children, let's examine two of the major problems – poor quality breathing and hyperactivity – that can interfere with sleeping and learning.

POOR QUALITY BREATHING (SNORING AND ALLERGIES)

If you've ever suffered through a head cold, I'm sure you'll agree that when you can't breathe easily during sleep, you can't sleep easily, either. In turn, this makes you sleepy during the day, which can affect your mood and performance. When the cold finally disappears, you feel like your 'old self' again, and your mood improves as does your performance. Some children experience the same type of disrupted sleep *every night* due to snoring or allergies.

Snoring

Two of the world's leading sleep researchers, Drs Christian Guilleminault and William C. Dement, published a landmark paper in 1976. This was the first careful study of how impaired breathing during sleep destroys good quality sleep. At Stanford University School of Medicine, they studied eight children (seven boys and one girl, aged 5 to 14 years) all of whom snored. Here's how their symptoms were described:

All eight children snored loudly *every* night and snoring had been present for *several years*. Snoring started in one child at age 6 months and while the snoring in most children was originally intermittent, the snoring eventually became *continuous*.

Daytime drowsiness Five of the eight children experienced excessive daytime sleepiness. The report noted that: 'The children, particularly at school, felt embarrassed by their drowsy behaviour and sleep spells and tried desperately to fight them off, usually with success. To avoid falling asleep, the children tended to move about and gave the appearance of *hyperactivity*.

Bed wetting   All the children had been completely toilet-trained, but seven started to wet their beds again.

Decreased school performance   Only five of the eight children had learning difficulties, but all the teachers reported lack of attention, hyperactivity, and a general decrease in intellectual performance, particularly in the older children.

Morning headaches   Five of the eight children had headaches only when they awoke in the morning; the headaches lessened or disappeared completely by late morning.

Mood and personality changes   Half the children had received professional counselling or family psychotherapy for 'emotional' problems. The report noted that: 'Three children were particularly disturbed at bedtime: they consistently *avoided going to bed, fighting desperately against sleepiness.* They *refused to be left alone* in their rooms while falling asleep and, if allowed, would go to sleep on the floor in the living room.'

Weight problems   Five of the children were underweight, and two overweight.

Overall, we have a picture here of impaired mood and school performance that deteriorated as the children grew older or as the snoring became more continuous or severe. Sleep is definitely not bliss for these children!

But was this a new discovery? Not really. As I will discuss further, most snoring children have enlarged adenoids, which medical texts as far back as 1914 acknowledge can disrupt sleep and cause behaviour problems:

> Restlessness during the night is a prominent symptom; the patient often throws the covers off during the unconscious rolling and tossing which is so characteristic . . . Daytime restlessness is also a characteristic sign. The child is fretful and peevish or is inclined to turn from one amusement to another . . . The mental faculties are often much impaired . . . difficult attention is very often present. The child is listless and has difficulty in applying himself continuously to his play, studies, or other tasks, of which he soon tires. He has fits of abstraction.

The increased motor activity or physical restlessness

during sleep, the distractability, and the 'difficult' attention described in this 1914 report of children with enlarged adenoids are characteristic features of children who have been diagnosed in more modern times as 'hyperactive'.

A 1925 study from the Department of Preschool and Elementary Education at Kansas State Agricultural College included enlarged adenoids and tonsils as a physical cause of poor sleep. So educators also were aware of this problem a long time ago. Even a major paediatric professional journal as far back as 1951 cited 'difficulty in breathing, such as seen with extreme enlargement of the adenoids' as a common cause of 'infantile insomnia'. In truly severe cases of enlarged adenoids and tonsils, affected children appear to be mentally retarded, and have retarded physical growth or short stature, and even enlargement of the right side of the heart.

In one study of children who had documented difficulty breathing during sleep, the following problems were observed in addition to snoring:

'Breath holding', 'stopping breathing' during sleep
Frequent night-time wakening
Breathing through an open mouth
Sleeping sitting up
Excessive daytime sleepiness
Difficulty concentrating
Bedwetting
Decreased energy, poor eating, weight loss
Morning headaches
Hyperactivity

Some parents also have described to me their child's apparent 'forgetting to breathe' during sleep. Their child's chest is heaving, but during those moments of complete airway obstruction, air flow is stopped. These periods are called 'apnoea'. With only partial airway obstruction, though, excessively loud snoring throughout the night is the result. In either case, it's the poor *quality* sleeping that's the culprit, causing daytime sleepiness, difficulties in concentration, school and behavioural problems, decreased energy, and hyperactivity . . . even though the *total* sleep time may be normal!

Why, then, has children's snoring practically been ig-

ignored? Are there more snorers around today? Perhaps yes, because surgical removal of tonsils and adenoids up until recently has been a very popular procedure for recurrent throat infections and this also 'cured' snoring children. And, perhaps yes, because the air we breathe is increasingly polluted and our processed foods increasingly allergenic, causing reactive enlargement of adenoids or tonsils in more of our children. This brings us to allergies, a second major cause of poor quality breathing.

Allergies

Allergies frequently are suggested among items typically listed as signs and symptoms characterizing snorers. Here's a list of symptoms from one study of children with difficulty breathing during sleep conducted at the Children's Memorial Hospital in Chicago:

Snoring
Difficulty breathing during sleep
Stops breathing during sleep
Restless sleep
Chronic runny nose
Mouth breathes when awake
Frequent common colds
Frequent nausea/vomiting
Difficulty swallowing
Sweating when asleep
Hearing problem
Excessive daytime sleepiness
Poor appetite
Recurrent middle ear disease

Perhaps the 'chronic runny nose' and 'frequent common colds' are due to allergies.

Allergists have long associated sensitivity to environmental allergies or food sensitivities to behavioural problems, such as poor ability to concentrate, hyperactivity, tension, or irritability. Terms such as 'tension-fatigue' syndrome or 'allergic-irritability' syndrome are used by allergists to describe children who exhibit nasal or respiratory allergies, food allergies, and behavioural problems. It is possible that allergy causes behavioural problems in many children by producing swollen respiratory membranes, large adenoids, or large tonsils which partially obstruct breathing during sleep. The difficulty these children experience in breathing during sleep causes them to lose sleep and thus directly causes fatigue, irritability and tension.

Also perhaps due to allergies, large adenoids or tonsils can partially or completely obstruct breathing during sleep as well as cause hearing problems or recurrent ear infections. So, either because of the actual enlargement of the tonsils or because of the underlying allergies that cause swelling of the membranes in the nose and throat, these children suffer from frequent 'colds' – runny nose, sneezing, coughing and ear problems.

Snoring revisited

We've seen so far that children who snore aren't getting the best quality sleep. Now we'll see that generally they aren't getting as much, either. Another study of snorers carried out at the Children's Memorial Hospital showed that children with documented obstruction to breathing generally slept less than normal children. At about age 4 years, the night sleep durations were only 8½ hours in affected children, and 10½ hours in normal children.

In another study which I performed, also at the Children's Memorial Hospital, the affected snoring children were somewhat older, about 6 years of age, and their total sleep duration was only about *½ hour less*. They also had longer duration of night wakings, went to bed later and took longer to fall asleep after going to bed. These affected children had snoring, difficult or laboured breathing when asleep, or mouth breathing when asleep. Parents described problems in their snoring children as overactivity, hyperactivity, short attention span, inability to sit still, learning disability or a non-specified academic problem. And as we've seen, just a chronic sleep deficit of only ½ hour per night might cause impaired intellectual development.

Even in infants, snoring might be a problem. I studied a group of 141 normal infants between 4 to 8 months of age. In these infants, 12 per cent had snoring and 10 per cent had mouth breathing when asleep. These snoring infants slept 1½ hours less and awoke twice as often as infants who did not snore.

In another study of infants about 4 months of age, cow's milk allergy was thought to be the cause of brief night sleep durations and frequent awakenings. Other studies have suggested that cow's milk protein allergy can cause respiratory congestion.

Please Note
Although snoring reflects difficulty in breathing during sleep, this is *not* related to Sudden Infant Death Syndrome or 'cot' death.

The night waking in these snoring infants and the restless, light sleep in older children probably represent *protective arousals* from sleep. As we learned in an earlier chapter, these arousals mean that the child awakens or sleeps lightly in order to breathe better! When awake, they breathe well, but the brain's control over breathing is blunted during deep sleep stages. So, to prevent asphyxiation and perhaps even death, these children awaken frequently, cry out at night, and have trouble maintaining prolonged, consolidated, deep sleep states. Here, the crying and waking at night and resistance to falling asleep are caused by a valid medical problem – not a behavioural problem, not nightmares, not a parenting problem.

Important Point
All children sometimes snore a little, and frequent colds or a bad hay fever season might cause more snoring, which usually does no harm. But consider snoring a problem when it progressively gets worse, is chronic or continuous, disrupts your child's sleep, and affects daytime mood or performance. About 10 to 20 per cent of children snore frequently.

Not all children who snore a lot have all of the problems listed above. Differences among snorers can probably be explained by differences in the severity and duration of the underlying problems. Also, I have encountered many monster snorers with minimal problems, because they habitually take very long naps or have been able to go to bed much earlier than their peers. In other words, there are snorers and there are snorers! Some, like myself, have never been studied, and except for occasional nightmares – like the ones of asphyxiation, drowning, or strangulation I have when sleeping on my back – do not suffer adversely from snoring. Other snorers are not so fortunate because their snoring is more severe due to enlarged adenoids or tonsils.

The reason that attention recently has been focused on this problem of enlarged adenoids and tonsils is because sleep researchers only lately have proven that breathing actually is disordered during sleep. This is an important point, because when the child opens his mouth, the tonsils do not necessarily *look* enlarged! In fact, the adenoids and tonsils may cause partial airway obstruction in some children during sleep only because the neck muscles naturally relax and the airway thus narrows. In other words, the basic problem in some children might not be big adenoids or tonsils, but rather too much relaxation in the neck region during sleep.

Locating the problem

Try to suck through a wet drinking straw . . . you can't, because it collapses. When we breathe in, the air flows into our lungs and active, neuromuscular forces keep our neck from collapsing like a wet straw. Sometimes things don't work well during sleep, and our neck muscles lose their tone. Sometimes the major problem involves the tongue; the tongue does not stay in its proper position during sleep and flops backwards, causing upper airway obstruction.

Think of this as a neurological problem involving the brain's control over the muscles during sleep. The result is that the airway is not kept open while the child sleeps. If it's a neurological problem, then consider the possibility that there are other asssociated neurological problems: difficulty in concentrating, poor school performance, excessive daytime sleepiness, or hyperactivity. If the major problem involves the tongue or neck muscles, removing the tonsils or adenoids might not help. So, determining the cause of the problem is obviously important before considering surgery.

Children who snore and have many of those problems listed above that are associated with poor breathing during sleep often have abnormal x-ray pictures of the neck when viewed from the side. Obviously, the most common abnormality is enlargement of adenoids or tonsils and a simple x-ray might tell the entire story. But some children who snore might have normal x-ray pictures, and will require other studies designed to document airway obstruction; this is important to pursue before clinical problems develop.

Studies used to document obstructive breathing problems during sleep include actual measurements of respiratory flow through the nose, skin oxygen levels, and the carbon dioxide concentrations in the expired air during sleep. Another type of sleep study, called fluoroscopy, has been used to visualize the level of obstruction. Computerized tomography or CT scans during sleep also have been used to measure the cross-sectional area at different levels of the airway to determine the anatomic location of the airway narrowing.

Electrocardiograms are useful because in severe instances, the right side of the heart shows sign of strain. This right heart strain can lead to pulmonary hypertension in long-standing cases.

Pulmonary hypertension also occurs with massive obesity in the 'Pickwickian Syndrome'. In *The Pickwick Papers* an extremely fat boy is pictured as standing motionless, barely awake and feebly snoring. Massive obesity itself apparently causes difficulty in breathing.

Finding the answers

If the tonsils or adenoids are causing significant airway obstruction, they should be removed. Sometimes a surgical procedure to correct an abnormal nasal septum solves the airway problem. Tracheostomy or creating a breathing hole in the neck occasionally is needed when the obstruction is due to airway closure or narrowing not caused by enlarged adenoids or tonsils. During the day, the hole is closed and covered by a collar. Oral devices are now becoming available which keep the tongue from flopping backwards, when that's the major problem.

Weight reduction to correct obesity and management of

allergies may be crucial non-surgical treatments in some children. The management of allergies might include a trial of a diet without cow's milk, making the bedroom dust-free by using large air purifiers, reducing moulds by using dehumidifiers, or getting rid of pets. Nightly administration of decongestants or antihistamines sometimes are needed to reduce the allergy symptoms. Often, intranasal steroids sprays are used to keep the nasal airway open and this treatment avoids side-effects of decongestants taken by mouth. A 'snore ball' which is a small glass marble or half of a rubber toy ball sewn or attached with a Velcro strap in the midback region, will prevent a back snorer from sleeping on his back.

Enjoying the cure

When treatment restores normal breathing during sleep, the loud snoring, daytime sleepiness, morning headaches and all other problems either *disappear* or are *reduced!* Sleep patterns and electrocardiogram abnormalities return to normal. These changes are rapid and dramatic. For example in one report, a 13-month-old-boy had a standardized development score of 11 months before surgery, but during the five months after surgery, his score had jumped to the 20-month level!

In every study, the harmful effects of unhealthy sleep were shown to be partially or completely reversible.

Major Point, Again
Sleep deficits may directly cause behavioural developmental or academic problems. These problems are reversible, when the sleep deficits are corrected (see Figure 8, p. 84).

One word of caution, once children are cured of their snoring or their allergies are under control, if the problem has been long-standing, then bad social or academic habits or chronic stresses in the family will still require the continuous attention of professionals, such as psychologists, tutors, or family therapists. The treated child is now a more rested child, however, and he is now in a better position to respond to this extra effort.

Figure 8

OBSTRUCTIVE SLEEP APNEA

Snoring, difficult breathing or
mouth breathing when asleep

DISTURBED SLEEP

Abnormal sleep schedule
Brief sleep durations
Sleep fragmentation (protective arousals)
Nap deprivation
Prolonged latency to sleep

BEHAVIOURAL, DEVELOPMENTAL & ACADEMIC PROBLEMS

Reversible

We have a third and final group of children, not usually
thought to be related to snorers or children with severe
allergies, with similar academic problems and characteristic-
ally poor sleep patterns to study in this chapter. Educators
and parents have used different terms to describe these
children but the current popular diagnoses are 'attention
deficit disorder' or 'hyperactivity'.

HYPERACTIVE CHILDREN

Restless sleep, increased amounts of movement during sleep,
or increased motor activity during sleep have been documented in hyperactive children. Could these children be
cranked-up from chronic, poor sleep habits starting in
infancy?

I studied a group of boys at age 4 to 8 months; only boys

were included, because most hyperactive school-age children are boys. The infant boys in my study also had active sleep patterns – they moved throughout the night in a restless fashion with many small movements of the hands, feet or eyes. They also had difficult-to-manage temperaments: they were irregular, withdrawing, had high intensity, were slowly adaptable, and were negative in mood. This temperamental cluster also is thought to be common among hyperactive children. The results of my study showed that infant boys at age 5 months with more difficult temperaments and active sleep patterns also had *briefer attention spans!* Maybe their motors were racing so fast, day and night, that they couldn't sleep quietly at night or calmly concentrate for prolonged periods when awake during the day.

Another study I did was performed on pre-school children, at age 3 years. It also showed that children who had increased motor activity when awake had a physically active sleep pattern. The children with active sleep patterns were more likely to be described in the following terms from the Conners' Questionnaire used to help diagnose hyperactivity:

1. Restless or overactive
2. Excitable, impulsive
3. Disturbs other children
4. Fails to finish things he starts – short attention span
5. Constantly fidgeting
6. Inattentive, easily distracted
7. Demands must be met immediately – easily frustrated
8. Cries often and easily
9. Mood changes quickly and drastically
10. Temper outbursts, explosive and unpredictable behaviour

Figure 9 (p. 86) summarizes my research suggesting how a transformation could take place from a colicky/difficult temperamental boy with *brief sleep durations* to a hyperactive, school-age child. The upgoing arrows mean that high ratings for rhythmicity signify irregularity and high ratings for persistence signify short attention spans. These infants traits are replaced by hyperactivity and increased intensity as the child becomes more fatigued. As infants, they were negative

Figure 9

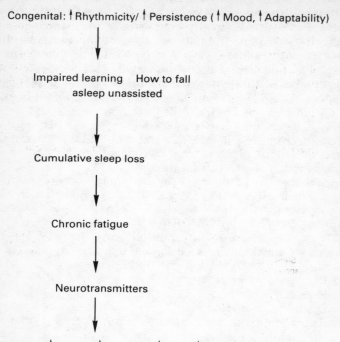

Congenital: ↑Rhythmicity/ ↑Persistence (↑Mood, ↑Adaptability)

Impaired learning   How to fall
asleep unassisted

Cumulative sleep loss

Chronic fatigue

Neurotransmitters

Acquired: ↑Activity/ ↑Intensity (↑Mood ↑Adaptability)

in mood and slowly adaptable due to brief sleep durations, and they remained so at age 3 years.

These children never learned how to fall asleep unassisted and accumulated a chronic sleep loss, which caused chronic fatigue. As previously discussed in the chapter on Disturbed Sleep, this long-lasting fatigue turned them on, made them more active night and day, and interfered with learning.

Learning may suffer, then, in children who do not sleep well, because they breathe poorly during sleep or sleep too little and in turn suffer from chronic fatigue which causes hyperactivity.

Figure 10 (p. 87) summarizes this entire cycle. It shows

that crying and sleeping problems present at birth can trigger parental mismanagement as discussed in the last chapter. Parental mismanagement or breathing problems during sleep can cause disturbed sleep, elevated neurotransmitters, and a more aroused, alert, wakeful, irritable child. This turned-on, 'upcited' state directly causes even more disturbed sleep, because of heightened arousal levels. It also may indirectly cause parents to misperceive their child as not needing much sleep.

Figure 10

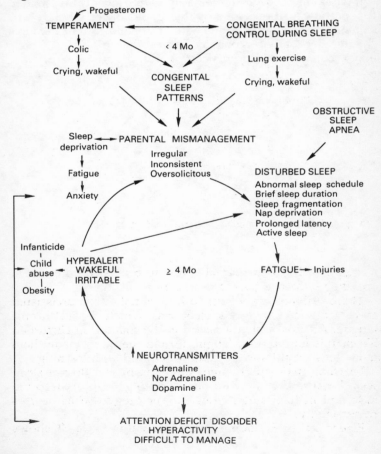

All these factors in combination – the fatigued child who is too alert to sleep well, plus irregular, inconsistent fatigued/anxious parents – conspire to produce a child who may find it difficult to concentrate, who may seem hyperactive, or who may have behavioural problems that make him difficult to manage. These school and behavioural problems make the parents even more anxious, and the cycle continues on, and on . . . Of course, there may be other causes of school problems or hyperactivity, but disturbed sleep appears to be *one* cause that is both preventable and treatable.

In later chapters, we'll look at how to prevent this circular trip or how to break out of this cycle, if you already are experiencing these problems with your child. But in the next chapter, let's briefly consider some other problems which may occur when children sleep poorly.

6 How Tired Children Suffer: Overweight and Overinjured. Will I Hurt My Child?

The previous chapter discussed how lack of sleep or poor quality sleep over time may lead to chronic fatigue and how this fatigue interferes with your child's development, learning, or academic performance. This may be sufficient grounds to convince you that establishing healthy sleep patterns are an important part of parenting.

On the other hand, you may feel that school issues will be taken care of later when your child is older and that for now, at a more tender, younger age, you want to give full expression to your natural feelings of love, care and nurturance. You may want your young child to experience complete, or almost complete, freedom, and to grow up naturally without artificial constraints, such as sleep schedules. You may see your role as unselfishly providing a soothing, comforting response whenever your child whimpers or cries. You may really have no strong feeling or desire to establish sleep patterns by setting regular nap times or bedtimes or getting your child to sleep in his own bed.

If everyone is getting the sleep they need, then fine. There is no problem. But if your lifestyle or disinclination for orderly home routines creates a tired child, or a tired *family*, then consider some of the other impacts – beyond the behavioural and learning problems – you may experience as a consequence. Let's look at three major concerns: injuries, weight problems, and abuse.

INJURIES

Injuries occur to children of all ages. Some can – or should – be prevented, some cannot. Examples of preventable injuries include leaving a 4-month-old infant alone on a changing table from which she falls, poisonings occurring when safety seals are not used or medicines are left lying around, or electrical shocks from uncovered wall sockets. A non-preventable injury is truly an 'accident'; for example, those resulting from an earthquake or a lightning bolt. The truth is though – and I realize that this sounds harsh to many parents' ears – most so-called childhood 'accidents' are really preventable injuries that occur because of parental neglect or the lack of parental forethought. They can be a consequence of home routines that create tired children – and tired families.

But wait, what about the child's responsibility? Is there such a thing as an 'accident-prone' child? To determine if traits within the child cause him to suffer frequent injuries, various studies have examined babies before any injuries start to occur. After a child has had several injuries, a 'halo' effect develops and adults are more likely to perceive traits in the child – clumsiness, lack of self-control, etc. – that 'explain' why he has had so many injuries.

One such study included 200 babies who were evaluated between 4 and 8 months of age. Some of the infants were difficult to manage. As we saw earlier, these infants were called 'difficult' because they were irregular, low in adaptability, initially withdrawing, and negative in mood. During the next two years, difficult babies were much more likely to have cuts requiring sutures than babies with the opposite or easy-to-manage temperaments. This study showed that during the first two years of life, about one-third of the difficult children had cuts deep or severe enough to require stitches, while only 5 per cent of easy babies had similar cuts.

Remember also my data – at 4 to 8 months of age, the difficult babies slept about 3 hours less than easy babies, and at age 3 years, the difference was about 1½ hours. By age 3, the briefer the sleep, the more active, excitable, impulsive, inattentive, and easily distracted they appeared – the perfect description of an 'accident-prone' child. Little wonder, then that these tired children fell more often sustaining deep cuts.

Obviously, for both the 'difficult' kids and all other children, chronic fatigue can lead to more injuries, such as cuts and falls. More sleep is the remedy.

Another study which supports this fatigue/injury connection included over 7,000 children who were 1 to 2 years old. They compared those who frequently woke up at night with those who slept through the night. They defined night waking as waking 5 or more nights a week plus one or more of the following: (1) waking 3 or more times a night, (2) waking for more than 20 minutes during the night, or (3) going into the parents' room. Among the night wakers, 40 per cent had injuries requiring medical attention compared to only 17 per cent of the good sleepers. The parents of the children who were night wakers reported that they immediately went to their child when they heard a cry to prevent further crying. There was a tendency for the mothers of the night wakers to feel more irritable in general and 'out of control'. One sign of family tension was that these mothers felt unable to confide in their husbands and the association of marital difficulties with disturbed sleep has been mentioned in many studies.

Maybe the parents who don't supervise sleep patterns to meet sleep needs are the same ones who don't supervise children at play to protect physical safety. The message is clear – if your child is often injured, it's not necessarily because he is careless or clumsy – he may simply be exhausted!

OVERWEIGHT

Difficult-to-manage children fuss and cry a lot. One way to respond to their demands is to put food in their mouths. This certainly quiets them. Coincidentally, it also might ensure their survival in times when food is scarce, as was shown to be the case among the Masai people of East Africa during drought conditions in 1974. But in a study conducted in a white, middle-class Pennsylvania paediatric practice, the more difficult babies there tended to be fatter babies. Perhaps this sets the stage for obesity in later years.

In my own paediatric practice, fat babies are almost always tired babies. That's because their mothers have incorrectly attributed their babies' crying to hunger instead of crying from fatigue. They are always feeding their babies, and telling me that their babies can't sleep, because they're always hungry! So, overfeeding a crying child to keep him quiet may cause unhealthy obesity. In many ways, this could be thought of as a mild form of child abuse.

Such overfeeding may have begun innocently enough, usually at 3 to 4 months of age when nutritional feedings in the middle of the night give way to recreational feedings. Later, the bottle or breast is used as a pacifier, and the frequent sipping and snacking cause excessive weight gain. Please try to become sensitive to the difference between nutritive and nonnutritive feeding. Overdoing milk or juice bottles is a common way babies learn to not 'like' eating solids. After all, they are getting calories so they have no appetite for solid foods when they are older.

Q: If I give my child a bottle at naps or at bedtime, will I make him fat? When should I not include a bottle in the bedtime ritual?

A: Most babies and even older infants are comforted by sucking or sipping a bottle before falling asleep. There is no harm in doing this and there is no particular age when you should stop as long as: (1) you hold the baby, so he drinks in your arms, (2) the rate of weight gain is not too fast, and (3) frequent or prolonged feedings are not part of a sleep problem.

CHILD ABUSE

Let's get one ugly fact out in the open so we can see what our true feelings are. No more pretending. When we are very, very tired of hearing our baby cry at night we would like to shut him up. We don't act on our feelings, we don't harm our babies. But at night time, the thought might have occurred to us: 'What if I weren't so much in control, might I . . .?'

The tired, difficult-to-manage infant, whose howling at night will not stop becomes a target or 'elicitor' for abuse or even infanticide. Crying is the behaviour which seems to trigger child abuse in some parents, and crying at night, instead of sleeping, is the historical setting for infanticide.

As discussed in the section 'Loving the dead: the ambiguity of lullabies', from her book, *Infanticide*, Maria W. Piers writes:

Children, as everybody knows, can be very trying. They exhaust their elders and in that sense appear to be enemies. Often, the only thing that keeps these elders from desperate measures is the fact that the little ones must eventually and periodically go to sleep. Anton Chekhov gives a good illustration of this problem in his story, 'Sleepyhead'. A young nursemaid, who is supposed to watch and rock a baby in the cradle, is so overcome by exhaustion that she knows only one desire: to drop off to sleep. Since her little charge will not be comforted and does not stop crying, she kills the child. The story ends as follows:' . . . and having smothered the child, she drops to the floor and, laughing with joy at the thought that she can sleep, in a moment sleeps as soundly as the dead child'.

Chekhov's nurse does not, to say the least, present the standard image of the loving caretaker. On the contrary, the cliché with which everyone is familiar is that of a mother and father bending over a crib, deeply moved by the sight of the 'sleeping angel'. Even so, it is the child's very helplessness that moves us. Sleeping children cannot make us angry by refusing to obey, or frustrate us by rejecting our affectionate advances. They cannot assert themselves or retaliate or, indeed, make demands on us that are impossible to meet. When they drop off to sleep, we can love them unambivalently.

Many an ancient lullaby refers to this yearning for the passive, lovable child. Here is a German lullaby with this theme.

Sleep, Baby, sleep.
See the grazing sheep?
One is black and one is white

And if my baby won't go to sleep,
He'll feel the black sheep's bite.

The message is clear: being asleep equals being good. Could it be that being permanently asleep is even better?

It could. And some lullabies are quite explicit about it. The famous 'Hushaby Baby' –

Hushaby Baby
    On a tree top,
When the wind blows,
    The cradle will rock;

When the bough breaks,
    The cradle will fall.
Down tumbles Baby,
    Cradle and all.

Here is another death-threatening traditional English lullaby:

Baby, baby, naughty baby,
Hush, you squalling thing, I say.
Peace this moment, peace, or maybe
Bonaparte will pass this way.

Baby, baby, he's a giant
Tall and black as Rouen steeple,
And he breakfasts, dines, rely on't
Every day on naughty people.

Baby, baby, if he hears you,
As he gallops past the house,
Limb from limb at once he'll tear you,
Just as pussy tears a mouse.

And he'll beat you, beat you, beat you,
And he'll beat you all to pap,
And he'll eat you, eat you, eat you,
Every morsel snap, snap, snap,

Michael Wigglesworth, a seventeenth-century colonial American poet, also knew what would happen to crying babies:

But get away without delay,
Christ pities not your cry:
Depart to Hell, there may you yell,
And roar eternally.

So when your baby gets all cranked up late at night with her desperate, angry, or relentless screaming, when she should be asleep, and you feel like a tightly wound spring, don't be surprised if you feel that you want to 'get even' or 'shut her up for good'. If you and your child don't get the sleep you need, you may have experienced these intense feelings of anger, resentment, or ill-will towards your child.

Do not hesitate to talk to your health visitor or your GP if you feel the need for help. Alternatively, contact one of the following organizations:

CRY-SIS
c/o Zeta Thornton
63 Putney Road
Enfield, Middlesex
(01 882 4720/886 5848)

COPE – Prevention of Family Strain
19–29 Woburn Place
London WC1H 0LY
(01 278 7048)

Organization for Parents Under Stress
(OPUS)
Great Carr Farm
Kirkby Misperton
Moulton
North Yorkshire
(065 38 6256)

The next part will describe how to avoid creating this nightmare situation in the first place and how to get back to peaceful, silent nights if you are now locked into struggles with your child at sleep times.

Part III   How Parents Can Help Their Child Sleep Well

In the previous part, I discussed how parental mismanagement of sleep habits can develop when the baby cries too much at night, how the bright child might not fully develop his mental gifts because of chronic sleeplessness, and how the tired child might become obese or suffer from frequent injuries, either intentional or nonintentional.

But none of these grim scenarios need be played out in your home. You can help your child sleep well!

In this part, I will discuss how you can establish and maintain healthy sleep patterns throughout childhood, and will deal with the normally occurring events that tend to disturb sleep. Also, I will teach you how to solve sleep problems if they are already present. Finally, a chapter by an adult psychologist, Patricia Della-Selva, will explain why some of you might have difficulties in establishing good sleep patterns in the first place or correcting sleep problems that have become ingrained.

Onward now to more peaceful nights . . .

7 How to Help Your Family Enjoy Peaceful Nights: Establish Healthy Sleep Habits

If you have started to read this book here, please stop. The first three chapters explain what is meant by healthy and unhealthy sleep, and explode some of the common myths surrounding it. After reading those chapters, you'll then see that the material presented here makes good sense. I will try to guide you step-by-step through different ages and stages of childhood as well as common disruptive events (holidays, illness, etc.) that all children experience, and what you can expect healthy sleep to be in each category.

The material presented in this chapter will help you establish healthy sleep habits in your child, and the next chapter will explain how to correct unhealthy sleep habits if already present.

THE NEWBORN

While recovering from labour and delivery or the after-effects of anaesthesia, you may begin to experience new feelings of uncertainty, inadequacy, or anxiety. This is perfectly normal. However, hospital schedules can serve to exacerbate these feelings. In hospitals without total 'rooming in', an artificial time schedule is imposed on baby-care activities. This is determined by changes of nursing shifts, visiting hours, and measurements of vital signs, not by your baby's whim.

But please relax and throw away your clocks; feed your baby when she seems hungry, change her when she's wet, and let her sleep when she needs to sleep. Full-term babies sleep a lot during the first several days. They also eat very little and often lose weight. This is all very natural and should not alarm you. Don't confuse sweetness with weakness.

Presumably this calm, quiet period during the first days is somehow synchronized with the need for a few days to pass before breast milk comes in. Babies sleep a lot, 15 to 18 hours during these first few days, but usually in short stretches of 2 to 4 hours. These sleep periods do not follow a pattern of day or night transitions, so get your own rest whenever you are able.

Remember
Your baby has no circadian rhythms or internal biological clocks, so you can't set your baby to clock time.

Helpful Hints
Unplug your phone when feeding
Unplug your phone when napping
Unplug your phone when your husband is with you
Consider a 'relief' bottle (one bottle a day of water, formula or expressed breast milk) if you are breast-feeding

WEEKS 2 TO 4
All babies are a little hard to read during these first few weeks, but you *will* learn. Most activities such as feeding, changing nappies, and soothing to sleep occur at irregular times. Don't expect a scheduled baby, because the baby's needs for food, cuddling, and sleep occur erratically and unpredictably. When your baby needs to be fed, feed him; when he needs to have his nappy changed, change him; and when he needs to sleep, allow him to sleep.

What do I mean by 'allow him to sleep'? Try to provide a calm, quiet place for your baby if he sleeps better this way. Many babies are very portable at this age and seem to sleep well anywhere. You're lucky if your baby is like this, and you're even luckier if your baby is one of the few that has long night sleep periods. Most babies don't sleep for long periods at night.

Studies have shown that for babies a few weeks old, the longest single sleep period may be only 3 to 4 hours and it can occur at anytime. Colicky babies may not even have single sleep periods that are this long, but premature babies may have longer ones.

Strategies such as changes in the amount of light or noise don't appear to influence babies' sleep patterns much now. In fact, specific styles or methods of burping, changing, or feeding do not seem to really affect the baby.

Major Point

This is the time to enjoy doing things *with* your baby. Do that which gives you both pleasure.

Holding
Cuddling
Talking and listening
Walking
Bathing
Sleeping together

A change will occur in all babies during this first few weeks and you should prepare for it. When your baby is about to fall asleep or just about to wake up, a sudden single jerk or massive twitch of his entire body may occur. Sometimes the eyes appear to roll upward when the drowsy baby drifts into a deeper sleep. This is normal behaviour during sleep–wake transitions. Also, all babies become somewhat more alert, wakeful and aroused as their brain develops. You may notice more restless movements such as: shuddering, quivering, tremulousness, shaking or jerking, twisting or turning, and hiccoughs. There may be moments when your sweet little baby appears impatient, distressed, or agitated . . . for no identifiable reason. THIS IS NORMAL NEWBORN BEHAVIOUR.

During these spells of unexplainable restlessness, the baby may swallow air and become windy. Often he appears to be in pain; sometimes he cries, but you can't find any reason for it.

1. Do whatever comes naturally to soothe your baby; don't worry about spoiling your baby or creating bad habits.
2. Use swings, dummies, or anything else that provides rhythmic, rocking motions or sucking.

If you find that your baby sleeps well everywhere and whenever she is tired, enjoy your freedom while you can. A time will come when you will be less able to visit friends, shop, or go to exercise classes, because your baby will need a consistent sleep environment.

Q: I've heard that my baby should not sleep in the carrycot in my room next to me because it will spoil him.
A: Nonsense. For feeding or nursing it makes it easier for both of you if your baby is close. When your baby is older, say 3 or 4 months, both of you may sleep better if your baby is not in your room. Anyway, the number of night feedings then is usually none or one.

WEEKS 5 TO 8
Many parents find this time particularly frustrating. Your baby may irritate and exhaust you, because of her increasing amounts of wakefulness or fussiness.

Remember
Your baby's immature nervous system lacks inhibitory control. The brain will develop inhibitory capabilities as it matures, but this takes time . . . things usually settle down after 6 weeks of age.

She may give up napping altogether and to make matters worse, when awake she may appear to be grumbling all day. You may feel battered at the end of each day; you may be at your wit's end . . .
Here is an account of one mother's first 8 weeks:

MY FIRST BATH IN 8 WEEKS

'Today my baby girl, my first (and probably only) child, Allyson, is 8 weeks old. I celebrated by taking a relaxing bath – my first uninterrupted bath since her birth. Of course, she woke up just as I was drying myself but I have learned to be grateful for all small pleasures.
'Allyson doesn't sleep much, and when she's awake she's usually either crying or feeding. It's been a little better the past week, but she still sleeps very little: 6 to 8 hours at night

and 2 to 4 hours during the day. And since I can't bear to hear her cry, that means she spends most of her time on my breast where, mercifully, she can always be soothed. I feel as if I've merged with the brown corduroy chair where I nurse her.

'Lately she's good for a couple of 10 to 20 minute "play periods" (on the floor, on her back and me leaning over her, or on the changing table while I change her nappy). I can't hold her and play with her; she's always squirming to get at my breast. So, anyway, she's on my breast 10 to 12 hours a day. As my gay hairdresser said when I related all this to him: "Well, honey, I guess you can kiss *one* erogenous zone good-bye." How true. The first week my nipples bled (I did my Lamaze breathing during feeding, then they scabbed over, and now not even during her most violent writhing spells do I feel a thing. When she twists her head with my nipple in her mouth, my nipple just stretches like a rubber band. No problem. (By the way, hydrocortisone ointment saved my life.)

'Given Allyson's behaviour (constant crying or "fussiness" and constant desire to feed, or at least "hang out" at my breast), I naturally concluded that my baby was starving, that I did not have enough milk for her. If I did have enough, surely she would fall asleep and *stay* asleep. Obviously, I thought, she was waking after a few minutes, or half an hour if I were lucky, because she was hungry. A weighing at the doctor's, where I learned that she was in the 75th percentile for growth (at 3 weeks) did not reassure me. I remembered after the weighing that she had drunk about 8 to 10 ozs of formula on the way to the doctor's office. It was the only way to keep her quiet in the taxi and in the doctor's waiting room, so I thought this must have misrepresented her true weight. And I continued to worry . . . and feed around the clock.

'This brings up another worrisome aspect of Allyson's behaviour – she would gulp down any bottle anyone would give her. She once drank 10 ozs of formula immediately after having sucked at my breast for 45 minutes. Of course, a few days later I conducted an "experiment" and let her drink about the same amount of formula, then put her to my breast – where she sucked away for about an hour.

'At one time I thought she just had a great need to suck, but she spits out any dummy my husband and I have tried to give her (and we've tried every kind in existence). I was again left with the conclusion that my breast milk supply was insufficient, and that the only way my baby could satisfy her hunger was to breastfeed almost constantly, until she finally slept from pure exhaustion.

'Throughout all this, I received a steady stream of "advice" from friends and relatives about how my baby was obviously hungry and how I should put her on the bottle immediately. Also it was suggested that I: (1) start the baby on some cereal to help fill her up, (2) stop smoking; it was probably ruining my milk, (3) handle the baby more gently, (4) bounce and jiggle the baby more to help her pass the wind that she had in such abundance, (5) get a lamb's skin for her to sleep on (we did; it gave her a rash on the side of her face she slept on), (6) RELAX; the baby was probably picking up on my tension, (7) take her to this place where infant massage was taught (I didn't; someone said they turned out the lights there and burned incense and I already went through that in the sixties in college, thank-you-very-much), (8) stop drinking milk and eating cheese and put the baby on soya formula for the 3 to 5 bottles she was getting per week, and (9) buy a swing so the rocking motion could help soothe her. Well, we did get a swing when she was 3 weeks old, and she hated it at first. But we got her used to it a minute at a time, and now at 2 months, she's good for up to 20 minutes. She even fell asleep in it twice!

'Anyway, most of the above advice was heaped on me all at once by the many relatives who gathered in my home town when Allyson was a month old for my mother's funeral. How I survived my mother's unexpected death, my anxiety about my baby's behaviour (which at that time was unexplained), the fatigue, the hormonal changes *plus* all this unwanted advice – I'll never know. Why I did not abandon breast-feeding, I will never know. I came close at the 6-week mark, but my doctor encouraged me to persevere just a few more weeks, and I did.

'A second trip to my home town when Allyson was 6 weeks old convinced me I needed to discuss my baby's behaviour at length with the doctor. A new batch of relatives who were actually staying in the house with me could not believe how much she cried or how much I nursed, they assured me that this was not normal, that something was definitely wrong, and I should see a doctor.

'I had, of course, previously talked to the doctor by phone. The first phone call was made to him at home on a Sunday afternoon – the first full day I was home from the hospital with the baby. She had been very sleepy in the hospital, but awoke at dawn the first day home screaming. The doctor told me all babies had fussy periods and that it would get better. A week later, I called to tell him how much time I spent with her at my breast to calm her, and again I was told it would get better. In the meantime he suggested the hydrocortisone ointment, which really helped my nipples heal fast. When she was 3 weeks old, I called again. That's when the doctor asked me to bring her in for a weighing, at which time he pronounced her to be a normal, healthy baby with some bad fussy spells that would eventually pass. I started to think I was a real wimp for being upset about what all mothers must go through, so I decided to grit my teeth and wait it out. At my doctor's suggestion, I hired someone to take care of the baby three afternoons a week so I could get out of the house, and that helped tremendously.

'Weeks 3 to 7 – when I didn't know what was wrong or why I was so upset by her crying, when I kept hearing it was "normal" – were absolute hell. I "lost control" only three times though. Once was one Sunday when my husband left to play golf all day and Allyson was particularly wild. I found myself shaking her carrycot and screaming "SHUT UP" into her little helpless, screaming face. (Of course, I then immediately picked her up and put her to the breast, convulsed with guilt.) Another time was at the funeral home for my mother's visitation. I had Allyson camouflaged sucking at my left breast, so she would not scream and disturb everyone else. All I could think of was that I wanted to get away from my baby so I could sob and grieve for my mother ALONE. I couldn't, so I got somewhat hysterical, which I'm sure was interpreted by everyone else there as my way of grieving. Little did they know how angry I felt toward this little baby glued to my chest. The third time was in the doctor's office on the day I finally went in for a consultation. Allyson was 7 weeks old, and I was convinced I had something other than the normal "fussy" baby. In the waiting room my reserves of strength were nearly exhausted by a woman who asked me where my child was. When I told her I was there just to talk to the doctor about my child's excessive crying, she said something about how I must be a first-time mother, and said I was probably the "nervous type" and my baby sensed this. She also said she worked in a hospital maternity ward and asked me what kind of formula I used when not breast-feeding. When I told her, she said, "A-ha"!, like, of course, that was the answer to the problem. I did my best to ignore her, but then, at about the same time, two women with babies walked into the waiting room. One baby was 18 days old, the other looked about Allyson's age. Both women were holding their babies in their arms quite calmly waiting to be seen by the doctor. Their babies seemed content to be held. They weren't asleep; they were just lying there, moving their heads around and looking. It hit me that in the nearly two months since my baby was born (with the exception of the two and a half days in the hospital and part of the first day at home), I had *never* been able to simply hold my baby like that. I repeat (and I am NOT exaggerating): I had *never* been able to simply cuddle my baby, unless she was feeding. I started to cry right there in the waiting room, and couldn't stop.

'When I talked with the doctor, he said it did seem my baby was "colicky", and I took his book home to read. Finally I found descriptions by other mothers of babies like mine! I was not alone. I came to understand how sleeping problems, like those of my baby, are probably related to colic, and how although my baby *appears* to be hungry, she really isn't. I also learned how there's nothing that I can do for my baby that I'm not already doing, and so I might as well turn some of my energy around and start taking care of myself. Truly, I believe that in the case of a colicky baby, who in most cases cannot be treated for her condition, it is the MOTHER who needs "treatment" or help and to this end I suggest:

1. Get out of the house an hour or two a day, MINIMUM.
2. When out of the house, try to get some physical exercise to burn off the tension.
3. Don't feel guilty about doing anything that makes you feel good. (In my case, it's smoking – which I resumed

after cutting down to practically nothing during pregnancy.)

4. Socialize as much as possible outside the home, but for God's sake stay away from people when you're with your baby. Discourage visitors. You don't need the inevitable nonsense advice; it will just make you more anxious and confused.

5. Keep a diary or log of your baby's sleeping–feeding habits. One day, when you're especially tired you'll find yourself thinking in despair that your baby's behaviour is getting much worse, but when you look at your diary you'll find this is probably not the case – it's just *you* who are more fatigued than the day before, and things are looking blacker.

6. When the baby is asleep, go to sleep yourself, unless you're doing something for your own peace of mind. Sleep is so important. I'm convinced that only women who have had babies, doctors on call and possibly victims of Viet Cong sleep deprivation torture can understand how lack of deep, long sleep periods can make you do and say things you couldn't possibly have thought you were capable of.

'Well, there's hope, I guess. Baby Allyson is slowly getting better. My husband and I have adapted somewhat. I continue to put her to my breast whenever she needs consoling, which is most of the time. During her several "catnaps", I put her down and rush around the house doing whatever it is that needs doing with two hands (grating cheese for spaghetti for dinner, making the bed, taking a shower, etc.). Then, while she is nursing on my left breast during the day, I do everything I can with my right hand (browning the meat for spaghetti, dusting, brushing my teeth, even going to the bathroom). It's a challenge for me to have the house picked up, myself looking presentable and something started for dinner by the time my husband comes home from work. It's kind of a game I play with myself, getting everything done that needs doing during the day. It is important to me that I feel I have accomplished something, however mundane, besides feeding my baby and changing her nappies. That's how I keep myself going. My husband has been great. He cuts my meat for me at dinner, for example, so I can eat with my right hand while she's feeding on my left side. That way we can both eat in peace, without having to hear her heartbreaking wails.

'And things are getting better. Last night (I saved the best news for last) she woke up from a three-hour nap, fed calmly and wasn't fussy for several hours afterward. She didn't go back to sleep, but she didn't cry either. Later that evening she slipped back into her old ways, but I got to HOLD her and play with her for over an hour, then she stayed calm in the swing for a while.

'And I got my bath this morning.'

Allyson dramatically and permanently improved within several days after her 8-week birthday. Perhaps she went through severe, unexplained fussiness between the fifth and eighth week. Colicky babies behave this way for 3 to 5 months and unlike Allyson, often a portion of their crying is inconsolable. Whether we call Allyson's behaviour fussiness or colic makes little difference, because the baby's behaviour and our responses are so much the same.

Try to remember not to let the routine of bathing, nappy-changing, dressing, and feeding grind you down. All are essential parts of looking after your baby, but they are not sufficient and do not by themselves constitute 'caring for your baby'. Smiling at your baby is important, even if your baby doesn't smile back.

Remember
PRACTISE SMILING

At about 6 weeks of age, or 6 weeks after the expected date of delivery for premature babies, your child will start to return your social smiles.

If you are lucky to have a calm baby who appears to have regular sleep periods, please prepare yourself for changes resulting from your child's increased social maturation. The social smiles herald the onset of increased social awareness and it may come to pass that she will now start to fight sleep for the social pleasure of your company. This is natural!

(Please skip ahead to the next section which describes my '2-hour guideline' which will help prevent your early bloomer from fading fast.)

In addition to the onset of social smiling at about 6 weeks of age, night sleep becomes organized so that the longest sleep period predictably and regularly occurs in the evening hours. This sleep period is now about 4 to 6 hours long. If your baby has colic, the longest sleep period might be less than this.

Other issues may be important to consider if you feel overwhelmed or angry dealing with a wakeful/crying infant:

Maternal employment   'How can I go back to work after maternity leave when I've had so little fun with my baby, when I'm so tired, when my baby needs me so? . . . but I promised them; they've kept my job open, my career was just starting to take off. . .'

Marital stresses   Your husband may be jealous that you are spending so much time day and *night* with your baby. He may be angry and imply that your baby-care skills or breast milk are somehow inadequate, causing the baby to cry too much or sleep too little.

Bed-sharing   Sleeping in the parents' bed may have become a workable solution in the first few weeks, because the closeness, warmth, and ease of nursing helped everyone sleep better. Problems may arise now, because the mother has positive feelings toward her baby, wants her baby close, but also wants some uninterrupted sleep. But the mother might want to use the baby's presence in their bed to avoid dealing with pre-existing marital problems. Or she may want the baby out of her bed to enjoy privacy with her husband at night, but she fears that this is selfish. Obviously this ambivalence creates a fertile ground for mixed feelings, confusion, and fatigue.

Feeding   If breastfeeding is the only or best way to calm your baby, how can you go back to work? If you only feed, how can your husband be sensitive and helpful at night to give you a break? Let's look a little closer at some of the issues revolving around feeding.

DIFFICULTY FEEDING AND SLOW WEIGHT GAIN

Some fussy babies are terribly hard to breastfeed and some really do not get enough nourishment resulting in slow weight gain. Even the most patient and determined mother sometimes wonders if it's worth the effort. Here you are, ignoring your own post-partum aches and fatigue, trying to soothe and nourish your baby in the most intimate way you can. What is the result? Often it is a tense, thrashing armful who arches her back, cries and gasps, sucks so hard your toes curl up, then jerks her head back and forth, sucks in rapid bursts, kicks, flails, and continues to cry. One mother describes this 'cry–suck' routine as 'she pulls away as if stuck by a pin; then she dive bombs at the breast!'. Is this the rewarding bonding experience you have heard so much about?

A GUIDE TO BREASTFEEDING

If you decide to keep breastfeeding your fussy baby, several techniques can make it easier. The following suggestions come from Ellen McManus, a breastfeeding counsellor for the Association for Women's Health Care Ltd in Chicago. They have helped many mothers succeed at this challenging task.

You should check the baby's position at the breast:

1. Get yourself comfortable and then have the baby brought to you.
2. Have the baby's head placed in the bend of your arm. Turn her on her side, belly to belly with you. Then take the baby's arm which is closest to you and gently pull it down to your waist or around your back. This lets the baby get closer to the breast.
3. Put your fingers under your breast, with your thumb on top as a guide.
4. Dip your nipple downwards and tickle the baby's bottom lip. Watch for the baby to open her mouth wide and then centre the nipple and put the breast into her mouth. Make sure that a good portion of the areola (brown part

of the breast surrounding the nipple) gets into her mouth. This is very important; if the baby sucks only on the nipple your milk supply will fall and your nipples will be very sore.

5. After the baby has latched on and is sucking well, pull her up and in toward you. This will open the air passages to the baby's nose.

Always bring the baby up to you. Never bend over – this creates a sore back, sore nipples, and a poor suck. Use pillows and blankets to get into a comfortable position. You will especially need pillows to support the arm that is holding the baby.

Timing feeds

Is your baby fussy most of the time? In this case, feed her whenever she seems hungry during the day, but consider not feeding at night (say between 10 pm and 6 am). During these hours, someone else will have to feed the baby a bottle containing expressed breast milk or formula. A sustained, predictable rest at night is very important to maintain your milk supply during this stressful time. It will restore the strength you need to cope with your fussy baby during the day, and you will get a break at night. When your baby outgrows the fussiness, you can consider changing strategy and begin to feed once or twice during the night.

Does your baby have a predictable fussy period instead of crying all the time? Many fussy babies are at their worst in the late afternoon or evening. In this case, feed on demand during the day and night except during the fussiest period. For those 3 to 5 hours of crying, take a break. Ask someone else to hold, carry, and feed the baby. If no family member is available, hire somebody. (You should always have your hired caretaker to help at the time when the baby is at her worst.) You may want to use this time to sleep – out of earshot of the crying, of course. But at least once a week you should leave the house. Visit friends, go swimming, take an exercise class, go to the movies. Relax! Do not do errands, they will only tire you.

Remember

You are the source of your baby's strength and nourishment. Taking care of yourself is an indispensable part of taking care of your baby. You cannot maintain an adequate milk supply if you are exhausted, tense, or under stress. Rest and relax – for you and your baby's sake.

BABIES WITH SLOW WEIGHT GAIN

Sometimes, despite a mother's best efforts, a fussy baby who is being breastfed (and even receiving supplementary formula feedings as described above) will not gain weight well – less than 5 ozs (150 gms) each week. If this happens, you might be tempted to offer unlimited formula after each breastfeed. But you should know that unlimited formula feedings nearly always lead to weaning. This is because the child will suck less often and less vigorously at the breast, you will soon produce less milk, and as the cycle continues will eventually find that you have stopped breastfeeding altogether.

Certainly your first concern should be giving your baby adequate nutrition, so that she gets her weight up. But you can do this while building up your own milk supply. The secret is shorter, more frequent feedings, followed by a *measured* amount of formula. Consult with your doctor, and try this 3-week plan:

First week During the day, feed the baby every 2 hours and then give 2 ozs (60 ml) of formula. At night, feed the baby whenever she wakes up and again give 2 ozs (60 ml) of formula each time. After each daytime feeding, use a breast pump to empty your breasts completely. Refrigerate whatever milk you get. Do not be concerned if you pump only a small amount of milk – it's the extra stimulation that is really important. You will find this schedule quite time-consuming, but it is only for a short time.

Second week Assuming that the baby has a good weight gain, feed again every 2 hours during the day and pump your breasts afterwards. This time, give 2 ozs (60 ml) of formula or expressed breast milk only after *every other* feeding. The nighttime programme is the same as for Week 1: feeding on demand followed each time by 2 ozs (60 ml) of formula or expressed breast milk.

Third week   Feed every 2 hours during the day. Supplement these feedings with a bottle only if the baby becomes really fussy after feeding (this may be the latter part of the afternoon especially). At night, feed the baby when she wakes up and then give 2 ozs (60 ml) of formula. It may no longer be necessary to pump your breasts after daytime feedings. If your baby is gaining weight, and if she has six to eight really wet nappies during a 24-hour period, you can assume that your milk supply is now adequate and you can stop pumping.

Depending on your baby's size and vigour, you may have to spend longer than a week at each stage. Your doctor can help you decide about this. You will feel better knowing that your baby is receiving enough supplementary formula to gain weight and stay healthy. As you worry less, you will produce more milk. It will not be long before you can dispense with the supplementary feedings altogether.

Also, encourage the baby to take both breasts at a feeding. Feed 5 minutes on one side, then 5 minutes on the other, then 5 minutes back at the first and 5 minutes more on the second. This is a total of 20 minutes. Switching back and forth makes possible more than one let-down in a feeding period, and also gives the baby the creamier, calorie-rich 'hind-milk' from the breast.

TAKING CARE OF YOURSELF

All nursing mothers – whether their babies are calm or colicky, gaining weight well or slowly – need to take very good care of themselves. Your diet should be between 2,300 and 2,500 calories a day. The baby consumes anywhere from 600 to 1,000 (your fussy baby is probably at the high end). And you are probably more active than you realize, and consuming a great many extra calories yourself.

In addition, you should drink 5 to 8 pints of liquid a day; this can be soup, water, juice, or milk. You do not have to drink milk to produce milk, although you do need to keep up your intake of calcium.

Guard against stress and fatigue, they can definitely hurt your milk supply. Are you exhausted from sleepless nights with the baby? Are you eating erratically, because of the baby's unpredictable schedule? Do you have responsibilities other than caring for the baby? Any nursing mother – and especially one with a fussy baby – should simplify her life radically. Try and find someone who can help in the house and do the errands. Let your husband help with the baby during the fussiest times and at night. Pay special attention to keeping things simple after 4 pm; this is when most households become busy, when a mother's milk supply is down, and when many fussy babies 'wind up' for the evening.

If you rearrange your priorities for as long as your baby's fussiness lasts, you will find that you have enough milk, enough strength, and enough good cheer to nurture your baby through this brief but trying time.

As the 6-week peak of fussy/wakefulness passes, your baby will start to settle down more and more. She will become more interested in objects such as mobiles, toys and playing games and her repertoire of emotional expressions will dramatically increase.

If you are lucky enough to have an easy baby, you may have already noticed sleep patterns have become somewhat regular. You may try to help your baby become more regular by putting her down to sleep after about 2 hours of wakefulness when she appears tired. If she cries for 5–10–20 minutes, it will do her no harm and sometimes she may drift off to sleep. If not, console her and try again at other times. Try to become sensitive to her *need* to sleep. The novelty of external stimulating noises, voices, lights, and vibrations will more and more disrupt her sleep so try to have her in her cradle when she needs to sleep. Go slowly and be flexible.

Here is an account from one mother who needed to get her child's sleep more scheduled before she went back to work. Trying her methods with a more irregular, fussy child probably wouldn't work at this early age and shouldn't be tried. But an easy baby often responds quickly to sleep-training strategies around age 6 weeks.

'We never dreamed we would be faced with a baby whose internal clock thought day was night and night was day. Oh, it didn't happen right away. In fact, the first few weeks were spent feeding and changing nappies in between David's naps. He was blissful, and I tried not to worry every time he did something new and different. At the same time as I was beginning to relax and feel YES everything was going along normally, David became more alert. Ron and I thought and knew it was a great step in his development. We looked forward to his periods of wakefulness as a time to interact with our son, and David began to discover his world around him. But a pattern began to develop. David didn't want to go to bed at night.

'At first, we were happy to have David's company for the evening. But the stretch of hours became longer and longer and it was obvious to us that David was not as happy as we were to be awake. We began to try everything. The bouncy seat, the rocking infant seat, the swing. The swing worked – perhaps too well. David slept in the swing, propped up with rolled up nappies. Then, when it was time for bed, David cried.

'So I nursed him, rocked him, walked with him, gave him to Ron to be walked, tried to feed again, tried the dummy, walked some more. And on and on into the night. We took David for rides in the car and that usually helped. And we called the doctor.

'The doctor listened to what we were going through and assured us that, first of all, this was normal for some babies. He suggested putting David in his Snugli and going for a walk, rides in the car, patience and lots of love for our baby. David was really too young to go through sleep training at 6 weeks. Most babies respond to training at 3 or 4 months, he told us. So, Ron and I resigned ourselves to some more of the same. Luckily Ron was a night owl and I was an early bird. He stayed up with David most nights, waking me for feedings when necessary (about every 2 hours). It helped, too, that Ron did most of his work out of the house. I relied on him and he on me and we shared all the tasks (except, of course, feeding). Even though our friends shared their stories of sleepless nights with us, we really understood we were not alone the night Ron was taking David for a ride in the car at

2 am, pulled up to a stop light and turned to see a woman in the car next to him with a baby strapped into a car seat in the back, she was trying to get her baby to sleep too. Ron had visions of sleepy parents at stop lights all over the world, trying to get their babies to sleep.

'At the doctor's suggestion we tried to keep David up a little longer during his daytime wakings, hoping that we could turn his little inner clock around. But David would not cooperate. Just as he refused to go to bed at night, he wouldn't keep awake for anything during the day. We felt we were losing the battle. I can remember some nights standing over his cradle, crying in exhaustion. Too tired and angry to hold him, just needing a break. I think the anger was the most difficult emotion all this sleeplessness brought out. How could I be angry at this little helpless baby that I loved so much? It took a while (and a lot of guilt) before I realized that it was OK to be angry as long as you don't take it out on the baby.

'David was now 2 months old and I began to panic because my maternity leave would soon be over. I could barely stand up most of the time, I was so tired. I also wanted to continue to feed David whenever I would be home. I knew we had to do something before I went back to work. So we called Dr Weissbluth and made an appointment to see him.

'First, the doctor checked over David's physical condition. He was in perfect health. Then we talked. Dr Weissbluth explained we would have to make some changes in the way we handled David's sleep periods. David was to have a quiet, darkened room when sleeping. No more night light, music, etc. Naps should be at least 45 minutes to 1 hour. If he got up sooner, we were to leave him until he got the rest he needed. Instead of letting David stay up late, we were to put him in bed between 7 and 9 pm. No rides in cars, pushchairs, swings, etc. where sleep occurred for the time being. David needed to learn that rest came in his cot. The doctor explained that sleep from motion was not restorative, which was what David needed now. And then the hard part – when we put David down for the night we were not to go to him if he began to cry. Only if he had at least 45 minutes to 1 hour of sleep and he was scheduled to be fed. Older babies can turn around in about three days, the doctor explained. If after three days there was no improvement we should abandon the training for a few weeks and try when David was older. We were assured that three days of crying himself to sleep would in no way harm our baby, but to go on any longer without improvement would be unfair, to David and to us.

'We decided to start that next Monday, since Sunday was Mother's Day and I knew that while we were ready to begin the grandmothers would rebel if we limited David's time with them. Early on Monday I called the doctor to make sure I had his instructions straight. (Turns out I didn't, but I didn't know that until Tuesday.) We agreed that I would call the doctor daily for the next few days to report on David's progress. Ron and I took a deep breath and braced ourselves for the days to follow.

'Poor David. That first day I woke him after he napped for an hour instead of letting him sleep for as long as he wanted. The doctor later explained that you should never wake a sleeping baby; the baby will know when to wake up. But in spite of my mistake, the day went quite well, that is until that night. For some reason, the night before David fell asleep on his own at 7 pm and slept through the night. I hoped that he would repeat the cycle and that somehow, as if by magic, he would have straightened himself out. Wrong. That night Ron had to work late and out of the house. I fed David at 9 pm and by 9.30 he was asleep in my arms. I tiptoed him into bed and crept back to the living room and turned on the intercom. It was quiet until 9.45 when I heard David sucking his fingers. I thought, OK he'll get back to sleep soon, when at 10.00 the crying began. David cried until 12.30 – two and a half hours. For every cry I heard I shared his frustration, anger and seemingly pain. And I was angry – at David, the doctor, myself and Ron who unfortunately wasn't there to keep me going. David slept until 6.45 the next morning when I woke him to feed.

'The morning wake-up was planned and agreed to with Dr Weissbluth, the idea being to get David to wake before I left for work so that I could feed him. David seemed fine; I was exhausted. It was really an emotional night. I was having doubts about proceeding with the remaining two days, but my morning call to the doctor gave me one more day's courage. He assured me that, first of all, my 1-hour nap wake-ups did not ruin anything. He was encouraged that

David slept through the night and told me that the 2½ hours of crying was normal.

'So Tuesday, I let David wake himself up. I found out that the poor little thing was really cheated out of some sleep the day before. He took 2- to 3½-hour naps that day, but his schedule was rather loose. At 8.30 that night when he woke up I fed, bathed and played with him until he had one last feed and I put him in bed, although not asleep, at 10.50. This time he cried from 10.50 until 11.15 – only 25 minutes? Could it be this easy? I was very encouraged. Weeks of David's inability to get to sleep at night seemed to be at an end. Even Dr Weissbluth seemed surprised at David's progress. Once again, he slept through the night.

'Although we were still unsuccessful at getting David to bed early, the periods of crying himself to sleep were getting shorter. On day three, he cried 21 minutes and not another peep until the next morning,

'Just when Ron and I began to let out our breaths David put us back in our places. Day four, David cried for nearly an hour and a half. My spirits dropped. Was it just a temporary setback or were the last three days just a fluke? When I called the doctor that next morning he told me to continue the training. David will have some off days, he explained. The great strides we had taken over the past few days were important and showed that David could and would accept some training. We may not yet get perfection, but our success should not be denied. Keep it up and check back with him in a few days.

'David had his good days when he would only cry for 5 to 10 minutes and then his bad days when the crying would go on for up to 45 minutes. Ron and I were really beginning to understand David's needs and wants. We found that if we responded too quickly, assuming he wanted to feed, he became irritable and difficult to feed. Those were the nights the crying seemed to go on for ever. Thank goodness Ron was around to keep me from running at David's every whimper. The poor thing would have never got any sleep.

'We continued to check in with Dr Weissbluth, but less frequently. At the end of our third week of sleep training David, Ron and I really had our acts together. Ron and I could tell when David was ready to call it a day and we didn't push him to stay up any later than he wanted. David had developed an unusual way of confirming his need for sleep. When we put him in bed, he would lay his little head down, put his fingers in his mouth and suck his way to sleep. If he began to cry, he refound his fingers and would pacify himself back to sleep. At 8 months, he still lets us know he's tired by putting his fingers in his mouth.

'When Ron and I started the sleep training we kept a log of David's wakings and sleepings. We still do; not because he's still in training – we've established reasonable bedtimes and sleeping patterns – but with my return to work and Ron's busy schedule, we are better able to understand David's moods, hunger patterns, etc. when the childminder lets us know what's happened during the day.

'Do we regret having trained David at such an early age? Well, Ron and I realize that his training took a bit longer because he was so young. And, I wish that I had been able to take a bit more time off from work to be with David, but that just wasn't possible. No, we have no regrets. David became a happier baby. By putting some structure in his day, he became more relaxed and in return so did we.'

MONTHS 3 TO 4

Let's consider the ways in which your child has changed. The increased smiles, coos, giggles, laughs, and squeals light up your life. Your child is now a more *social* creature. She is sleeping better at night, but naps may still be brief and irregular.

Become sensitive to her *need* to sleep and try to distinguish her *need* to sleep from her *wanting* to play with you. She would naturally prefer the pleasure of your company than be left alone in a dark, quiet, or boring bedroom. Therefore, she will fight off sleep to keep you around.

In addition to your presence providing pleasurable stimulation, her curiosity about all the new and exciting parts of her expanding world will disrupt her sleep. How interesting it must be for an infant to regard the clouds in the sky, the trees moving in the wind, the noise of barking dogs, or the rhythms of adult chattering.

Become sensitive to the difference in quality between brief, interrupted sleep and prolonged, consolidated naps. Your child is becoming less portable. As her biological rhythms evolve for day sleep, your general goal is to *synchronize your caretaking activities with her biological needs*. This is no different from being sensitive to her need to be fed or changed.

When she needs to sleep, try to put her in an environment where she will sleep well. As she continues to grow, you probably will notice that she will sleep poorly outside her own cot.

Warning, Again
The crying baby may be hungry or just fussy, OR the crying baby may be TIRED.

I have examined many children who cried with such intensity and persistence that their mothers were sure that they were sick. During their crying or fussing, they may swallow air and become very windy. It is tempting to assume that their formula doesn't agree with them or that they have an intestinal disease – but only at night? These children were healthy, but tired. Not only did they cry hard and long when awake, they also cried loud and often during sleep–wake transitions.

Most of these children are tired from not napping well. They are not napping well, because they're getting too much outside stimulation, too much handling, or too much irregular handling.

Sleep Strategy
Plan to put your child somewhere semi-quiet or quiet to nap after she's been awake for about 2 *hours*.

Q: If I put my child to sleep after about 2 hours of wakefulness, how long should she sleep?

A: The naps may be short or long without any particular pattern. This variability occurs because that part of the brain which establishes regular naps has not yet fully developed. Watch for signs of tiredness to help you decide whether a particular nap was long enough.

The 2-hour limit is an approximation. Often there is a magic moment of tiredness when the baby will go to sleep easily. She is tired then, but not overtired. After you go past 2 hours, expect fatigue to set in. When she is up too long she will tend to become overstimulated, overaroused, irritable, or peevish. Please don't blame changes in weather – it's never too hot or too cold to sleep well.

Overstimulation
When the duration of wakeful intervals is too long, the child becomes overstimulated. Overstimulation does *not* mean that you are too intense in your playfulness.

BECOME YOUR CHILD'S TIMEKEEPER

Watch the clock during the day and expect your baby to need to sleep after about 2 hours of wakefulness. Use whatever soothing method or wind-down routine works best to comfort and calm your baby. This may include a scheduled feeding, non-nutritive 'recreational' nursing, swings, rocking chairs, dummies.

After a while, you may notice a partial routine or a rough pattern of when your child's day sleep is best. It may then come to pass that based on: (1) your child's behaviour, (2) the time of day, and (3) the duration of wakefulness, you reasonably conclude that your child *needs* to sleep. However, she may *want* to play with you. Have the confidence to be sensitive to her need to sleep and leave her alone a little to let her sleep. How long do you leave her alone? Maybe 5, 10, or 20 minutes.

No rules. No regulations. No rigid schedules.

Simply test her once in a while to see whether when left alone for a while she goes to sleep after 5 to 20 minutes of protest crying. If it fails, pick her up, soothe her, comfort her and either play with her or try it again then or later on. This approach is appropriate for children a few months old who are biologically immature, but later, such inconsistency may well produce unhealthy sleep habits. Be flexible, but also become sensitive to your child's need to sleep.

You are giving her the opportunity to develop *self-soothing* skills. She is being allowed to learn how to fall asleep unassisted. Some children learn this faster than others, so don't worry if your child seems to always cry up to your designated time. Perhaps, she is too young. Try it again another time.

Always going to your child when your child *needs* to sleep, robs him of sleep. Never even letting your child cry might reflect a confusion in your mind between the healthy notion of allowing your child to be alone sometimes versus abandonment.

MONTHS 4 TO 8
As months 3 to 4 blend into months 4 to 8, behaviour does not change sharply. But none the less, a distinct shift occurs at about age 4 months. Increased sociability permits more playfulness and game-like interactions between you and your infant. Your child may roll over, sit well, imitate your voice with babbling, or respond quickly to your quiet sounds. This increased social interaction certainly makes having a baby more fun.

Warning: The Empty Vessel Myth
Your baby is not like an empty vessel that you can fill with love, warmth, hugs, kisses, and soothing until it is full, thus leading to satisfaction, blissful contentment or undemanding repose.

Infants really do enjoy your company, they thrive in response to your laughter and smiles. The more you entertain them, the more they want to be amused. So it is natural and reasonable to expect your baby to protest when you stop playing with her. In fact, the more you play with your child, the more they will come to expect that this is the natural order of things. Nothing is wrong with this, except that there are times when you have to dress your baby or leave her alone and she might resist the partial restraint or curtailment of fun and games. Or you might have to dress yourself!

Leaving your baby alone protesting for more fun with you while you get dressed is not the same thing as abandonment.

Leaving your baby alone protesting for more fun when your baby needs to sleep is not neglect. You have become sensitive to your child's need to sleep, and she is now old enough to set her clock at a healthy sleep time. Our goal is to synchronize our caretaking activities with her needs: her need to be fed, to be kept warm, to be played with, and her need to sleep.

Figure 11

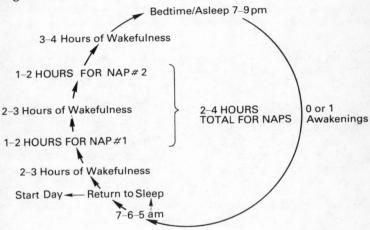

TEACH YOUR BABY TO SLEEP OR PROTECT HER SLEEP SCHEDULE

Let's look at how to teach your child to sleep well and to protect a naturally developed healthy sleep pattern. As discussed previously, the four elements of healthy sleep are: (1) the duration of night sleep, (2) the schedule of night sleep or the time when sleep begins, (3) consolidated versus fragmented sleep, and (4) naps (see Figure 11).

The wake-up time   Babies tend either to wake up early, at 5 to 6 am, and after a brief feeding or nappy change, return to sleep. This is a continuation of night sleep, not a nap. Or, babies wake up later to start the day. The wake-up time seems to be a neurological alarm clock in these young infants that is somewhat independent of that part of the brain which puts them to sleep or keeps them asleep.

Warning

You cannot change the wake-up time by:

1. Keeping your baby up later.
2. Feeding solids before bedtime.
3. Awakening your baby for a feed before you go to sleep.

Item number 3 seems insensitive anyway – how would you feel if someone woke you from a deep sleep and started to feed you when you were not hungry?

Morning wakeful time Focus now on the intervals of wakefulness. After about 2 hours for 4-month-olds or 3 hours for 8-month-olds, put your baby down in her cot for a mid-morning nap. Plan a wind-down or nap-time ritual of up to 30 minutes. You decide what you want to do; bath, bottle, breastfeed, lullaby, massage . . . but limit it. Hours of holding your baby only produce a light or twilight sleep state, which is poor quality sleep. At the end of your pre-determined nap-time ritual, whether your baby is asleep or awake, put her in her cot. She may now cry a little, a lot, or none at all.

Liberate Yourself

'I cannot tell you what a *liberating experience* it was to be able to put my baby down in her cot before she fell asleep in my arms.'

She may now cry a little, a lot, or none at all.

The temperamentally easy child cries very little and the routine is repeated for an early afternoon nap.

The temperamentally more difficult child, who may have also been a very fussy or colicky infant, might now cry a lot. The premature baby may cry a lot also, and the following approach might be delayed until 4 months after the expected date of delivery.

Mid-morning nap We will consider a sleep period to be a restorative nap if it is about an hour or longer. Maybe 40 to 45 minutes is sometimes enough, but most babies in this age range sleep at least a solid hour. Certainly sleep periods under 30 minutes should not count as naps.

Once you have determined that your baby is going to take a nap, and you are enforcing a nap-time, then leave your baby completely alone to allow your baby to: (1) learn to fall asleep unassisted, and (2) return to sleep unassisted until she has slept about an hour in an uninterrupted fashion.

You are responding sensitively to her need to sleep by not providing too much attention. You are decisive in establishing a routine, because you are upholding her right to sleep. Be calm and firm.

Important Point
Consistency promotes *rapid* learning.

Your baby will pick up on your calm/firm attitude and by ignoring her protest for the pleasure of your company, she will learn quickly not to expect it *at this nap-time*. You are not abandoning your child in her moment of need; you give her all the attention she needs when she is *awake*. But now, she needs to be alone to sleep,

Naturally she will protest and cry.

Q: How long do I let my baby cry?
A: Until she sleeps uninterruptedly for about an hour.

Q: Even if she cries for 1 or 2 hours?
A: Yes, even 3 or 4 hours.

Q: Even if she cries through her usual midday meal?
A: Yes.

Q: What's wrong if I quickly check my baby when she first cries and I give her her dummy or roll her back to her stomach? She always immediately stops crying and returns to sleep.
A: 'Checking' for soothing at about 4 months of age may not interfere with naps or night sleep in some infants. But please be careful, because eventually all babies learn to turn these brief visits into prolonged playtimes. This learning process may develop slower if it is the fathers who do the checking and provide minimal intervention.

Midday wakeful time Expect your baby to be ready for another nap after 2 or 3 hours of wakefulness. In general, avoid long excursions which might lead to mini-snoozes in the car or park.

Early afternoon nap This nap should usually begin before 3 pm. Please remember, this is an outline of a reasonable, healthy sleep pattern. Not a set of rigid rules to blindly enforce. There is nothing magic about 3 pm or any other time in this sleep schedule. You'll have to make some adjustments to fit your own individual lifestyle and family arrangements.

If the duration of crying and sleeping associated with the mid-morning nap puts you way past 3 pm or if your child has prolonged crying starting before 3 pm at the onset of the early afternoon nap and is continuing well past 3 pm, then to get things going, forget this nap. And put your baby down for the night early at 5, 6 or 7 pm.

If your baby naps well in the afternoon, again it should be about an hour or more, then go out afterwards and enjoy this longer afternoon period of wakefulness.

Healthy Sleep Rule
Never wake a sleeping baby!

Afternoon wakeful time This is the time to go on longer excursions, errands, or shopping trips. Many mothers will give their baby solid foods during this time. Exercise classes and outings to the park may be longer during this wakeful period.

Q: How long should my child nap?
A: You should ask yourself, does my child appear tired?

If your baby is tired late in the afternoon or early in the evening, this *might* indicate insufficient naps. A possible solution is simply to put your child to bed earlier at night. Keeping a baby up past her time of tiredness produces fatigue, lost sleep, and sleep deprivation, and will ultimately lead to resisting falling asleep or night waking. This may be especially a problem when a working parent or parents come home late, feeling guilty about being away from the family so long. Once the baby is 6 months or older it would be a mistake to encourage a third, brief nap around 5, 6, or 7 pm, as all that happens is that the baby's energies are recharged so she is better able to fight off night-time drowsiness. The bedtime hour then starts to migrate closer and closer to midnight. This leads to an abnormal sleep schedule, and the result is the equivalent of sleep deprivation.

Warning
One parent who persists in keeping the baby up past the child's natural time to sleep may be using this 'play time' with the child to avoid unpleasant 'private time' with the other parent.

Bedtime/asleep Remember, you are establishing an orderly home routine and enforcing a bedtime hour. You are not forcing your child to sleep. When your child seems tired and needs to sleep, you will establish her bedtime routine . . . whether she likes it or not. This may be the first time, but it is certainly not the last time you will ignore your child's protests. At some future time you will teach other health habits, such as hand-washing or tooth-brushing. You will protect her physical safety by not allowing unreasonable risks involving playground equipment. You won't let his protest crying discourage you if you know he might fall from too high a jungle gym. You will not overly shield him, you cannot protect him from all dangers. You cannot expect him to never be alone.

Now is the time to let him learn to fall asleep at night by himself and return to sleep at night, and to learn that being alone at night in slumber is not scary, dangerous, or something to avoid. Keep everything calm and not too complicated as you go through a bedtime ritual. Fathers should be involved, because babies now know that they cannot feed them and any protest crying is likely to be less intense or shorter.

Once down, down is down. No matter how long she cries, please do not return, until your baby falls asleep. Little peeks or replacing dummies might sabotage your efforts, because partial reinforcement has enormous teaching power.

Important Point

1. When the duration of protest crying is open-ended, not limited, learning to fall asleep unassisted takes place.

2. When you put a time limit on how much protest crying you can tolerate or accept before going to the baby, you teach the baby to cry to that time limit.

Overnight In this age range, many babies accept naps without protest and fall asleep at night without difficulty. These easy babies still might waken once in the middle of the night. I consider this behaviour normal, natural, and not worthy of change, as long as it's only a brief event and not a prolonged playtime.

Choose the one time when you'll go to feed your baby and change his nappy and don't go at any other time. (Please review the earlier discussion on 'arousals' in the first chapter, if you are puzzled why babies sometimes get up frequently throughout the night.)

Remember
You are harming your child when you allow unhealthy sleep patterns to evolve or persist – it's as unhealthy as feeding an unbalanced diet.

GENERAL COMMENTS

Most mothers will partially synchronize feedings to sleep patterns, so that the child is fed around the time he gets up in the morning, around the time (before or after) the two naps, around bedtime, and one other time. In other words, bottles or breastfeedings now occur 4 to 5 times per 24 hours. Frequent sips, snacks, or little feedings throughout the day are not necessary. Gradually your child will begin to learn to associate certain behaviours on your part with certain times of the day, in certain places and his sensation of tiredness with falling asleep. This learning process, when started at about 3 to 4 months of age, usually takes only about three days.

Stranger-wariness or stranger-anxiety may be present in

some babies by about 6 months of age and with this new behaviour, some mothers even note some separation anxiety. The child shows distress when her mother leaves her. I do not think this occurrence of separation anxiety in the child directly causes more difficulty for the baby to fall asleep unassisted. I have observed that these babies learn to sleep well as rapidly as any other babies when their mothers leave them alone at sleep times. The problem is that some mothers also suffer from the thought of separation and will not leave their children alone enough at sleep times to allow healthy sleep habits to develop. (This will be discussed further in the chapter by Patricia Della-Selva see pp. 190–204.)

A major problem in implementing this sleep schedule is that it is *inconvenient*. Many mothers resent the fact that their babies are less portable. It is inconvenient to change your lifestyle and be at home twice a day so that your baby can nap. When parents initially suffer through but accept inconvenience and build up a large sleep reserve by keeping their child well rested, irregularities and special occasions which disrupt sleep usually produce only minor and transient disturbed sleep. The recovery time is brief and the child responds to a prompt re-establishment of the routine.

When parents are unwilling to alter their lifestyle so that regular naps are never well maintained, then the child always pays a price. The child's mood and learning suffer, and recovery times following outings or illnesses take much longer. These parents often try many 'helpful hints' to help their child sleep better. I'm not sure any or all of these types of items can ever substitute for maintaining regular sleep schedules. Parents in my practice who have utilized regular sleep schedules have rarely, if ever, found these items to be useful.

Bureau of 'helpful' hints of dubious value
to soothe baby to sleep
Lamb's wool skins
Heart-beat sounds
Womb sounds
Elevate head of cot
Maintain motion sleep in swings
Continuous background noises

Change formulas or eliminate iron supplement
Change diet of nursing mother
Feed solids only at bedtime

Summary

Babies seem to respond quickly at this age to a somewhat scheduled, structured approach to sleep. If you can learn to detach yourself from their protest crying and not respond reflexively by rushing in to her at the slightest whimper, she will learn to fall asleep by herself. For one mother who had managed to do this, the benefits for mother and child were captured in her remark, 'She now goes down like warm butter on toast!'

MONTHS 9 TO 14

Strong-willed, wilful, independent-minded, stubborn, head-strong, uncooperative. Sound familiar? These are often the words parents use to describe their toddlers. You may observe that your child is simply less cooperative. A psychologist might use the term 'noncompliant' to describe this lack of cooperation, but the psychologist would also point out that these behaviours go hand-in-hand with the normal, healthy evolution of the child's autonomy or sense of independence. Usually, the experts tell us, the times when you should expect the most difficulties or so-called 'oppositional-behaviours' are at dressing, mealtimes, in public places, and at bedtimes. Since this is the beginning of the 'stage' of autonomy (noncompliance), some experts claim that it is natural for this *independence/stubbornness* to cause resistance in going to sleep or to cause the appearance of night wakings. I will explain later why I think this 'stage' theory is an incorrect interpretation.

Children in this age-range also often develop behaviours described as social hesitation, shyness or fear of strangers. They also might cry or appear in distress when their mother leaves them alone in one room as she goes to another room or upon leaving the child with a babysitter. Psychologists call this behaviour 'stranger-wariness', 'stranger-anxiety' or 'separation-anxiety'. So if a child developed increased resistance in going to sleep at night at this 'stage', some experts might say that the 'separation-anxiety' or *fear* of being apart or away from mother was the direct cause. I also think that this is an incorrect interpretation.

NAP DEPRIVATION

When parents have invested their efforts to build up a reservoir of good quality sleep, occasional disruptions due to illnesses, trips, parties, or holiday visits cause only minor disruptions of sleep. These children require only brief recovery periods before getting back on form. But when parents allow poor quality sleep patterns to emerge and persist, then there is a gradual accumulation of significant sleep deficits. Now even minor disturbances create long-lasting havoc.

Nap deprivation seems to be the major culprit, in this age range, in ruining healthy sleep patterns. Look, it's only natural that you want to get out more and do more things with your child. And, oh, what a kid he is! Full of new social charms, so cheerful, and walking now . . . why not stay out together and enjoy the good weather at the park or beach? It's your first summer together. Who wants to stay indoors anyway on such a gorgeous day?

But as naps slip and slide, a trend of increasing fatigue develops. First, she develops a little more crabbiness, irritability, fussiness, maybe only in the late afternoon or early evening. You might think it's normal for children this age to be easily frustrated or sometimes bored. Then she starts to get up at night for the first time ever, 'for no reason'. Later, maybe following a cold or day-long visit with grandparents, she starts fighting going to sleep at night and you wonder why night sleep is a new problem in your house.

When you re-establish the healthy regular nap routines, the night sleep problem corrects itself. I have seen this over and over again. Although noncompliant behaviours still exist and although separation-anxiety is unchanged, the night sleep problem corrects itself when nap routines are restored. That's why I think nap deprivation (which causes fatigue, in turn causing increased alertness/wakefulness/arousal) is the culprit behind disturbed night sleep, not a particular 'stage'.

Reminder

Boredom may be masked tiredness. If your baby's motor
is idling and she's not going anywhere, maybe she's just
tired.

Normal naps

You may think that your baby now only needs one nap, but
most babies really do need two naps in this age range. One
clue that some mothers have noticed is that their babysitter
can 'get two good naps', but 'I can get only one or none'. The
child is obviously more rested after the sitter leaves and the
mother wonders how the sitter 'does it'. Well, children are
very discriminating at this age. They know that the sitter,
following parents' instructions has a no-nonsense approach
and will put them to sleep on a fairly regular schedule. But,
with Mum, maybe if I protest long or loudly enough, maybe
she'll come and we'll go out to play. After all, sometimes it
works.

As long as your child retains the expectation that you will
come to her and take her out of her boring, quiet room, she
will fight naps.

Routines that comfort your baby include rocking, soft
lullabies, stroking, patting or cuddling; maintain these routines so that your child learns to associate certain behaviours
occurring at certain times in a familiar place with the
behaviour called 'falling asleep'.

Helpful Hints for Comforting

Soft, silky, furry textured blankets, dolls, or stuffed
   animals in the cot
A small soft blanket over forehead or placed in the hand
Dim night light
Breastfeed to sleep

Nurse to sleep?

There is nothing wrong with letting your baby suck herself to
sleep, when there is no sleep problem. Most breastfeeding
mothers in my practice do this all the time. If you have
difficulty in letting your child ever learn to fall asleep

unassisted so that your child always falls asleep at the breast, and your child has disturbed sleep, then breastfeeding to sleep might be a part of the sleep problem. It may reflect the kind of separation problems discussed in the chapter by Patricia Della-Selva (see pp. 190–204).

But most mothers breastfeed their babies for soothing and comfort, and they either fall asleep at the breast or they don't. In either case they are put in their cots when they *need* to sleep and sleep comes. I think that this intimacy between mother and infant is beautiful, and in itself, breastfeeding to sleep does not cause sleep problems.

Q: Do I roll my child over to her favourite sleeping position when she wakes up? Do I help her get down when she stands up and shakes the cot's railings?

A: Do you like playing these games with your child at night? What do you think you teach her when you go to her at night to roll her over or help her down?

Q: Won't she hurt herself if she falls down in her cot? She can't get down by herself.

A: No.

Try to be reasonably regular by watching the intervals of wakefulness, not necessarily by watching clock time. For example, try not to get locked into a fixed or traditional bedtime hour but vary the bedtime hour depending on duration of naps, when the second nap ended and indoor versus outdoor activities. Often the 9- to 14-month-old needs to go to bed earlier because of increased physical activity in the afternoon.

When you are somewhat organized, planned, or programmed regarding sleep schedules, sleep is accepted and expected. But don't feel you have to be this way for feeding or other infant-care practices! When mothers are creative, free-spirited, and permissive regarding solid – but wholesome – foods, feeding goes well. So try to cultivate opposite attitudes: restrictive for sleep, permissive for feeding solids.

MONTHS 15 TO 23

During this age-range, you can expect your child's schedule to be reduced from two naps a day to only one. This transition, however, may not be smooth. You might have a few rough months when one nap is not enough, but two are impossible. Here are some tips to consider making the transition easier:

Schedule a single nap, accept some tired behaviour in the afternoon and put your child to bed earlier that night.

Declare some days as two-nap days and other days as one-nap days depending on when she awakens, how long the morning nap lasts, scheduled group activities, or the time you want your baby to go to sleep at night. Flow with your baby and arrange naps and bedtimes to coincide with baby's need to sleep as best you can.

Obviously, any combination of parents' scheduling for their convenience and baby's need to sleep can determine nap patterns. If you are a napper yourself, you may protect your child's nap schedule differently from another parent who does not customarily take naps.

Q: How long should my child nap?
A: Does your child appear well rested? You be the judge.

All of us have good days and bad days, but if you notice a progression towards more fussiness, brattiness, tantrums, ask yourself, is my child also tired?

FEARS

Nightmares, monsters, fear of separation, fear of darkness, fear of death, fear of abandonment . . . don't fears at this age cause disturbed sleep? By age 2, 3, or 4, many experts tell us that night fears are common. Thunder-storms, barking dogs, lightning flashes, and many other events over which we have no control might frighten our children. If your child has been a good sleeper up to now, you should expect any disturbed sleep triggered by these events to be short-lived.

Reassurance, frequent curtain calls, doors open, night lights or a longer bedtime routine will help your child get over these fears. Some child-care experts believe severe sleep disturbances are caused by night fears. Usually though, these children had never slept well at younger ages and their current sleep problem is simply misinterpreted as directly caused by an age-appropriate 'stage'. Don't worry . . .

If your child has been a good sleeper up to now, the disturbances related to fearful events will be brief and infrequent.

ROUTINES AND SCHEDULES

At about 2 years of age, most children go to sleep between 7 and 9 pm and awake between 6.30 and 8 am. A single nap between 1 and 3 hours occurs in over 70 per cent of children. Try to be *reasonably* regular according to when your child is tired or clock times with nap-time and bedtime routines, and consistent in your behaviours for bedtime rituals. There are no absolute, rigid, or firm rules, because every day is somewhat different. *Reasonable* regularity and consistency implies *reasonable* flexibility. Be aware of how your lifestyle helps or hinders your child's sleep patterns. As natural as seasons change or tides rise and fall, there will be changes due to growth and rearrangements in relationships within your family.

REGULAR BED

One rearrangement is moving your child to a 'big kid's' bed. There is no special age when you should make this change. As long as the cot is large enough, you should not feel that she must be placed in a regular bed by a certain age. Many parents will do this around the second birthday.

If the move to a regular bed is associated with frequent nocturnal visits, curtain calls, calls to help to go to the bathroom, or calls for a drink of water . . . think before you act. A habit may slowly develop so that she learns to expect you to spend more time with her putting her to sleep or returning her to sleep.

Imagine what would occur if a babysitter gave your 2-year-old sweets every day instead of a real lunch? You discover your child might protest and cry, but do you give in and give the expected sweets? No. If you are spending too much time at night when she should be sleeping, consider what you are doing to be 'social sweets' – not needed and not healthy for your child. Be firm in your resolve to ignore the expected protest from your child when you change your behaviour.

Remember
Don't confuse these issues:
Needs versus wants
A sad cry versus a protest cry
Being abandoned versus being alone

YEARS 2 TO 6

Between 2 and 6 years of age, most children still go to sleep between 7 and 9 pm and awaken between 6.30 and 8 am. Naps gradually decrease in duration and few children are still napping after 5 years. Sleep problems and disturbed sleep usually do not develop in those children who previously had been good sleepers.

The major problem occurs when parents push their children too soon into pre-school, nursery school, or other scheduled activities. They are overprogrammed, and naps get scheduled out before the child is ready.

Remember
A missed nap is sleep lost forever

With increased mental and physical stimulation, some parents provide partial compensation by shifting the bedtime to an earlier hour. Working parents may not accept this solution, because it shortchanges their playtime with their children. When you sign up your child for courses, classes, or activities, another solution to prevent sleep deficits is to simply enforce a policy of declared holidays: once or twice a week he stays home and naps. Or he engages in more unstructured, low intensity, quieter activities.

YEARS 7 TO 12

School-aged children are sleeping less as the bedtime hour gradually is shifted to later hours. Most 12-year-old children go to sleep around 9 pm; the range is about 7.30 to 10 pm. The range for total sleep duration for most 12-year-old children is about 9 to 12 hours. This data, from a large survey of middle-class families I performed a few years ago, and the data from an ongoing study at Stanford University are in close agreement. Researchers there have shown that the prepubertal teenager needs 9½ to 10 hours to maintain optimal alertness during the day.

Warning
As your preteen grows older, he will need *more* sleep,
not less to maintain optimal alertness.

If healthy sleep habits are not maintained, the result is increasingly severe daytime sleepiness.

RECURRENT COMPLAINTS

Many children in this age range complain of aches and pains for which no medical cause can be found: abdominal pains, limb pains, recurrent headaches, and chest pains. Children who suffer from these pains often have significant sleep disturbances. Stressful emotional situations thought to cause these complaints include real or imagined separation of or from parents, fear of expressing anger that might elicit punishment or rejection, school, social, or academic pressures, or fear of failure to live up to parents' expectations.

These are real pains in our children, just as our tension headaches are real pain. When we work too hard or sleep too little we might have ordinary tension headaches. All laboratory tests or studies during these episodes of tension headache will be normal. So will all the tests be normal in our children who have similar somatic complaints. Performing laboratory tests should be discouraged, unless there is a strong clinical sign pointing toward organic disease. The reasons that tests, to 'rule-out' obscure diseases, should be avoided is because of the pain of drawing blood, irradiation, expense and most importantly the possible result of creating in the child's mind the notion that he is really sick – otherwise, why would my parents and doctor subject me to so many tests or examinations? Also, a slightly abnormal test result, not indicating pathology but just a little too high or too low, might lead to more and more tests . . . all of which in the end turn out to show basically normal results.

HOW TO HANDLE COMMON DISRUPTIONS TO HEALTHY SLEEP PATTERNS
There are, inevitably, events which might significantly disrupt your child's healthy sleep habits. Here are some examples.

MOVING

The only thing worse than moving is moving with children. You pack, they unpack. You clean up, they make a mess. You are harassed; the children upset. However, your general goal at such a time should be to maintain as regular and consistent a pattern as reasonably possible for the children, both before and following a move to minimize the disruption from the children's point of view. If your child is young, say under a year of age, quickly re-establish the bedtime rituals and sleep patterns that worked best before the move. Be firm and after a day or two for adjustment to the new surroundings, ignore any protest crying which may have evolved from the irregularity and inconsistency during the move.

If your child is older, say a few years, go slower. Fears of newness, excitement over novelty, uncertainty regarding further changes may create resistance with naps, difficulty falling asleep at night, or night waking as new problems. Be gentle, firm, and decisive. Reassurance, extra time at night, night lights, and doors open may have a calming or soothing effect. Be somewhat consistent in controlling this extra comfort so that the child does not learn that it is completely open-ended. For the older child, consider using a kitchen timer to control the amount of 'extra' time you are going to spend with him. The timer helps the child to learn to expect that mum or dad will leave for the night after a *predictable* time period. Anxiety or fear in this child regarding the move is natural, normal and not something which should unduly alarm you. After several days, start a deliberate social weaning process to encourage a return to your old, healthy sleep habits. Gradually reduce the duration on the timer. This should usually take no longer than several days in most instances.

HOLIDAYS

Think of a holiday with your child as only a sort of semi-holiday. After all, you may spend a lot of time babysitting among the palms and on sun-drenched beaches. I have spent many hours building simple sand castles, watching one non-swimmer helping on the castle architecture with one eye and watching another non-swimmer jump over small waves with the other eye. This intense concentration is not very relaxing!

Try to flow with your child, be flexible if you want to, forget schedules, try to have as much fun as possible and don't worry much if your kids become tired. Irregularity and spontaneity are part of what make holidays fun.

But when you return home, you know – back to the basics; it's home camp again with all the regular routines. Within a few days, if you are firm, consistent, and regular . . . they will learn quickly that the holiday is over. If your child had been well rested prior to this holiday, expect only one rough, crazy recovery day of protest crying. Trying to gradually soothe your child back to her previous good sleep routine over several days often fails because the child fights sleep for the pleasure of your soothing efforts.

FREQUENT ILLNESSES

Night wakings routinely follow frequent illnesses. First, let's have a clear understanding of what is happening. Videotapes of healthy young children in their homes at night show that many awakenings occur throughout the night, but the children usually return to sleep without help. Fever can alter sleep patterns and can cause light sleep or more frequent awakenings. So it is not surprising that a painful illness with fever, such as an ear infection, causes an increased number of night wakings. These more frequent and prolonged arousals often require your intervention to soothe or calm the child back to sleep. Your child might now begin to associate your hugging, kissing, or holding at night with returning to sleep. This learning process might then produce an alteration in the child's behaviour or expectations that continues long after the infection passes. Now we have a problem; usually it's called 'night waking'.

Actually, waking at night is *not* the problem. As we have seen, spontaneous awakenings are normal, as are increased awakenings with fever. Naturally, parents should go to their sick children at night. The real problem now is the child's learned inability or difficulty in returning to sleep unassisted, when the child is healthy and not bothered by pain or fever.

You should view this development as an unhealthy habit. Now you know that prolonged and uninterrupted sleep is as health-promoting a habit as are other health habits, such as teeth-brushing or hand-washing. How can you now reteach your child to develop her own resources to return to sleep after awakening? Remember, parents are teachers and we teach health habits, even if the child might not initially cooperate or appreciate our efforts. Here are three options:

Option One You might decide that since the child is frequently ill and you can't let him down when he needs you, you will always respond and wait for the child to 'outgrow' this habit. The problem with this option is that the awakenings initially tend to become more frequent, because your child learns to enjoy your company at night. After all, who wants to be alone in a boring, dark, quiet room in the middle of the night? Eventually, months or years later, the child sleeps through the night and the parents can congratulate themselves for always having attended to their child's crying at night. You have, however, paid a price. Parents following this course of action often become sleep deprived, chronically fatigued, and occasionally feel resentful towards the child for not appreciating your dedicated efforts. Additionally, the sleep fragmentation and sleep deprivation in the child often produce a more irritable, aroused, agitated, hyperexcitable behaviour in the child, *because the child is always fighting chronic fatigue and drowsiness*.

Option Two You might try to go to your child at night only when he is really sick and to leave the child alone at night when he is healthy. This is a hazardous strategy that often fails, because you are often uncertain whether frequent illness represents painful, serious problems or minor common colds. After all, at 7 pm you might decide that your child has only a minor common cold and that you are going to ignore his crying, but by 2 am you begin to worry about the possibility of an ear infection. Is it still reasonable to ignore the crying? What usually occurs is intermittent reinforcement: you sometimes go to your child and sometimes you do not. This behaviour generally teaches your child to cry longer and louder when he awakens at night, because the child learns that only loud and persistent crying will bring his parents. Quiet or brief crying often fails to get the parents' attention.

Option Three Enlist the help of your doctor so you can achieve a clearer distinction between non-serious common colds and more distressing or disturbing illnesses. Generally speaking, the child's playfulness, sociability, activity and appetite during the day are good clues; common colds do not cause much change in your child's behaviour when awake. Then, in a planned and deliberate fashion, your child is left alone more and more at night, so that he learns to return to sleep without your help. When an acute illness develops that is associated with high fever or severe pain, of course, do that which most comforts the child, both night and day. But when the acute phase of this illness is over, start again to give the child less and less attention at night. Remember, most children sleep through most common colds and with your doctor's help, you can learn to distinguish between habit crying occurring with a common cold and more painful crying associated with a serious and painful, acute infection.

MOTHER'S RETURN TO WORK

Some adults develop a sensitivity to children's needs and appreciate the benefits of regularity, consistency and structure in child-care activities. And some do not. The quality of the caretaker is what is important. Not whether it is or is not the biological parent.

Do not assume that when the mother returns to work outside the home, your child will automatically suffer in the quality of her sleep habits. Keep data, track the schedule of naps when cared for by someone else, watch for signs of tiredness in the early evening that might suggest nap deprivation, and become aware of your own feelings.

Please don't let your need to be with the baby because you have been away during the day cause you to keep your child up too late, to reinforce night wakings for sweet nocturnal private-time with your baby, to cause nap deprivation at weekends when you cram in too many activities. Please don't let household errands, chores, or non-essential social events rob you and your child of unstructured, low intensity playtime.

Practical Point

To help your child sleep better during natural changes such as holidays, moves, or your return to work, try to build an environment of familiarity by using certain cues *only* for sleeping:

The same bumper pads
The same music box
The same stuffed animal or blanket
A lamb's wool blanket
A spray of perfume

The child will then learn to associate these sensations with falling asleep and this will help reduce the disruptive effect of the novelty of the new surroundings. None of these items will work in the absence of regularity and consistency of parent-care.

Summary

As we have seen, different ages during childhood carry with them predictable, characteristic changes. But many unpredictable events occur, too. Don't assume that your child will necessarily reach a 'stage' during which he will not sleep well. Don't assume that some disruptive event necessarily will cause permanent or enduring disturbed sleep. Parents who say that 'all terrible twos fight sleep' or attribute teething pains, the arrival of a new baby, or moving as the cause of longstanding sleep problems are only making excuses. If you are a parent of a child with unhealthy sleep, the next chapter will help you correct the problem.

8 Return to Peaceful Nights: Correcting Unhealthy Sleep Habits

So far we've learned about healthy sleep and unhealthy sleep. Now it's time to discover how to help your child get a better night's sleep. If you've just turned to this section to read through the 'how-to's, though, please stop. Go back to the beginning of the book, because:

1. If you understand the difference between healthy sleep and unhealthy sleep, you'll be better able to determine: (a) whether there's a problem with your child's sleeping or with your preconceptions about how a child should sleep, and (b) what are reasonable, age-appropriate goals to try to reach.

2. If you determine that a part of the problem includes *parental mismanagement*, then the treatment or changes I suggest will be more palatable to you. Changes in home routines, especially involving non-sleepers, often bring forth feelings of uncertainty, guilt, or fear that your child will reject you. We don't want these feelings to prevent you from helping your child to learn to sleep better.

This chapter will start with early infancy and examine sleep problems at different ages. Sleep disturbances often involve combinations of problems, such as too little sleep at night, irregular or too brief naps, fragmented sleep or waking up at night, or abnormal sleep schedules. Treatment strategies that are aimed at correcting only one problem area while ignoring others usually fail, because the child remains overtired. So we need to attack sleep problems on all fronts.

Remember
Fatigue is the main enemy.

THE FIRST 3 TO 4 MONTHS

Every baby behaves differently during these first few months. Your own baby most likely will fall somewhere in between these two extremes.

EARLY BLOOMERS . . . WHO FADE FAST

These are placid, easy-to-manage infants who are quiet angels during most nights. Sure, they may have a fussy period in the evening, but it's not too long, intense, or hard to deal with. They appear to sleep well anywhere and anytime during the day, and quite regularly at night. In fact, the *early* development of regular, long night sleep periods – starting well before age 6 weeks – is a characteristic feature. These kids are very portable and parents bask in their sunny dispositions, particularly when social smiling begins at about the 6-week mark.

But shortly, dark clouds may gather. The baby starts to have some new grumbling or crabbiness that does not occur only in the evening, like the classic 'sundown' syndrome. In fact, the quiet evenings might now be punctured by new, 'painful' cries suggesting an illness. Or it might now take longer than before to put him asleep. What has happened to your sound sleeping baby?

Answer: Irregularity of sleep schedules, nap deprivation, a failure to become sensitive to your child's need to sleep.

Remember
It may sound like a 'Catch-22', but the more rested your child is, the more she will accept sleep and expect to sleep.

After about 6 weeks of age, the best strategy is to try to synchronize your caretaking activities with your baby's own rhythms. You should try to re-establish healthy sleep habits by removing the disruptive effects of external noises, lights, or vibrations. Although it may be inconvenient for you, try to have your baby home in her cot after *about 2 hours* of wakefulness. Consider this 2-hour interval of wakefulness to be a rough guide to help organize the day into naps and wakeful activities.

Be careful, But . . .
No set schedules
No rigid rules

Expect your tired child to protest when you put her down to sleep. This is natural, because she prefers the pleasure of your soothing comfort to being in a dark, quiet, boring room.

Keep in mind the distinction between a protest cry and a sad cry. You are leaving her alone to let her learn to soothe herself to sleep – you are not abandoning her.

Here's a very common question at this stage:

Q: How long should I let her cry?
A: Start with 5, 10 or 20 minutes. Try to make a decision whether your child is tired based on: (1) your child's behaviour, (2) the time of day, and (3) the interval of wakefulness – how long she has been up.

When you have decided she is tired, put her down to sleep – even if she doesn't want to sleep. Sometimes she'll fall asleep and sometimes she won't. When she doesn't, pick her up, soothe and comfort her and then at some future time, try it again. You may try it again after several minutes or you may decide not to try this again for several days.

Remember, this baby had once been a good sleeper and now is fighting sleep for the pleasure of your company. At those times when she needs to sleep, but wants to play with you, your playing with her is robbing her of sleep.

Keep a log or diary as you go through these trials to see if any trend of improvement occurs. Here's one account from a mother of a 12-week-old:

'To leave a baby crying and not pick her up goes against human nature. However, after three days of teaching her to sleep, and having to listen to her crying and being helpless – her hysteria was almost completely solved!

'It started at just 12 weeks – she was so fatigued, she would cry for hours -- screaming completely out of control, scratching her head, pulling her ears. Holding her didn't help, so it wasn't hard not to pick her up -- she screamed anyway.

'Instituting a new day schedule was easy -- *as soon as* she started getting cranky, I *rushed* her to her cot for a sleep. She would watch her mobile, and then sleep for *hours* at a time. The first week she was so tired, that she only stayed up 30 to 50 minutes at a time and slept 3 to 4 hours in between. The key for me was to get her down before she got *really* upset.

'The afternoon was when she was awake the longest, and then it was hard getting her to sleep at night. The first few nights under our new régime were the worst. Positive reinforcement from my doctor was important then. I had to hear several times that this "cure" was the best thing to do.

'The first night under our new strategy, my husband laid down on the floor in her room (I guess to make sure she didn't choke), while I sat crying in our living room. Finally, after *45 minutes* she was *quiet!* Hurray! Each night she cried less and less, and I handled it better and better. After a week, hysteria was gone! Sure she cried, a little, sometimes, but now she was on a schedule. She napped two or three times a day, 2 to 4 hours at a time, and slept 12 to 15 hours a night. Sleeping promotes more sleep, and makes it easier to fall asleep. It's a "Catch-22".

'Also writing down the sleep patterns helped, too. For one week, I kept track of every time I put her down and every time I picked her up from her nap. At the end of the week, I noticed a distinct pattern. She fell into it herself!'

COLICKY INFANTS

The other 'extreme' in behaviour for babies up to 3 or 4 months of age are colicky infants. As we have seen, these are intense, difficult-to-manage infants who tend to be very wakeful during the day, irregular when they do sleep, or stimulus-sensitive. Because of their irregularity and alert–aroused state, it doesn't make sense to try to schedule their sleep. They are hard to read. Most parents have difficulty telling whether they are hungry, fussy, or plain tired. So leaving them alone is confusing to everyone. I have already discussed the best ways of handling such babies earlier in the book, so see pp. 58–9.

FROM 4 MONTHS TO THE FIRST BIRTHDAY

Children are now very sociable and are well aware of the effect that their behaviours have on us. Don't *underestimate* their competence and ability to learn at these early months!

The key to correcting sleep problems during this age is to establish and maintain the sleep patterns discussed in the previous chapter for children 4 to 8 months of age (see pp. 122–30). That pattern does not change much up to age 12 months, so you can use it as your goal or guide up to her first birthday.

The major sleep problems between 4 to 12 months develop and persist, because of the inability of parents to remove themselves as reinforcers of bad sleep habits. Some parents don't see themselves as interfering with an important learning process in their child, namely learning how to soothe themselves to sleep unassisted. The failure of our children to develop their own resources to fall asleep, and stay asleep, by themselves is the direct result of some parents' failure to give their child the opportunity to learn self-soothing skills. In other words, some parents can't leave their kids alone long enough for them to fall asleep by themselves.

LOCUS OF CONTROL

When your baby was younger, she slept when she needed to. She controlled your relationship with her, in the sense that you met her *needs* whether you wanted to or not. You didn't let her go hungry simply because you didn't want to feed her. You didn't let her stay wet because you didn't want to change her. Her needs controlled your behaviour.

But from now on, a shift should occur so that *you* are in charge. For example, when she is older, you may decide not to provide food simply because she wants it. You will not risk her physical safety by letting her climb too high on a tree simply because she wants to. And you will not let her stay up to play when she needs to sleep. What then are we to do when our child does not cooperate, and cries because she does not *want* to go to sleep when she *needs* to sleep?

There is disagreement among those who write for the popular 'baby' magazines. Some reports describe what happens when children cry who are left alone at night to sleep:

He fails to learn the basic trust or confidence he needs to feel secure in his new world. He will not develop a strong sense of security. You teach the child he has no control over what happens if his cries go unanswered. It gives him the feeling that there's nobody out there who cares. He may become a passive, ineffective person or he may become angry or hostile. There is no such thing as too little sleep for your baby. He will get as much sleep as his body requires.

Other articles in these and similar magazines say:

Get an early start. Down is down. It is not hard-hearted. We all benefit when we are all well-rested. If you want to get uninterrupted sleep for your baby, you will need to let your child cry.

As one of the leading journalists in this field wrote, after her third child:

The trick was that after eight years of parenthood, my husband and I have discovered . . . [that] the first sound does not mean that a baby needs to be picked up immediately.

Warning
Please don't wait eight years to learn what experts have long ago discovered.

'LET CRY', AN AGREEMENT OF 'EXPERT' OPINIONS

While the popular press may give all types of conflicting advice from a variety of sources, expert opinion is solidly together. In fact, all evidence accumulated by a wide array of child health specialists concludes that 'protest' crying at bedtime will not cause permanent emotional or psychological problems. In plain fact, the contrary is true. For example, Dr D. W. Winnicott, a leading paediatrician and child psychiatrist, emphasizes that the *capacity to be alone* is one of the most important signs of maturity in emotional development. In his view, parents can facilitate the development of the child's ability to soothe herself or himself when left alone. Please don't confuse this with abandonment or, on the other hand, use this notion as an excuse for negligence.

Margaret S. Mahler, a prominent child psychoanalyst, has identified the beginning of the separation–individuation process whereby the infant begins to differentiate from the mother at 4 to 5 months of age. This is the age when children naturally begin to develop some independence from her.

Drs Alexander Thomas and Stella Chess, two American child psychiatrists, followed over 100 infants through young adulthood. One item they examined was regularity or irregularity of sleep and how parents responded. They wrote:

> Removal of symptoms by a successful parent guidance procedure has had positive consequences for the child's functioning and has not resulted in the appearance of overt anxiety or new substitute symptoms . . . The basic emphasis [of the] treatment technique is a change in the parents' behaviour.

Please don't fear that when your child cries in protest at night because he is being allowed to 'practise' falling asleep, this crying will later cause emotional or psychological problems. By itself, it will not.

Mothers or fathers who in general do not feel loving or empathetic towards their child, who are insensitive or emotionally unavailable to their children, who have a lack of warmth or affection towards their child, later come to the attention of professionals. Consequently, some psychologists or psychiatrists take the attitude that parents should be encouraged to *never* let their child cry for fear of encouraging a cold parent–child relationship. As a general practice paediatrician, however, I don't share this view, because I see all kinds of parents seeking paediatric care, not just those who have problems. The vast majority of parents are loving and sensitive to their child's needs. These parents should not fear letting their child cry at night for the specific purpose of learning to sleep.

A key question here:

Q: How long do I let my baby cry?
A: To establish regular naps, healthy sleep schedules, and consolidated sleep overnight, there is no time limit.

Remember
If we place an arbitrary limit on the duration of crying, we train our child to cry to that predetermined time. When it is open-ended, the child *learns* to stop protesting and to fall asleep.

Another key question:

Q: Why is it good for him to cry for hours; why not wait until he is older and more reasonable?
A: Crying is not the real issue. We are letting him alone to forget the expectation to be picked up, to learn to sleep. We allow him to cry, but we are not making him cry in the sense that we are hurting him. When he is older and still not sleeping, it will be harder for him to learn how to sleep well. The sleep that is lost while he is growing up is physically unhealthy, just as is too little iron or vitamins in his diet.

Q: But, I still think the crying has to be harmful.
A: Not necessarily. In fact recent studies have proven that *crying produces accelerated forgetting of a learned response*. So when he cries he may more quickly unlearn the expectation to be picked up. Therefore, when trying to stop an unhealthy habit, crying may have some benefit because crying acts as an amnesiac agent.

Let's look at several of the most common unhealthy sleep habits at this age, and the proven, effective strategy to deal with each one:

(1) ABNORMAL SLEEP SCHEDULE

When the bedtime hour and sleep periods are not in synchrony with other biological rhythms, we don't get the full restorative benefit of sleep. Please refer to Figures 5 (see p. 18 and 6 (see p. 18) for age-appropriate times when children fall asleep or awaken.

At any age, abnormal sleep schedules often lead to night wakings and night terrors in older children. The schedule often gets shifted to a too-late bedtime hour because: (1) Mum or Dad, returning late from work, want to play with their baby; or (2) parents deliberately keep their baby up late to encourage a later awakening in the morning.

The strategy for bringing sleep schedules back to normal is based on developing an age-appropriate wake-up at 6 or 7 am; a nap in the mid-morning; a nap in the early afternoon starting before 3 pm; and a bedtime at 7 to 9 pm.

Remember
You are enforcing an age-appropriate nap-*time* and
bed*time* schedule. Your child may not cooperate initially
by falling asleep immediately. Don't give up.

When your child does not sleep at his nap-times, he is left alone until you think that he has had about an hour of uninterrupted sleep. When starting this, for the first few days, the afternoon nap may be skipped if the duration of morning crying and morning sleeping puts you into the mid or late afternoon. At bedtime, he is put down after your bedtime ritual and not attended to until between 5 and 7 am. No matter how long or how loud he cries.

Studies have shown that when sleep disturbances are associated with abnormal sleep schedules the control of the wake-up time may be sufficient to establish a healthy 24-hour sleep rhythm. In other words, you set the clock in the morning!

Here's an account of one mother who left my office determined to set the clock that night and not wait until the morning!

'Our son did not like to sleep. In fact, if it can be said that babies are born with an aversion to any particular thing – for Ryan, sleep was it.

'From the day we brought him home from the hospital, he had shown himself to be a night owl. By the time he was 4½ months old, he was down to one nap a day. He didn't sleep through the night (and in my book, that's 8 hours straight or better) until he was 10 months old, and that lasted for only one night.

'Not knowing any better, Ryan being our first child, I thought that this kind of behaviour was perfectly normal for a majority of babies. When other mothers would talk about their children sleeping through the night at 3 months of age and napping twice a day for 2 hours or better at a crack, I figured that it was either so much idle boasting or their children had some sort of neurological disorder. But when our paediatrician told me at Ryan's 8-month check-up that it was not normal for a child his age to go to bed at 1.00 am and sleep until 10.00 am, I started to realize that we had a problem. The thought of my husband and I looking like "Dawn of the Dead" rejects from years without sleep was not a pretty one.

'We put Ryan to bed at 9.00 that evening and, as expected, he started to cry. We shut his door and went into the living room, closing two more doors between the baby's room and the living room in an attempt to muffle what were now becoming very loud screams. After a half-hour had passed, the crying was more muffled but continued, so I headed for Ryan's room to "reassure him". "Don't go in there now," Tom suggested. "He'll just get worked up again if he sees you. Do something else for a while." I could see the logic and agreed to hold off. A half-hour later, I cracked the door open and again heard the crying. But now I could hear something else mixed in. Ryan was talking to himself. In a very hurt tone he was babbling and complaining between the sobs. My heart was breaking. "My God," I said to Tom. "Now he's going to grow up hating us. I have to go to him." For the second time that night, Tom talked me into leaving the baby alone.

'The next 15 minutes seemed like 15 hours, but the next time I opened the door, there it was . . . SILENCE. I could finally look in on Ryan without undoing all that we had just accomplished. So as not to waken him with its squeaking, I opened the door with great caution, tiptoed into the room and clicked the light on at its dimmest setting. In this low light and from across the room, I saw what appeared to be Ryan's blanket hanging over the side of his cot. As I moved closer to remove it, however, I discovered that it wasn't the quilt draped over the side – it was Ryan. Our son had fallen asleep standing up!

'The next night we again put him in bed at 9.00 and again he fell asleep standing up. But this time he only cried for one hour. The third night, he cried for 25 minutes and fell asleep lying down.

'These days, with few exceptions, he cries for only a few minutes before falling asleep. He also usually wakes up smiling, thus dispelling any fears I once might have had that he would grow up to hate us for letting him "cry it out".'

(2) NAP DEPRIVATION

This is a common occurrence between 9 and 12 months of age. These children are fearless, full of grace and confidence, very explorative. Doing things together is simply a lot of fun. Unsure of when a child naturally needs only one nap, some parents try to get by with one nap before their child is ready. Afternoons full of activities help smooth over rocky moments of heightened emotionality or grumpiness. Also, Dad returns about then, so there is a loving play-period early in the evening.

The fatigue from nap deprivation leads to increased levels of arousal/alertness, and this causes difficulties in falling asleep or staying asleep or both.

The treatment strategy involves: re-establishing the early afternoon nap by focusing on the midday interval and making sure this wakeful period is not too long; making sure the afternoon nap does not start too late in the afternoon in order to protect a reasonable evening bedtime; and consistency in the nap-time ritual.

Remember

As long as your child *retains the expectation* that she can get around you and play during nap-time, she won't nap well. If she *thinks* she can outlast you, she won't give up her protesting.

It's not uncommon for a child to sleep well at night, but not nap well, especially in the afternoon. At night, it is dark, everyone is more tired, parents want to be regular with bedtimes because they, themselves, want to go to sleep. During the day, it is light, everyone is more alert, and parents are more irregular, because they want to run errands or enjoy recreational activities.

So during a retraining period, it's easiest to establish good night sleep and easier to establish regular morning naps than afternoon naps. Don't expect improvement to occur equally at all times.

Practical Point
If the afternoon nap is needed but your child fights sleep the most then, consider shortening the midday interval of wakefulness and start the afternoon nap earlier. Perhaps, you were allowing him to stay up too long and he was getting overtired and overaroused.

An additional element regarding nap quality is whether the mother likes to nap or not. Naps are valuable for our children and the most important factor in maintaining or re-establishing naps is being regular. This does not mean being regular in the afternoon according to clock time, but regular means maintaining fairly regular intervals of midday wakefulness that can vary somewhat based on the length of the morning nap. Otherwise, as one mother said, 'Sometimes she gets overtired and can't get off to sleep.'

This means that when a child has disturbed sleep and an abnormal wake-up time, we might decide to (a) control his schedule by waking him up earlier so that the naps and bedtime hour all occur earlier or (b) shortening the intervals of wakefulness before naps and bedtimes so that the bedtime hour is earlier. When our children are well rested and have no disturbed sleep, an early wake-up hour may be inconvenient but not necessarily changeable!

(3) BRIEF SLEEP DURATIONS

If your child is on an apparently normal sleep schedule and napping well, you might presume she is getting enough sleep. Overall, she doesn't look tired. But around 10, 11 or 12 months she starts new night waking. What is happening? Many times, physical and perhaps mental activity increase around 9 months. The child now is moving around more, exploring more, becoming more active and independent.

If the customary bedtime hour had been around 8 or 9 pm before the onset of night waking, I have observed that night waking will often disappear when the bedtime hour is now shifted earlier by ½ or 1 hour. Usually this change is easy for the baby; sometimes it is hard to accept for the parent who returns home late from work. Small changes in sleep patterns sometimes make big differences in sleep quality when the result corrects a chronic sleep deficit.

(4) EARLY AWAKENINGS

Most children 4 to 12 months of age go to bed between 7 and 9 pm and awake at 5 to 7 am. Some also get up once around the midnight hour for a brief feeding. This pattern is very common, but many parents don't like the idea of getting up so early! In this age range, it seems that the wake-up part of our brain is like a neurological alarm clock.

It's very regular and I don't think we can ignore crying in well-rested children at 5 or 6 am, simply because we don't want to get up so early. They are *well-rested* children, having slept overnight and it seems unreasonable to expect them to simply go back to sleep. If, in fact, they are well rested, then I would suggest a prompt, brief, soothing response so that hopefully both child and parent can return to sleep. But sometimes, the child starts to wake up in a new pattern at 4 am or to wake up at the usual 6 am and *not* respond by returning to sleep after a prompt, soothing parental response. These kids are *really* up and want to play, yet they are often *not* well rested. When the parents put these children to bed *earlier*, they sleep in longer because they are more rested and are thus able to sleep better.

Methods which usually fail to prevent
early awakenings
Keeping your baby up later at bedtime
Waking him for a feeding when you go to sleep
Giving solid food late at night

If your child is near his first birthday, you might consider some of the items discussed in the next section for older children.

(5) DIFFERENT SLEEP PATTERNS

Sleep patterns are as varied as children themselves, family sizes, and parental lifestyles. One 5-month-old child briefly awoke at 6 am and promptly returned to sleep until 10 am. A long midday nap occurred from 12 noon to 3 pm and a brief nap from 5 to 5.45 pm. Between 7.30 and 8 pm the child went to sleep for the night, until about 6 the following morning. This child was well rested, and the midday nap coincided with his older brother's single nap. For the time being, this pattern met both children's sleep needs. By 6 or 7 months, this child developed a more common mid-morning and early afternoon nap.

Warning
A temporary disturbance or mild variation in sleep schedules, nap patterns, amount of sleep, or early awakenings may not be changeworthy. But if chronic or severe problems cause your child to become tired, then do try to help your baby become more rested.

(6) NIGHT WAKINGS

In this age-range, night wakings typically are normally occurring complete arousals from sleep associated with: (1) post-colic disturbed sleep, (2) partial airway obstruction during sleep, (3) general disorganization of sleep with chronic fatigue, or (4) parental reinforcement only at night.
We've discussed the first three items in earlier chapters.

Let's now consider the child who naps well, has a reasonably normal sleep schedule, and does not appear overly tired, but simply gets up too often and/or stays up too long in the middle of the night. We want to help this child learn how to soothe herself to sleep unassisted when she wakes up. This skill also will help her fall asleep at bedtime, so the two strategies outlined here can also be used when the problem is *'prolonged latency* to sleep', or as commonly known: *fighting going to bed*. The first technique, called *fading*, is a more gradual approach, while the second, called *extinction* is an abrupt, 'cold turkey' solution. Let's look at how each works, and their pluses and minuses.

Warning

Do not attempt to correct unhealthy sleep habits unless you see ahead a clear period when you are in control. Perhaps you may decide to wait until your spouse is away. Don't trust most relatives or babysitters to do as good a job as you can to correct unhealthy sleep habits. Also, if your child's sleep improves during a re-training period but suddenly he becomes worse, appears ill or in pain, let your doctor examine him for the possibility of an ear or throat infection.

Fading

A gradual approach to reduce the number of night wakings until the baby can return to sleep independently is called a 'fade' procedure. Over a period of time, you gradually reduce your efforts at night, so that your child takes over for himself and falls asleep or returns to sleep by himself. This is like teaching your older child how to ride a bike. You first provide balance and support and gradually withdraw your efforts as the child gains confidence and skill. Here is an example of a fade-sequence to eliminate night wakings:

Respond promptly, spend as much time as needed
Father gives bottle or mother doesn't feed
Change from milk to juice
Dilute juice to only water
No bottle

No pick-up
No singing, talking, verbal communication
Minimal contact, petting, hand holding
No eye contact, sober, unresponsive face
No physical contact, sit next to child
Move chair away from cot towards the door
Reduce time with the child
Delay response

The apparent advantage of gradually weaning the child from prolonged, complex contact is its seeming gentleness. A disadvantage is that it does span several days or weeks, during which many brief crying spells may occur. The major reasons why this approach usually only partially succeeds, or fails completely, are: (1) unpredictable, real-life events interfere with parents' best plans and schedules; (2) parents do not appreciate the enormous power of intermittent positive reinforcement that maintains the behaviour ('I'll just feed him this one time!'); and (3) parents' resolve weakens from their own fatigue and sometimes impatience. Here is an account of one mother's attempt to use a gradual approach:

'Lauren was 8 months old when I finally sought help from the doctor; her sleep schedule could only be described as unbearable.

'When we brought her home from the hospital after birth, she would have a very long, wakeful period in the evenings from about 8 pm to 1 am. We can't say that she was colicky, as she was really quite pleasant most of the time. Only about once a week did she have an extended crying spell during which she would be inconsolable. Most other evenings, she would breastfeed often and sometimes fall asleep for a few minutes at a time, but would awaken as soon as put down. The great thing was that once she fell asleep at 1 am, she would sleep until 6 or 7 am. We thought she was terrific for a newborn. (During the day she would stay up for about half an hour to 2 hours between naps of varying length.)

'The problems started when we tried to move bedtime up (after about 3 months of age). We started being able to get her to sleep around 11.30 pm, but she would always wake once in the middle of the night, sometimes twice. Usually after feeding, she would fall back to sleep, but often she would end up spending the rest of the night in our bed. If I tried to put her back into her cot, she would wake up instantly and have to be nursed again. Interestingly enough, if we let her stay up until 1 am, she could still make it through the rest of the night. For fleeting moments, we actually considered moving to the Orient where her body clock might coincide better with the time zone!

'At around 7 months or so, we decided to try feeding her and putting her back in her *own bed* consistently. That's when the trouble really began! She would wake up every few hours, and it would take 1½ to 2 hours to get her back to sleep. By now she had learned how to stand up, and I think that made it even more difficult for her to settle down.

'The other thing she did was to fall asleep easily at about 9 pm and wake up ½ hour later, inconsolable. Eventually (after feeding, rocking, etc.), she would perk up and become very pleasant and often stay up and play happily for anywhere from 2 to 4 hours. Any attempt at putting her to bed was met with great resistance. Even letting her stay up until 1 am no longer guaranteed us the rest of the night's sleep. She would awaken at least twice during the night no matter what! It was no longer necessary to move to Japan – now we were considering the land of the midnight sun!

'At the same time, naps were totally irregular and unpredictable. She would sometimes sleep 20 minutes – sometimes 2 hours – usually 20 minutes.

'When I saw the doctor, she was about 8½ months old and and sleeping no longer than 2 to 3 hours at a stretch at night. When I explained that I was one of those people who didn't think I could let my baby cry herself to sleep, he recommended a plan of action that involved a gradual withdrawal process that would stretch out over 7 to 10 days. The response to her waking was supposed to be consistently prompt, but there was to be less handling of the baby at each step of the plan. One stage of the plan was to respond to her middle-of-the-night crying by entering her room, but trying to leave her in her bed. Singing, talking and stroking her were OK.

'On the night that we reached that point of the plan, I could soon see that there would be no way she would lie down and calm down enough to fall back to sleep. She just stood in her cot and got angrier and angrier that I wasn't picking her up. Of course, I eventually picked her up and put her to the breast; and she fell back to sleep in my arms; and, of course, as soon as I placed her back in her cot, she woke up. At this point, I realized that I'd been with her for 1½ hours (3.30 am to 5 am). On top of all this, my older daughter had woken at 1 am that night; and I had, so far, only managed to get one hour of sleep. Finally, exhaustion won out over patience.

'I put Lauren in her cot, kissed her goodnight, walked out and closed the door. She screamed for *45 minutes* and finally went to sleep. They were the longest 45 minutes of my life – longer than labour! But, it worked!

'The next few nights she slept all night – once we got her to sleep. And that was the next thing we needed to deal with. It was still pretty easy to get her to sleep around 9 pm, only to have her awaken in half an hour. A few nights after our first success, we decided to leave her alone when she awakened at 9.30. Well, that crying session, when we did it, lasted for about *35 minutes*. The next night she went to bed about 9 pm and got up at 7.30 am!

'Since then, that has been pretty much her night-time sleeping schedule. Occasionally she wakes up in the middle of the night, but only cries for about 2 to 3 minutes and goes back to sleep.

'Naps were still not too consistent at this time, but she has recently worked herself into a two-nap-a-day routine. She manages to get another 2 to 4 hours of sleep a day with those. She's always been a pretty pleasant baby, now she's almost all smiles all the time, because she's well rested.

'I can't tell you why it was so difficult for me to follow the doctor's advice right away about letting Lauren cry, except that I empathize with the baby completely and entirely. I kept thinking to myself that it must be horribly frightening for a baby, who is unable to communicate except through crying, to be left alone in a room to cry. What helped to convince me, however (in addition to utter, complete and entire exhaustion), was the realization that as long as I stayed in her room she screamed anyway. Walking, rocking, singing, etc. – none of these quieted her anymore – the only thing that calmed her was endless, non-stop nursing! I finally came to the conclusion that as long as she was going to be miserable crying anyway, she might as well be learning something positive from it – learning to go to sleep. Even now, if I stay in her room after I put her in bed, she stands up and cries; but as soon as I kiss her goodnight, walk out and close the door, she lies down and goes to sleep!'

Extinction (or going 'cold turkey')

When parents, however well-intentioned, stop reinforcing a child's night waking, the habit can be eliminated quickly. In fact, psychologists have shown that the more continuous or regular you had been in reinforcing the night waking during the first few months, the more likely it will be reduced rapidly simply by stopping it. The advantages of abruptly ending the habit of going to your baby at night are that the instructions are simple and easily remembered, and the whole process takes only a few days. But the seeming disadvantage is that a few nights of very prolonged crying are unbearable for many parents. This procedure strikes many people as harsh, too abrupt, or cruel. Those are personal value judgments, but bear in mind – this procedure is *effective*. It works.

Here is an account of one mother who decided to stop cold turkey in order to eliminate her child's night wakings. *Stimulus control* was also used, so that the child could nap well – in other words, certain behaviours in certain places at nap-time *and* bedtime (the stimuli) became associated with 'falling asleep'.

'One of the hardest things I've ever had to do'
'At six months of age, Stephen was strong, happy and healthy in every respect but one – he didn't sleep well. He did all his daytime napping in the car, the pushchair or our arms. If we put him in his cot, he awoke immediately and cried until we picked him up. His night-time pattern was different, but equally exhausting. He went to sleep in his cot promptly at 8 pm, but usually awoke within the first hour for a brief comforting and two or three times between 11 pm and 5 am for feeds.

'This routine was taking its toll. I was almost as tired as when Stephen was a newborn, and had no emotional reserve for handling everyday problems. I was sharp with the rest of the family and got angry if my husband was even 10 minutes late getting home from work. We needed to make a change.

'We discussed the problem with our doctor, and he suggested leaving the baby alone to cry both at naps and at night, but I just wasn't ready to do it. I hoped he would outgrow his sleeping problems. Two weeks later, I decided to try a limited programme of letting him cry at nap-time. Because I was still going to him at night, however, I think he was confused. After a week, he still cried for up to an hour before each nap. I felt depressed and even more discouraged than when he wasn't napping at all. But, at the same time, I knew we couldn't go back to the way things had been.

'We made another appointment with the doctor and for an hour, talked over all my anxieties about going "cold turkey" and letting Stephen cry at night. I wanted to know about all the "what-ifs" – what if he's afraid, hungry, too cold, too warm, uncomfortable from a dirty nappy, awakened by a noise outside? I wanted to raise every concern I had, no matter how insignificant it might seem.

'During that appointment, the doctor also explained to us the importance of regular day and night-time sleeping for babies, and how they need to learn to use their own resources for falling asleep. He said we were perpetuating Stephen's night waking habit by going to him whenever he awoke, and told us that sleeping problems tend to persist and even get worse. I began to see that I was doing Stephen a disservice, as well as myself, by continuing the pattern we were in. He needed the sleep as much as I did.

'The doctor gave us explicit instructions for instituting morning and afternoon naps and unbroken night-time sleeping. At the end of the appointment, I was full of resolve. Stephen was free of any illness, and we had the weekend ahead of us, when my husband would be around for support, so we decided to start that night.

'We put the baby to bed at 8 pm and he awoke the first time around 9.30. He cried for 20 minutes and went back to sleep. He awoke again around 2 and 4 am and cried about 20 minutes each time. When he cried at 6 am, I rushed into his room, anxious to hold him and be sure he was the same healthy, happy baby I had put down the night before.

'Over the next few days it was amazing to see how quickly he fell into the schedule we had set up for him. He cried 10 to 15 minutes several times, but never again for an hour. Now he naps regularly and sleeps all night, occasionally crying for 1 or 2 minutes during the night as he puts himself back to sleep.

'For the first two weeks after we began the programme I felt tense every time I put Stephen in his cot, wondering if he would cry a long time before falling asleep. Finally, I began to relax and unwind from the weeks of indecision and tension we had been through surrounding this problem.

'Letting my baby cry was one of the hardest things I've ever had to do. Now that the experience is behind us, however, I have no doubt at all that it was right. Both he and I are better rested, and he can enjoy outings in the car or pushchair without falling asleep and missing the activity. During his naps, I have time to do household tasks or simply catch my breath. I feel refreshed and delighted to be with him when he wakes up. At night, I look forward to several hours of uninterrupted rest, rather than falling asleep feeling tense and wondering when the first waking will occur.

'In a broader sense, too, this experience had value. It gave me more confidence in my abilities to handle tough issues as a parent and respect for my child's ability to learn and adapt to the guidelines I establish for him.'

Helpful hint when you skip midnight nappy changes
Use thick layers of zinc oxide *paste* on your baby's bottom so that no rash will develop if you do not go to him at night to change his nappy. Ordinary mineral oil will make removal of the paste easier in the morning. Or, consider using the extra absorbent disposable nappies specially designed for night-time use in this weight range.

Here are some other typical questions and answers for this age group:

Q: I've heard that if I breastfeed my baby to sleep, I'll create a night waking problem – is that right?

A: The issue is not whether to breastfeed to sleep or not but rather is nursing too frequent or night-time nursing part of a night waking problem. Please include breastfeeding, if you wish, in nap-time or bedtime rituals. But when you've spent the time you want to spend on such rituals, whether the baby's asleep or awake, put her down, kiss her cheek, say good night, walk away, lights off, close the door.

Q: Once I let my child cry a long time and she vomited. Won't I be trading one problem for another?

A: If the vomiting always occurs, I think you will want to always go in and clean her promptly and then leave her again. If the vomiting is irregular and occasional, you should try waiting until after you think she is deeply asleep before checking and then quickly cleaning her if needed.

Q: Won't she simply outgrow this habit? My doctor says to try these procedures later, if needed then, when she's a few years old. She'll understand more then.

A: Believe it or not, college freshmen, at age 18, who don't sleep well, had difficulties sleeping as infants, according to their mothers, as reported in one study. It seems that if she doesn't have the early opportunity to practise falling asleep by herself, she'll never learn to easily fall asleep by herself.

Q: Even if she won't outgrow this habit, what's really wrong with my still going to her at night?

A: Consider your feelings. Studies conducted at Yale University show that *all* mothers eventually become anxious, develop angry feelings toward their child, and feel guilt about maintaining poor sleep habits. These feelings may persist for years. True, you will also feel bad letting your baby protest cry. But this will last only several days.

Here's one mother's account of how she felt:

'The moment my daughter arrived home from the hospital, she exploded with a very bad case of colic. I took her to the doctor's office several times, only to be told there was "not a thing wrong, relax", and received several suggestions about breastfeeding and a pat on the back. All of these suggestions irritated me, and I felt as though I was being perceived as an anxious, first-time mother.

'After 12 weeks of crying at best and screaming at worst, we were evaluated by two child development specialists. I decided we should work with one until my daughter's crying and screaming settled down. We also saw a psychiatrist, who recommended medication and that we continue to be followed by the development specialists. In the meantime, our lives had become a nightmare. She cried most of the day and always screamed in the evening. To our horror, this behaviour had worked itself into the entire night hours also.

'By 5 months, we were referred to Dr Weissbluth for what was hoped to be a sleep disorder. I say hoped, because we were at the point of seeing a paediatric neurologist and having an EEG done. I was very frightened for my daughter, and my husband and I were exhausted. We had read *Crybabies*, and I was eager for the consultation. My daughter had definitely been cursed with colic. Could this now be wired exhaustion from a sleep disorder caused by the treatment for colic – rocking, swinging, motion all the time? It was.

'My daughter was old enough now to try "crying it out". It was the most difficult thing I've had to do as a new mother.

'The first night she screamed, choked and sobbed for 32 minutes. I remember I felt sick to my stomach and kept following my husband around reading parts of *Crybabies* out loud. It wasn't that he needed to hear any of it, but rather, I needed to hear the statistics and conclusions of Dr Weissbluth as an encouragement.

'The first two days weren't too terrible. However, the third and fourth were almost intolerable. She would cry through her entire nap-time. Then I would get her up to keep Dr Weissbluth's time-frame going. Her temperament after these episodes is only known to mothers who have been through the same ordeal! When she would scream for over an hour during a nap-time and in the evening, I felt cruel, insensitive and guilty.

'Three things kept me going. My husband's support; Dr Weissbluth's concern, encouragement and compassion; and the fact that I knew it had to be done – she had to learn to sleep.

'It took her about a week to catch on to the idea. The bags under her eyes faded, her sporadic screaming attacks stopped, and her personality was that of a predictable baby – a sweetheart when rested and a bear when she's past a nap or bedtime.

'I would offer these suggestions to other mothers and fathers who have to take this measure in order to teach their baby to sleep.

'You, as parents, have to understand and believe intellectually it is the right thing to do. Otherwise, your feelings of being cruel and guilt will overpower you, and you will give in. You must have the support of your spouse, as it will be too much of a strain on the two of you.

'You are doing what is best for your baby. It seems cruel and unacceptable as a loving new mother to let your baby cry. But it is a fact of parenting – many, many things will bring tears and protests in the years to come.

'Enlist the support of a sympathetic friend as much as you feel the need to. I found close telephone contact a tremendous help. Some parents may not need this close interaction, but many of us do.'

In our roles as parents, teaching our children to sleep may be the very first difficult task we have to undertake. Parents who do should feel a special sense of accomplishment, for it is a very difficult task! Those of us who have been through a baby with a sleep disorder know what misery is. But so does the baby, who is crabby and exhausted all the time. Once patterns and the practice of sleep are established, everyone benefits and finally life can be somewhat predictable again.

It *will* get better!

A few more typical questions and answers:

Q: Look, those are not going to be my feelings. I grew up in the peace-and-beads generation; everything is going to be beautiful in its own way. If you leave it alone. I believe in no interference with nature, de-control, and feeling good. I feel good, when I go to my baby at night.

A: Just consider the 'unnatural' effects of chronic sleep fragmentation on your child.

Q: I just don't think I can do nothing when my baby cries for me at night . . .

A: Letting your baby cry is *not doing nothing*. You are actively encouraging the development of independence, providing opportunities for her to learn how to sleep alone, showing respect for her capability to change her behaviour . . .

Q: Maybe you're right, but why do I feel that I just can't do it?

A: If you want to do it but can't do it, consider the following possibilities:

Why Can't I Let My Baby Cry?

1. *Unpleasant childhood memories* surface and remind you of your childhood loneliness, or feeling unwanted. Because your baby clutches you so tightly at night, it appears palpably obvious that he loves you and you don't wish him to grow up feeling unloved.
2. *Working mothers' guilt* from being away from the child so much.
3. *We already tried it and it didn't work* – maybe she was too young then, maybe you time-limited your inattention, maybe you unknowingly provided partial reinforcement.

Remember
Small, soothing efforts such as kissing the forehead, rearranging blankets, comforting and patting appear trivial to parents, but they interfere enormously with learning to fall asleep *unassisted*.

4. *I enjoy my baby's company too much at night*, because I'm not a good sleeper myself.
5. *If I don't feed my baby at night* she might lose weight.
6. *Never another baby*: in *My Child Won't Sleep* by Jo Douglas and Naomi Richman, they write: 'If you are feeling stressed, your child may respond by not sleeping so well. If the stress is related to difficulties between you as parents, you may think that your young child will not notice, but the chances are that he will. His way of waking at night and coming into your bed can be a way of preventing you from talking to each other and sorting out your problems, and his presence can act as a useful contraceptive.' Although written for older children

coming into your bed, maintaining baby's night waking
when the baby is younger might also serve the purpose of
avoiding marital problems. The next chapter will discuss
these issues in more detail.

Warning

When your over tired child first starts to sleep better
during a retraining period, he may appear, in the
beginning, to be more tired than before! You are
unmasking the underlying fatigue which previously had
been present, but which was hidden by the turned-on,
hyperalert 'upcited' state.

THE SECOND AND THIRD YEARS (12 TO 36 MONTHS)

Your child's developing personality and awareness of himself
as an individual means his second and third years will be a
time of testing, non-cooperation, resistance, and striving for
independence. Sleep problems in 12 to 36 month-olds are
related to this normally evolving stubbornness or wilfulness
in our children who now want to do their own thing, for
example: (a) to get out of their bed or cot at night, (b) to not
take naps, (c) to get up too early to play and, of course, (d) to
resist falling asleep and waking up at night. This last item
might have started during the first year and may now
continue during the second year as an ingrained habit. Let's
look at each of these major problems in turn.

GETTING OUT OF THE COT OR BED (OR, THE 'JACK-IN-THE-BOX' SYNDROME)

It's quite natural for 2 or 3 year-olds to climb out of their cot or
bed to check out the interesting things that they think their
parents are up to. Or maybe they just want to watch the late
late movie or have a bite to eat. Of course, what they like to
do most is to come to visit us and/or get into our bed. This not
only disrupts our sleep, but it also harms the child. Here's
how.

When the child has a naturally occurring partial arousal
during sleep, instead of soothing himself back to sleep, he
learns to force himself completely awake to get out of his bed

or cot. The result is sleep fragmentation – for him, and us, too. Here's a 5-step treatment plan to put your Jack back into his 'box' at night:

Step 1   Keep a chart, log, or diary to record key sleep events: time asleep, time awake, number of times out of bed, and duration of protest calling, fussing or crying. This will make you a better observer of both your child's and your own behaviour. The chart enables you to determine whether the strategy is working, and helps remind you to be regular according to clock times and consistent in your responses.

Step 2   Ask yourself, does my child behave as if he is tired in the late afternoon or early evening? If the answer is yes, then consider the possibility that naps are insufficient or the bedtime hour is too late. Deal with these problems at the same time you are working on his getting out of the cot or bed. If needed, keep data in your sleep chart regarding naps such as time he falls asleep, how long he slept during the day, how long he cried in protest before napping, and the interval between the end of his nap and when he went to sleep for the night.

Also, consider whether your child is snoring or mouth breathing more and more at night. Please review the section on snoring in Chapter 4 if this is now a problem.

Step 3   Announce to your child that there is a new rule in the house which is: down is down – *no* getting out of bed until morning. Tell him that you love him very much, that you need your sleep, and he needs to put himself back to sleep by himself; getting out of bed is not allowed. Tell him that when he gets out of bed, you are going to put him back to bed and you are not going to talk to him or look at his face.

Depending on whether he has just turned 2 or about 3, he may or may not understand what you are saying. But, he senses or understands that tonight, something different is going to occur.

Warning
Be *silent*, unemotional, appear disinterested or
mechanical. No more night entertainment!

Step 4   Place yourself somewhere where you can easily hear him get out of his cot or bed. Place a bell-rope on his door or your door, to signal you when he leaves his room or enters your room, or use an intercom if you must be out of earshot.

Every time you determine that he is out of his bed or discover him in your bed, gently place him back in his bed. *Maintain silence*. Plan not to sleep the first night as he may try – many, many times – to get back to his old style. Parents might want to alternate nights, so that at least someone gets some sleep. Do not take turns on the same night, because the child might think one parent will behave differently. Children learn quickly that there's no benefit in getting out of bed, so they stay in bed and sleep through the night.

Step 5   Every morning, shower the child with praise or affection for cooperating with the new rule. Perhaps offer a favourite food that was previously withheld or go on a special outing. Try small rewards for partial cooperation and larger rewards for more complete cooperation.

In addition to praising or rewarding your child when he cooperates, you might consider changing some of the routines when he does not cooperate. For example, past 15 to 18 months, you might close the door in a progressive fashion every time he gets out of bed. You can put three or four white tape marks on the floor and for the first three or four times he gets out of bed, the door is more and more closed until it is barely open or completely closed. If he stays in bed, the door is left open to the first tape mark. A similar progressive strategy could be used with brighter or dimmer night lights.

Expect this plan to reduce or eliminate the getting-out-of-bed routine dramatically within a few days, usually three or four. All you have to do is remove the previous night-time social interaction (whether pleasant or unpleasant) as a reinforcer to the habit of getting out of the cot.

Here are some typical questions and answers about this strategy:

Q: Won't he hurt himself when he climbs or falls out of his cot?
A: This is a common worry and often used as an excuse to go to your child or buy a 'big kid's' bed. But the truth is that

serious injuries simply do not occur when the child bumps on the floor as he lets himself down.

Q: Can the plan fail?

A: Yes, when both parents aren't committed, so that one partner passively or actively sabotages the programme. One father in my practice loved to sneak a bottle of formula to his baby once or twice a night. This caused the baby to suffer excessive wetness and a severe, persistent and painful monilial nappy rash. Only in the course of trying to eradicate the rash did his behaviour come to light. Failures also sometimes occur when the child is still chronically fatigued from too late a bedtime hour or nap deprivation.

Q: What if he stays in his cot but cries?

A: Letting your child cry when he protests going to sleep or staying in his cot is not the same as making your child cry as if you were hurting him. Leave him alone.

Warning, Again

Do not underestimate the enormous power of partial reinforcement to ruin your efforts to overcome your baby's habit of getting out of the cot. If you are not silent or discuss getting out of bed when it is occurring, your social behaviour reinforces the behaviour.

One family instituted this five-step programme when their daughter was 26 months old, after 26 months of poor sleeping. She always had difficulty in falling asleep and difficulty in staying asleep. Nicole always wanted to, and did, get out of her bed and go into her parents' bed. After the birth of Daniel, her brother, her parents decided that this had to stop.

Their records showed the following results:

Night 1: Between 8.13 and 9.45 pm – *69* return trips to bed. Slept until 8.30 am with one brief awakening at 2.15 am.

Night 2: Between 8.20 and 10.30 pm – *145* return trips to bed. Slept until 7.20 am with one brief awakening at 2.15 am.

Night 3: After 9.14 pm (bedtime) – *0* return trips to bed. Slept until 7.40 am awakening at 3.20 am.

That's it! From then on, the curtain calls at bedtime ceased. Furthermore, at naps the mother would now leave after 15 to 20 minutes of reading, whereas before, she had to stay in the room until Nicole fell asleep. The parents described her as easier in many ways: less resistance in dressing, less argumentative, more charming and better able to be by herself.

Remember
Problems may get worse before they get better during a retraining phase.

REFUSAL TO TAKE NAPS

Playtime in the park or shopping together is so much fun; who wants to take a nap? Ask yourself, is 'not napping' my *child's* problem or *my* problem: 'I have so many things I want to do.' Some parents simply find it too inconvenient to hang around the house so that their child can get their needed day sleep. But reflect on how 'inconvenient' it is to drag a tired child around while shopping! Please review the first section of this book, if you feel that naps are not that important.

Let's consider three common problems regarding naps: (1) two naps go to one nap, (2) resistance to one nap, and (3) no naps.

1 Two naps go to one nap　This normally occurs about 15 to 18 months, and many children naturally shorten one nap on their own (either morning or afternoon or alternately either nap). Most of these children do not appear to become very tired. Other children appear simply to actively resist the second nap, and because it was short anyway, many parents forget it. The result is a tired child late in the afternoon or early evening. If two naps are clearly impossible, but one nap is insufficient, then put your child to bed earlier. Do this even if this means that a working parent coming home late does not see the child then. You can get up extra early to have longer morning playtime with your child before you go off to work. Another solution is to declare some days a two-nap day and others a one-nap day depending on when she wakes up, her scheduled activities and her degree of daytime sleepiness.

2 *Resistance to one nap*   This often occurs after a special event, such as a day out, party, or holiday. There was so much excitement the day before, they don't want to miss anything again! Sometimes this becomes apparent because of unappreciated chronic fatigue due to an abnormal sleep schedule, brief night sleep duration, or sleep fragmentation. If these problems are present, work on them as you work on day sleep.

The trick in solving the problem of resisting a nap is judging when your child is tired, but not overly tired. This is usually after being up about 3 to 4 hours. If the interval is too short, she might not be tired enough. If the interval is too long, she might be overtired and not able to fall easily asleep.

Keep a sleep chart, log or diary; pick a time interval you think is right, and then put your child down in the cot at that time. *You* are controlling the nap-time. Spend the time you want, 10, 20, 30 minutes hugging, kissing, rocking, nursing to soothe your child. Then down is down . . . no matter how long he cries, don't go in until you think he has slept for about an hour without interruptions.

If your child has been quite well rested up to now, the crying may only be an hour or two. But if your child has had a background of chronic fatigue, prepare yourself for several hours of crying. Here's one mother's account of how her 14-month-old daughter responded:

'My daughter was 14 months old, ate poorly, resisted naps, woke 2 to 3 times in the night, needed to be rocked to sleep and was tired all the time. My husband and I were exhausted, angry, resentful, and blaming each other for the situation we were in.

'We were ambivalent, scared, concerned, and sceptical about letting her cry [as the treatment plan recommended]. We thought she would feel unloved and worthless, if no one responded to her.

'After only one episode of crying, she learned how to lie down and fall asleep on her own! It was very difficult listening to it, but when she woke in the morning smiling and kissing us good morning, we were reassured that she loved us. Now she naps regularly, sleeps through the night, eats better, plays better and is able to play a while in her cot before going off to sleep on her own.'

The more well rested the child is, the quicker you'll see improvement. A very tired child might require several days of training before he learns to nap.

Your goal is to establish a routine, so that the child learns to associate being left alone in a certain place, with a familiar, soothing routine and feelings of being tired – with taking a nap. No more playtime. No more games. Just sleep. Parents who would rather hold their child in a rocking chair, let them snooze on a sofa with one hand on their back, or catch catnaps in the pushchair are robbing their children of healthy sleep. This lighter, briefer, less regular sleep is less restorative; it's simply not as effective in returning your child's energy and attentiveness to its best levels.

3 *No naps*   If your child is a young 2-year-old, you might find that simply establishing a pattern, as described under the previous section on resistance to one nap and sticking with it works best. Especially if the duration of not napping was not too long. But if you have an older 2-year-old or a 2-year-old who hasn't napped for a long time or is very tired because of unhealthy sleep habits in general, try the methods described in the next section on how to re-establish naps in the older child.

Here's another common question:

Q: My child's problem is not refusal to nap or resistance to naps, but *irregular* naps. What's wrong?

A: If your child is well rested, it may be that you are in fact very sensitive to his need to sleep and place him in an environment conducive to sleep when he needs it. Differences in daily activities produce differences in wakeful intervals and differences in the durations and timing of naps. Perhaps you have an unrealistic expectation regarding regularity of naps according to clock times. If your child is very tired, he might be crashing at irregular times when he is totally exhausted.

Now let's look at a third major problem in this toddler age group.

GETTING UP TOO EARLY

The first question to ask is, how early is too early? If your child gets up at 5 or 6 am and is well rested, maybe this pattern is not changeable. Perhaps getting everyone together in a family bed at that hour will allow everyone to get some more snooze time. Often families have established the habit of giving the baby a bottle at this early hour, after which the baby returns to sleep for a variable period of time.

Bottles given early in the morning may help the child return to sleep, but if the baby is allowed to fall asleep with the bottle in her mouth, the result is decayed teeth. This will not occur if the bottle contains only water. Unfortunately, many parents go to their child at 4 or 5 am with a bottle of milk, and then let the baby feed herself.

Treatment for the well-rested child who has the early morning awakening-bottle habit is to first switch to juice, and then gradually over about a week dilute the juice to only water. Now that the child is drinking only water, place two water bottles at either end of the cot and point them out to the child at bedtime. If your child is not well rested, work hard to establish a healthy sleep pattern. In the morning, for either child, don't go to him until the wake-up hour.

Controlling the wake-up hour involves *stimulus control*. Place a digital clock in her room and set the alarm for 6 or 7 am *after* the expected spontaneous wake-up time. Then at the wake-up time *you* have decided, you bounce into her room, shower her with affection, open the curtains, turn on the lights, bring her into your bed, or give her a bath. Be dramatic, wide-eyed, and happy to see her. Point out the numbers on the digital clock and exclaim, 'Oh, see, it's time to start the day!' The child learns that the day's activities start at this time. The pattern on the digital clock acts as a *cue*, just as a green traffic light tells you to start moving. Before the wake-up time, she has her water bottles, but no parental attention.

The last major sleep problem centres on the bedtime hour and on waking up at night.

RESISTANCE TO FALLING ASLEEP/NIGHT WAKING

Cues can also be used to control the bedtime hour. Use a digital clock and say 'Oh, look, it's 7.00 (say, seven, zero, zero) – time for a bath.' After bath, hugs, stories, kisses . . . 'It's now seven, three, zero (7.30), time to go to sleep.' Lights out. Door closed. No returning or peeking. The child learns that after a certain hour, no one will come and play with him, so he falls asleep and stays asleep until the morning. He learns to amuse himself with cot toys or other toys in his room until the wake-up time.

If your child has had a long history of resistance to falling asleep or night waking, then read the earlier sections in this chapter and work on establishing a healthy sleep pattern in general. Prepare yourself for some long or frequent bouts of crying as you extinguish this habit. A fade procedure probably won't work if your child is chronically tired and has longstanding disturbed sleep; he'll outlast you. The following published account of a 'cold turkey' strategy in a 21-month-old boy shows that it is effective, that the improvement occurs over several days, and that the treatment has *no ill effects*. The account was published in a professional journal for psychologists, so please forgive the dry style of writing:

Case Report: The Elimination of Tantrum Behaviour
by Carl D. Williams

This paper reports the successful treatment of tyrant-like tantrum behaviour in a male child by the removal of reinforcement. The subject child was approximately 21 months old. He had been seriously ill much of the first 18 months of his life. His health then improved considerably, and he gained weight and vigour. The child now demanded the special care and attention that had been given him over the many critical months. He enforced some of his wishes, especially at bedtime, by unleashing tantrum behaviour to control the actions of his parents.

The parents and an aunt took turns in putting him to bed both at night and for the child's afternoon nap. If the parent left the bedroom after putting the child in his bed, the child would scream and fuss until the parent returned to the room.

As a result, the parent was unable to leave the bedroom until after the child went to sleep. If the parent began to read while in the bedroom, the child would cry until the reading material was put down. The parents felt that the child enjoyed his control over them and that he fought off going to sleep as long as he could. In any event, a parent was spending from ½ to 2 hours each bedtime just waiting in the bedroom until the child went to sleep.

Following medical reassurance regarding the child's physical condition, it was decided to remove the reinforcement of this tyrant-like tantrum behaviour. Consistent with the learning principle that, in general, behaviour that is not reinforced will be extinguished, a parent or the aunt put the child to bed in a leisurely and relaxed fashion. After bedtime pleasantries, the parent left the bedroom and closed the door. The child screamed and raged, but the parent did not re-enter the room. The duration of screaming and crying was obtained from the time the door was closed.

The results are shown in Figure 12. It can be seen that the child continued screaming for 45 minutes the first time he

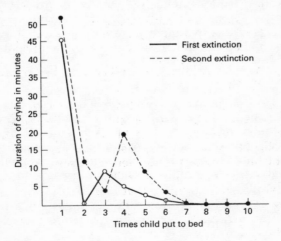

Figure 12 Length of crying in two extinction series as a function of successive occasions of being put to bed

(*Copyright 1959 by the American Psychological Association, reprinted by permission of the publisher and author*)

was put to bed in the first extinction series. The child did not cry at all the second time he was put to bed. This is perhaps attributable to his fatigue from the crying of Occasion 1. By the tenth occasion, the child no longer whimpered, fussed, or cried when the parent left the room. Rather, he smiled as they left. The parents felt that he made happy sounds until he dropped off to sleep.

About a week later, the child screamed and fussed after the aunt put him to bed, probably reflecting spontaneous recovery of the tantrum behaviour by returning to the child's bedroom and remaining there until he went to sleep. It was necessary to extinguish this behaviour a second time.

The figure showed that the second extinction is similar to the first. Both curves are generally similar to extinction curves obtained with subhuman subjects. The second extinction series reached zero by the ninth occasion. No further tantrums at bedtime were reported during the next two years.

It should be emphasized that the treatment in this case did not involve aversive punishment. All that was done was to remove the reinforcement. Extinction of the tyrant-like tantrum behaviour then occurred. No unfortunate side- or after-effects of this treatment were observed. At 3¾ years of age, the child appeared to be a friendly, expressive, outgoing child.

Here are some final questions for this age group:

Q: Does this mean that after my baby falls asleep I can never peek, never go in to soothe him or comfort him?

A: No. Only during the period when you are establishing a new sleep pattern is it important to avoid reinforcement. After your child is sleeping better and becomes well rested, there is nothing wrong with going into check on him at night.

Q: I took his older brothers out of their bedroom so his crying wouldn't disturb them. When can they go back into their old bedroom?

A: Allow several days or a couple of weeks to pass before making changes. The more rested the baby becomes, the more flexible and adaptable he will be. Changes then will be less disruptive.

Q: My 15-month-old child shows separation anxiety during the day. At night, she wants me to hold her and sit with her on the sofa until she falls asleep. How can I leave her alone at bedtime when she will be most anxious?

A: Stranger anxiety, stubbornness, or simply exhibiting a preference for parents' company over a dark, boring room might separately or in combination cause her to behave this way. Please understand that it is normal for children to feel some anxiety, and learning to deal with anxiety and not be overwhelmed by anxiety is a healthy learning process.

Let's not use separation anxiety in our child as an excuse for our own problems in dealing with a child's natural disinclination in not wanting to cooperate at the bedtime.

If there has been longstanding ambivalence or inconsistency regarding putting your child to bed at night, then the naturally occurring separation anxiety will only aggravate or magnify the problem. The same could be said of the naturally occurring *fears* of darkness, death, or monsters that older children around age 4 often express. For separation anxiety or for fears at night to be dealt with, we must understand that all children experience them, they can learn not to be overwhelmed by them at the bedtime hour by experiencing a consistent attitude of calm resolve in their parents at bedtimes. The routine of a set pattern in a bedtime ritual reassures the child that there is an orderly sequence: sleep will come, night will end, the sun will shine again, and parents will still be there smiling.

Warning

Don't hide behind excuses; there is always one handy! Some families use colic (0 to 6 months), teething (6 to 12 months), separation anxiety (12 to 24 months), the terrible-twos (24 to 36 months) and fears (36 to 48 months) to 'explain' why their child wakes up at night and has trouble returning to sleep by himself.

YOUNG CHILDREN: 3 YEARS OLD AND OVER

Three-year-olds may no longer have tantrum behaviours, but they may call parents back many times and clearly express their feelings of love for their parents or fears of the dark. Let's look at the problems that may occur in nighttime and daytime sleep habits, and some of the strategies we can use to deal with them.

NIGHT SLEEP

Here's one mother's account of how hard it was to ignore her 3-year-old child at night.

'Here's a quiz! What does every parent want to be, but most parents aren't? The answer is to be CONSISTENT. How many times has "one more time" turned into two or three more times? If we don't fulfil our promises to our children, then the inconsistency in our behaviour sparks inconsistency in their behaviour.

'My daughter Chelsea is almost 3 years old. Putting her to bed has always been an ordeal. At 18 months of age, she started to climb out of her cot anywhere from 75 to 100 times a night. The problem seemed to be solved with the advent of a "big bed". She now sleeps through the night, however, getting her to stay in bed and fall asleep is still an ordeal.

'I have yelled and screamed. I have used gates and locks on her door to physically keep her in her room. I have used treats as an incentive for positive reinforcement of desired behaviour. Unfortunately, the only consistent behaviour has been my inconsistency.

'You may ask, why? What is so hard about being consistent? I have thought about this and analysed and agonized over it for quite some time. I have concluded that consistency is difficult, because we look at it as a punishment rather than as a means to develop positive behaviour in our children.

'If Chelsea knows that I will put a gate on her bedroom door if she leaves her room, even once, then she will gradually conform and stay in her room. But, there is a catch! She eventually will start to challenge my consistent behaviour. One night she will appear in the living room and say. "Mum, I need a hug and kiss goodnight." As a parent, do you deny your child such a loving request and lock her in her room? So, you give her a hug and kiss and send her off to bed, again. Then, the next night she wants water and before too long, she's out of bed 3 or 4 times a night for hugs and kisses, water, band-aids, scary noises, you name it! Within a week, saying goodnight and falling asleep takes one hour or more. Now, we have to start all over again.'

As this mother said, 'Unfortunately, the only consistent behaviour has been my inconsistency.' In other words, when a behavioural approach fails with older children, it almost always is not a failure of the methods, but rather a failure of the resolve of the parents to implement it.

In one study of children about 3 years old conducted in Oxford, psychiatrists examined: (1) difficulty in going to bed (defined as requiring parents' presence until going to sleep in the bedroom or falling asleep downstairs before going to bed); (2) night waking at least three times a night or for more than an hour, or waking and continuing sleeping in the parents' bed; or (3) both. Treatment consisted of keeping a sleep diary for a week and establishing goals concerning the child's behaviour with the parents that included:

(a) Sleeping in his own bed;
(b) Remaining in his bed throughout the night;
(c) Not disturbing his parents during the night.

The treatment consisted of identifying the factors that reinforced the child's sleep problem, and then gradually withdrawing them or temporarily substituting less potent rewards. It was a 'fade' strategy, not a 'cold turkey' approach.

Here's an example of how they gradually reduced reinforcement: (a) the father reads a story to the child in bed for 15 minutes, (b) the father reads his newspaper in the child's bedroom until child falls asleep, (c) the child is placed back in bed with minimal interaction, and (d) gradual withdrawal of father from the bedroom before the child was asleep.

Another example they presented was: (a) parents alternate, but respond to the child, (b) no drinks are given but the child is held and comforted until he stops crying, (c) parent only sits by the bedside until he is asleep, and (d) less physical contact at bedtime.

Warning
At every stage of reduction of parental attention, expect
the problem to get worse before improvement begins.
That's because the child will put forth extra effort to cling
to the old style.

In the Oxford study, 84 per cent of the children improved.
Not surprisingly, the two factors that most likely predicted
success were *both* parental: the absence of marital discord and
the attendance of both parents at the consultation sessions.
Also, when one problem, such as resistance in going to sleep,
was reduced or resolved, other problems such as night
waking rapidly disappeared. And lastly, although half of the
mothers in this study had current psychiatric problems
requiring treatment, this did *not* make failure more likely.

I think this study points out the importance of working
with professionals who can provide parent-guidance advice
directed towards changing the child's behaviour without
dwelling on current psychological/emotional problems within
the mother or father. The exception, of course, is when *these
problems directly are related to marital discord or their ability to
maintain a behavioural management programme*.

In another study, the researchers included children who
took at least an hour to go to bed, awakened at least three
times a night or for more than 20 minutes, or who went into
the parents' bed. Treatment started with the parents record-
ing the present sleep pattern in a sleep diary. A therapist
worked with the parents to develop a programme of
treatment based on gradually reducing or removing parental
attention, adding positive reinforcement for the desired
behaviour, making bedtime earlier, and developing a bedtime ritual. Target behaviours were identified and an individual treatment programme was developed for each child.
Also, mothers were evaluated for psychiatric symptoms.
Mothers rated as showing psychiatric symptoms were more
likely to terminate treatment, again pointing out how stressful treatment can be. But for those families who completed
about four or five treatment sessions, 90 per cent of the
families showed improvement. The authors concluded that
'the evidence that children's night-time behaviour could thus
change so radically often within a surprisingly short time,

suggests that parental responses were extremely important in maintaining waking behaviour . . . A rapid achievement of improved sleep pattern with reduced parental attention would be unlikely if anxiety in the child or *lack* of parental attention were causing the sleep difficulty . . . Parents needed help in analysing goal behaviour into graded steps so that they could achieve successes. Once some success was obtained, the morale and confidence of the parents rose and they were reinforced in their determination to persist by the more peaceful nights.'

I have seen this over and over again; when you see even partial improvement, you gain confidence and you no longer feel guilty or rejecting when you are firm with your child.

Often it appears that the child is listening to the treatment plan in the office, because they often sleep better that very night . . . as if they knew something was going to be different! I think they are responding to the calm resolve and firm, but gentle, manner in their parents, which tells them that things are going to be different.

Q: Do I ever lock my child in her room?
A: Let's say that you've already tried patient reasoning, threats, criticisms, perhaps you've even tried spanking – which of course never works by itself – and all methods have failed. Also, let's assume that you are not working with a therapist to gradually reduce reinforcing behaviours. What's left to be done? Maybe a stiff door hook which, when locked, holds the door in a slightly open position but prevents opening or completely closing is the answer. The door is held locked in a slightly open position to protect his fingers from a crush injury. Completely closing and locking the door may be an overwhelming degree of separation for either you or your child.

What have you accomplished? You have established an unambiguous routine: the child knows that leaving the room after a certain time is unacceptable, and will *always* result in the door being latched in the slightly open position. The child learns that you mean business. The usual result is that after a night or two the child negotiates to stay in bed, and does, even if you do not lock the door. Also, you avoid the repeated prolonged stresses of your trying to separate physically from a child who is clinging to you or your trying to pull the door closed while your child is in the room trying to pull the door open.

Rewards are often used to encourage the child to co-operate. They must be items the child really wants. One mother placed a piece of chocolate, at night, after some cooperation, in a wicker basket which was under a special doll. Part of the motivation was the excitement of discovery in the morning when she looked for her treat. Paper stars on a chart may be used but they might be ineffective. One strategy that often works is withholding a favourite wholesome food and giving it only as a reward for cooperation. Other rewards might be small toys, surprise trips, or wholesome snack foods. By using a timer, you can give measured amounts of extra time for games, stories, TV, or free play.

Remember
Always reward even partial cooperation. Small rewards for small efforts, bigger rewards for more cooperation. Rewards are best given in the morning after awakening or immediately following a nap.

DAY SLEEP

You may conclude that life is impossible without your child taking a nap, but it is impossible to get him to nap. You've worked at sleep schedules, night wakings, resistance to sleep and things *are* better, but he also really needs a nap. Not necessarily a long one, but no nap at all is no good.

Some mothers have successfully re-established naps as a routine even when they have been absent or sporadic for several months. The method involves taking a nap with your child (at least initially): take her in to your own bed, dress yourself for sleep, and nap together. The idea is to make this a very comforting, soothing event. Try to be fairly regular according to clock time. Use a digital clock as a cue, and be consistent with the routine of a glass of warm milk and biscuits or reading from a favourite book. Try to fall asleep yourself. Tell your child what is expected of him; if he sleeps with you, then A occurs, if he rests quietly next to you but doesn't fall asleep, then B occurs. You decide what kind of reward A and B will be.

If he doesn't cooperate at all and jumps on the bed or runs around the room, then you might restrict or withdraw some pleasurable activity or privilege. If you are able to get him to nap with you, then eventually you'll want to try to shift his napping to his own room. This should be done in a graded or staged fashion. You might decide the next step is for him to be in his bed and you're in his room resting as long as needed. Rewards are now given *only* for this new behaviour. This process of reinforcing successive approximations to the desired target behaviour is called '*shaping*'.

OTHER IDEAS

Notions, theories, and opinions on how to prevent or solve sleep problems abound. It would be worth taking a closer look at some ideas published recently, and see how they stand up to the facts about children's sleep habits that have been reviewed in this book.

CHECKING: A METHOD OF HELPING FALL ASLEEP
(By Jo Douglas and Naomi Richman)

The Theory

Go into your child's room when he starts to cry and provide reassurance and comforting: 'A firmness of approach, without undue sympathy or contact, is necessary.' Then leave the room, even if he is still awake and continues to cry. Wait up to 5 minutes, then return and repeat the same procedure. Continue to do this, back and forth, until he realizes he will not be picked up . . . 'they normally fall asleep quickly'. This pattern of checking is repeated consistently each time your child cries and 'he should learn within 3 or 4 nights his crying no longer achieves the desired end of getting up'. This procedure is implemented after age one year, 'because of the vagaries of the first year'. They do not recommend totally leaving the child alone, because the distress to the parents is unbearable. They state that the advantage of checking is that 'the regular visits reassure you that your child is safe and well'. In other words, they think this is an *easier* approach for the *parents*, not a more *effective* approach for the *child*.

My Comment

I think checking would work well for some families, but not for those families who start off with a very tired child, perhaps one who had had colic, or for some mothers who have trouble separating from their child. It is equally unbearable *not* to pick up and hug or nurse – just once. And as we've seen, once is all it takes to start the habit all over again.

SHAPING AN INFANT TO SLEEP
(By Rita J. McGarr and Melbourne F. Hovel)

The Theory

This is a single case report that describes awakening a child 15 to 30 minutes before her expected early awakening. For example, if the child usually got up at 4 am, the parents would awaken her at 3.45. Then, when awake, mother would nurse or cuddle before putting back to bed. Maternal attention, they stated, was thus associated with falling asleep, not waking and crying. Next, the scheduled awakenings would be shifted later by 15- to 30-minute intervals. If the baby spontaneously awakens earlier, respond immediately and on the next night awaken her 15 to 30 minutes before that unscheduled awakening the night before. The goal is to increase the child's length of sleep and eliminate night crying. The child in the study was 3 months old.

My Comment

The data in this study looks good, but 'the parents declined to conduct a formal follow-up measure . . . they acknowledged that she occasionally spontaneously awoke earlier than 5 am . . . both parents reported that the procedures were difficult to employ'. In addition to no follow-up data, still getting up early, and finding the method hard to use, there is also the risk that the child learns to associate the cuddling and nursing with the immediately prior event, which was awakening.

FOCAL FEEDING . . . FOLLOWED BY WATER AND LOVE
(By Joanne Cuthbertson and Susie Schevill)

The Theory

Start on the third day of life by always feeding between 10 pm and midnight even if you have to wake her. This is called the focal feeding.

The staged procedure is recommended to start around 6 weeks (when night sleep organization spontaneously begins!) or later if baby has colic.

Night 1

Step 1: Have some water ready in a bottle.

Step 2: Focal feeding; awake baby between 10 pm and midnight. Get him back to sleep quickly.

Step 3: First spontaneous wake-up; father or assistant (not mother) change, wrap in blankets, settle back to bed. Do not now pick him up but sing, rock, offer a dummy, or rock the crib.

Step 4: (a) He fell asleep but now is up again, try to gain 'further stretching time' by playing with him in your arms, walk around.

(b) He did not fall asleep after 10 to 20 minutes, pick him up, play with him.

Step 5: Having stretched your baby as long as possible, offer the water that you prepared. They write, 'A baby will quickly abandon night-time awakenings if water and love are the only reward.'

Step 6: Change nappy, try to settle him back to sleep . . . then or later, feed him (formula or breastmilk).

Repeat this procedure for 3 full nights and if he is sleeping better and awakening initially at 5 or 6 am, let him fuss for 10 to 20 minutes. If he is not sleeping better, try this procedure again in a few weeks.

My Comment

In discussing this procedure with the first author, she told me that it worked 90 per cent of the time, but that there was no data or survey to validate that claim. It would be worthwhile to know whether both the temporal control part (focal feeding) or the removal of positive reinforcement (the water instead of milk) are needed or whether only one item would work as well. Then the procedure would be simpler to execute and in my experience, the simpler the procedure, the more likely that parents will stick to it.

PROPER ASSOCIATION WITH FALLING ASLEEP
(By Richard Ferber)

The Theory

A child associates certain conditions with falling asleep, such as being held in parents' arms, lying down on a living room sofa, or rocking in a swing. When put to sleep in a cot or bed, upon awakening, those certain conditions are missing so the child has difficulty returning to sleep. The progressive approach is to not respond to the baby's cry at night when she awakens in her cot for a brief period of time, say 5 minutes. After crying for 5 minutes, the parents return and stay in the room 2 to 3 minutes, but do not pick up or rock her. This is thought to reassure the parents and the child that all is well. Parents then leave, whether asleep or not, whether crying or not, and return in 10 minutes for the same brief interaction, if needed. After leaving, they would return again after 15 minutes of crying for a brief curtain call. They would return every 15 minutes for a brief encounter until the child fell asleep during one of their 15-minute absences. If no crying or mild whimpering, then no return. If the child awoke later that night with hard crying, they would repeat the original progressive routine of 5, 10, 15, 15, 15 . . . minutes of delay in response time. The second night would be a repeat performance except the progression would be 10, 15, 20, 20, 20 . . . The third night would be 15, 20, 25, 25, 25 . . . and so on. The child learns to associate falling asleep and returning to sleep in her bed or cot.

My Comment

Whether we call this approach developing 'proper associations' or 'learning self-soothing skills,' I'm sure this method can work. But the general problem is that it's very difficult to maintain any time schedule in the middle of the night for several nights in a consistent fashion . . . frustration and exhaustion often override planning and patience.

Summary

Children who don't sleep well usually have developed this pattern as a result of parental mismanagement, when allergies or airway obstructions have been ruled out. Too much attention, irregularity, or inconsistency in bedtime 'policy' and routines interfered with the development of healthy sleep habits. Accepting this responsibility is the first step in developing an appropriate treatment plan.

But as we've seen, there's quite a variety of options, and you may be uncertain whether you want to try a gradual, 'fading' approach or an abrupt, 'cold turkey' extinguishing approach. When you try to decide between gradual versus an abrupt approach in putting to rights your child's sleep habits, consider not only your own resolve, but also the external supports that you know you can count on.

Many parents start with a gradual approach, see partial success, but then get worn down and recognize their evolving inconsistency. Feeling a bit more confident and competent, many parents then shift directions to a more abrupt approach. But some parents cannot even start to correct their child's sleeping problems at all, because the same personal stresses revolving around the child's emerging independence, marital discord, and other problems within the parents that created the unhealthy sleep habits in the first place are still present. If you suspect this is you, the next chapter may help.

9 A Sleep Disorder – My Child?

By Patricia Della-Selva, PhD

What do we mean by a sleep disorder? To be honest, this is usually defined by the parent. When the child's sleep, or lack thereof, becomes troublesome to the parent, it gets identified as a problem. Because you are reading this book, you probably already have decided a problem may exist and are looking for help.

At some point in time, almost all children have trouble either going to sleep or waking at night. Perhaps they can't settle down after a particularly exciting day or have trouble saying good night following a separation from Mummy. Disruptions in a young child's life are bound to affect his eating and sleeping habits for a while, and we expect this. We comfort the child and it soon passes.

We had a recent example of this in our own home. My 2½-year-old daughter became fearful of being alone at night when we moved to a new house. She would call me back several times after being put to bed, wanting 'just one more song' or another 'night-night story'. I realized her need for extra assurance and provided it. After several weeks, she had settled into the house, but had got into the habit of calling me and resisting sleep. She would cry and say she was scared, but as soon as I'd arrive, she'd laugh. It became clear that she had learned how to get me to respond to her protests. I told her that she no longer seemed frightened, but just wanted to stay up late. I told her it was bedtime and that I'd see her in the morning. She was angry at being found out and put up quite a protest, but I remained firm and didn't return to her room. This isn't as easy as it may sound. She screamed on and off for 40 minutes and really tested our resolve, but we held out. It worked! The very next evening our regular routine was restored. If I hadn't been able to determine when she was really frightened and when she was play-acting, this could have dragged on endlessly.

The move to our new house was the obvious cause in this example, but many parents complain of chronic sleep problems in their children with no idea whatsoever regarding its cause. Since all children have trouble with sleep at some time in their early lives, we as parents need to find ways to handle it before it becomes a chronic problem. In preceding chapters, Dr Weissbluth has outlined clear, well-researched guidelines to help you and your family enjoy more silent nights. Some parents can't seem to make them work. What gets in their way?

WHOSE PROBLEM IS THIS, ANYWAY?

Let's begin by talking about the feelings that surface in you as your baby develops. Often, our own very early memories return when we become parents. Thoughts and feelings that may have been buried for years arise when we have our own babies. Sometimes, without even thinking, we find ourselves saying things we never dreamed we'd utter. We vowed not to be like our parents, but when asked 'Why?' for the tenth time by our curious 2-year-old, we find ourselves saying, 'Because I said so.' Sometimes old feelings about our own childhood get in the way of our being effective parents.

Some of this may be painful, but bear with me. If you can understand what you're feeling and where it's coming from, you'll be well on your way to resolving your baby's sleep problem.

While it seems to the casual observer that the problem of going to sleep is clearly the baby's, I have frequently found that the mother – as the baby's primary care-giver – subtly and unconsciously either encourages wakefulness or prevents the development of independent self-soothing in her child. Here is just one example.

A working mother who returned to work after a 3-month maternity leave felt very guilty about the limited amount of time she had to spend with her new baby. She kept him up late and always responded to his calls at night. At the age of

18 months, her son still failed to sleep through the night. Upon reflection, she admitted that she cherished these times alone with her baby and wouldn't want to see them end. Her need to have contact with her baby, and guilt over leaving him during the day, prevented her from allowing her baby to learn to sleep on his own. As our talk continued, she said her husband was now refusing to have any more children and she realized her son would be her only child. Now she clung to him and this period of 'babyhood' even more tenaciously, because she knew she would never again have the chance to experience this special closeness. She required some professional help to separate her needs from those of her baby and to learn to behave in his best interest, while dealing with her own feelings and problems in an appropriate way.

MARITAL PROBLEMS

Another type of problem that can contribute to a baby's sleepless nights is within the marriage itself. In fact, marital problems are frequently present in the families of the children I've seen who have sleep disorders. Often, the woman feels unloved and unappreciated by her husband and seeks solace in her child. This was dramatically demonstrated by one mother who would leave her husband's bed to go sleep with her baby, who was waking in the night. This mother's view was: my baby needs me, wants me and is happy to see me when I enter the room. This mother felt none of this warm, loving acceptance from her husband, so the lure of her baby's cry was too much for her to resist.

In this example, the mother's own needs coloured her judgment. Unconsciously, she was using the baby to soothe herself. But, she was convinced consciously that she was being a good mother by responding to every call. Her husband couldn't very well get angry with her for being such a devoted mother, so a confrontation was avoided. This points out the other crucial area of difficulty I've noticed in these mothers – their inability to express anger directly

ANGER

A third area where a mother's problems can contribute to her baby's sleep problems is the ability to express anger. Even successful professional women can feel dependent and frightened in an intimate relationship and fear that any expression of anger will disrupt or even destroy it. By being continually preoccupied with her baby, the woman expresses her anger and dissatisfaction with her husband in an indirect fashion. Not only is this destructive for the marriage itself, it also hampers the baby's development.

THE NEED TO BE NEEDED AND LOVED

As you can see from these examples, several themes recur again and again in these women. The central issue seems to be a strong need to be needed and loved. Some women have a poorly developed sense of self and are, therefore, overly dependent on others for feelings of self-worth. If their baby is unhappy and making a fuss, they feel personally inadequate and will do whatever is necessary in order to quiet him down – and make them *both* feel better. I have found, too, that many women fear being alone and need another's presence to feel safe. Nighttime can be especially difficult, and some women may go to their children for soothing and companionship if their husband is away or emotionally unavailable.

HOW ABOUT FATHER?

Why am I addressing myself to mothers? In this country, the great majority of babies are cared for primarily by their mothers. Even though fathers are more involved than ever, very few assume the role of primary caretaker. While both parents may discuss child-rearing practices, the mother is usually the one who implements these practices on a day-to-day basis either herself or supervising the baby's caretaker. This does not mean, however, that fathers don't influence their children or contribute to their baby's sleep problems.

Here are only a few cases that illustrate how they certainly can and do.

A mother came to me recently for advice regarding her 2-year-old son, who cried for 'Mummy' throughout the night and demanded her presence before returning to sleep. She felt this was becoming a real problem, and wanted to correct it. A plan was devised and she told her son that she would no longer be coming to him at night. The parents agreed to let him cry, if that's what it would take. But the father backed out after hearing his son cry for 10 minutes. He began to yell at his wife, saying, 'Are you really going to let him cry like this? If you don't go to him, I will!' Needless to say, the plan went down the drain and night waking continued.

Another father in a similar situation yelled, 'I have to work in the morning. I need my sleep. Go and shut him up!' As these examples illustrate, *both* parents have feelings about child-rearing, and they need to agree and *stick together* if their plan is going to work. I hope that both mothers and fathers will read this and work out a strategy for solving their child's sleep difficulties together. Children gain a great deal of security from the knowledge that parents are unified, rather than split, on important issues.

THE WHOLE FAMILY GETS INVOLVED

As the divorce rate has soared, remarriages have become commonplace and step-families are more prevalent than ever. When a new baby enters the picture, frequently the older siblings from the previous marriages have to deal with the new arrival. As a mother in this situation, you may worry that if you allow yourself to be absorbed with your new infant, the others will feel neglected and get angry. On the other hand, you may receive all sorts of advice from your older children about how to handle the new baby. You may try to please everyone, and end up feeling that no one is happy. One woman told me she continued to go to her baby at night long after she would have if he were her only child. She had teenage step-children in the house, and didn't want to keep them up. She went to her baby 'to keep him quiet'. Things certainly do get complicated in these situations, but solutions can be found.

It would be great if everyone could sit down, talk about the situation, agree on a solution and carry it out. But things aren't always so easily resolved. You, as parents, have to decide what's best and let the older children know about your decision. They should be told to abide by your wishes, even if they don't agree with them. They'll eventually get their turn at parenting.

WHOSE ADVICE DO I FOLLOW?

I've had many parents ask me how to determine which route to follow in this or other areas of child care. It seems as though every 'expert' has a different opinion and technique. Parents today are often alone in the demanding task of child-rearing, having moved away from their family and friends, and they rely on books and professionals for help. One mother said she understood the position being taken in this book, but worried about letting her baby cry, because she had read elsewhere that you should 'never let your baby cry'.

Some experts try to simplify the complex task of child-rearing by concentrating on one principle or guideline. Le Leche League provides both useful information and much needed support to nursing mothers. But, they oversimplify the task of development by using one parental response – that of offering the breast – as the answer to all dilemmas. They address the baby's need for love and nurturance to the exclusion of all other needs. Babies are complicated creatures and they need to be able to be alone, be angry, and even be sad at times without being forced into 'blissful union' with a mother who can't tolerate hearing her baby cry.

Recent research has been done on babies who are unable to fall asleep on their own and require holding in order to do so. It was discovered that the mothers of these babies wouldn't allow them to separate, to grow and to learn how to do things on their own. They discouraged the baby's attempts to soothe himself by sucking his thumb or using a dummy. These babies were described as 'addicted to mother's presence'. Some recent attention has been directed at adults who become addicted to their lovers. It's my suspicion that an addiction to mother, like the one described in this research, is at the root of this problem as well.

HOW CAN THEORY HELP?

We no longer need to rely on old wives' tales or the latest fashion in child-rearing advice to guide our behaviour with regard to child care. Significant strides have been made in research concerning babies over the past twenty years, and the findings can be of great help. It's my belief that most parents will respond when given clear, accurate information along with a feeling that they are being supported in this complex and anxiety-arousing job of parenting. In this light, let me briefly review what we know about babies and the process of separation as it unfolds in the first few years of life.

THE 'HATCHING PROCESS'

According to the research conducted by Margaret Mahler mentioned earlier, the first signs of individuation, or development as an individual, normally occur at the beginning of the baby's fourth month. Up until that time, baby and mother are as one. The infant is totally dependent on the mother for all his physical and psychological needs. Optimally, the baby's needs and the mother's ability to give are balanced. During the late stages of pregnancy and the first few months of extrauterine life, the normal mother finds that she is preoccupied with her baby. This allows her to tune into and get to know her baby in a special way. In addition to providing warmth and food, the mother provides the vital function of soothing the infant, who is being bombarded with stimulation from both internal (hunger) and external (noise) sources. By responding immediately to your baby's cry, you are providing a basis for trust essential in healthy emotional development. The result of a successful 'dance' between you and your baby is that the world is felt to be manageable rather than an overwhelming or threatening place.

The first few months   During the first few months of life, babies sleep a lot and do so according to their own needs and rhythms. Research suggests this cannot and should not be altered. When your baby is tired and fretful, he needs your soothing ministrations to lull him to sleep. Being left alone to cry is overwhelming for an infant. The baby is absolutely dependent on you for soothing and has no internal resources on which to rely. Only by having the soothing provided externally on a reliable basis will your baby eventually be able to internalize it, in order to calm himself and feel a safe, whole being even when alone.

Given the total dependence of newborn infants, one cannot speak of an infant without referring to and understanding the mother. The physical process of birth does not coincide with psychological birth. In her pioneering studies of mother-infant pairs, Mahler found that mothers' conscious and, more importantly, unconscious attitudes, had a significant impact on the course and outcome of the 'hatching' process that begins in the fourth month of life. At that time, bodily dependence decreases and the baby's focus gradually changes from the inner world to the world around him. The baby shows interest in objects and pursues goals. At this time your baby will start to push away from you in order to explore your face. He'll express active pleasure in the use of his entire body. If your baby has had an optimal experience of unity with you in the first, symbiotic phase of development, he will take your presence for granted and play confidently at your feet.

Some mothers find this first step toward independence painful, and interpret the baby's pushing away as rejection. While some become angry and withdraw emotionally, others cling to their babies and try to prolong the feeling of oneness they so enjoyed. It is these mothers who seem to have the greatest difficulty putting their babies down to sleep. They continue to feel that their babies must fall asleep before being put down. While they consciously feel this is essential for the baby, it has become clear, as I've explored these issues with them, that it is *their* need to feel needed that motivates their hanging onto the baby.

In the first three months of her life, my youngest daughter slept a good deal. She tended to wake up at around 6 am, and fall right back to sleep after being nursed. She'd get up again around 8 am, sleep again from 10 to 12 noon and 2 to 4 pm, and was in for the night at 7 pm. It seemed she was content to just eat and sleep. Between 3 and 4 months, she became far more sociable and playful. I noticed that she began to have difficulty falling asleep. At first we were perplexed, because the child who had always slept so much was now fighting sleep. All my holding and rocking seemed in vain. I soon came to realize that she was confused. Her growing awareness of the world and desire to explore it were at odds with her need to sleep. My typical method of holding her until she dropped off wasn't working, because her closeness to me was now stimulating her curiosity and desire to interact. Her lack of sleep was taking its toll, and she became very cranky. I decided that I needed to put her down in her cot when I saw signs of sleepiness. She cried for a minute or two, but the familiarity of the cot and the music from her mobile soon lulled her to sleep. It was clear she needed help regulating her sleep/wake cycles at this point in development, and she readily accepted the routine. Her waking hours were filled with active exploration of the environment, and her naps were consistent and restorative.

Was putting my baby down and letting her cry for a few minutes cruel? Would she feel abandoned and lose confidence in the world around her? This is what many mothers fear. In fact, by understanding the needs of a baby at this stage of development, you'll find that the opposite is true. You interfere with development when you fail to recognize your baby's growing ability to do for himself what you once did for him. This is where theory can help in a practical way.

About 4 to 9 months   It used to be thought that babies were totally dependent upon their mothers for a year or more. Now we know from research that they are able to do more earlier than we ever thought possible. At this age, a baby needs and responds to regularity in his day. By beginning to institute a reasonable nap schedule, you are making life predictable and reducing anxiety. Imagine how interminable a day must seem to a 4-month-old infant. By having a fairly routine day of meals, naps, play-time and bath you are providing a structure which can be internalized over time. Trying to impose a schedule on a 6-week-old infant will prove futile, but three months later the baby can respond to it. To be effective parents, we need to understand and respond to these changing capabilities in our babies. Yes, respecting your baby's need for regularity in his day may entail some sacrifice on your part. But adapting yourself to your baby's needs now, will lay the foundation for healthy development later.

This sort of adaptation to your baby's needs does not come naturally, and usually needs to be learned. A couple with children my own kids' ages proved a vivid example of this. Upon discovering the similarity in our family structure, we decided to get together with this couple and their children one afternoon. When nap-time came, I put my baby to sleep and rejoined the company. They were amazed that I could just put her down. They said their 6-month-old rarely napped. They attributed this to luck and heredity, but it became clear as the day progressed that the differences between the babies reflected the differences in the way they were handled. I watched as they talked, played with and fed their baby. When she began to cry, squirm and rub her eyes, they interpreted this as a need for more active intervention. They took her on their lap and began to bounce her up and down. This worked for a few minutes, but the crying returned. Then they tried pushing her back and forth in the pushchair. The baby was clearly tired, and all these attempts at entertainment were causing her to get more keyed up and less able to get the sleep she needed. Babies this age don't just fall asleep in the midst of commotion the way a newborn will. We need to understand their cues and respond accordingly.

What interfered with this couple's ability to recognize their daughter's crankiness as fatigue and put her to bed? I learned that both parents, professionals with demanding careers, worked full-time and wanted to be with their children as much as possible on weekends. As much as they complained about their children's lack of sleep, it was obvious that they enjoyed the extra time this afforded them. They were not able to separate their need for time with the children from the children's need for rest. They tended to pack weekends full of visits and activities. They wanted to take them to zoos and parks, and didn't want naps to interfere. What they failed to recognize was that the children were so fatigued that they couldn't enjoy or learn from these experiences. Their toddler would tend to pass out from exhaustion while riding in the pushchair. Accommodating to his needs might have meant forgoing day trips until he got a little older.

Some may say you are being overly protective if you schedule around your children, but for the first two years or so this is essential to their health and well-being. Some professionals undertake the role of parenthood with the same gusto and ambition that made them successful in their chosen field, but it is misplaced here. Children need to develop at their own pace and will suffer if pushed to do too much, too soon. This is the other extreme of the overly protective mother we discussed earlier.

A 'love affair with the world' The next stage of development, referred to as the 'practising' phase, ushers in what's been called by Mahler the infant's 'love affair with the world'. It lasts from approximately 10 to 15 months. The baby's increased motor skills and exploration of the environment make this an active time, one in which sleep difficulties often arise. The baby is so taken with the world and his ability to affect it, that he won't willingly retreat. Many parents subscribe to the notion that the child knows best and will sleep when tired. I've seen parents use this excuse to justify allowing their infants to go all day without a nap. Research tells us that babies of this age continue to require naps and reasonable bedtimes, but they also may require more help in settling down than they did several months ago. Why is this? Your baby is increasingly able to determine cause and effect. You'll notice babies of this age will play endlessly with those toys where they can vividly experience the effects of their actions. This newfound ability also will affect your baby's relationship with you. Their desire to control the world, including you, is more powerful than their desire for sleep. So, it's up to you to help your baby turn off the world and go to sleep.

One mother, whose baby had always been a great sleeper, suddenly had a problem during this stage of development. The infant refused naps and prolonged sleeptime at night by calling mother back each time he was left in his cot. The first step in tackling the problem was to understand it. The baby was exercising his newfound powers of control by calling his mother back when he wanted her. It was an ongoing peek-a-boo game! She decided it was time for her baby to learn the limits of his control. *She* decided on a reasonable sleep schedule and, following a lullaby, would say to her son, 'It's nap-time now. I'll see you in a couple of hours.' At night she'd say, 'I'll see you in the morning.' While a prolonged period of screaming and protest was anticipated, it only lasted 10 minutes that first night and 5 minutes the second night. How can this be explained? Did this 9-month-old understand what mother was saying? Obviously he didn't comprehend the words, but his mother had spoken his language – one of action, and her attitude – one of calm assurance – relayed the message. This sort of assurance is very important, because babies pick up on their mothers' feelings. They will respond to any tension or ambivalence they perceive. Rather than being traumatized, as some parents fear, this baby seemed happier than ever. Bedtimes were no longer a struggle, and both parent and child were able to enjoy this special closeness before bed without dreading a confrontation.

I have found that refusing to set limits and continuing a struggle with going to bed over a period of weeks and months has a more damaging effect to the parent–child relationship than a few nights' crying in the process of establishing good sleep habits. There is an added benefit to settling this problem as soon as it arises. First of all, it's easier to get rid of a habit that's just forming than one that's well established. Most importantly, though, is the fact that a well-rested child enjoys his waking hours and can be at his best all day.

Now we'll get back to the task of development. Weaning your baby from his total dependence on you is the central issue when the baby is 10 to 15 months old. Weaning means more than the gradual elimination of the breast. It signals the start of baby's identity as a separate individual. Both sadness and anger can, and frequently do, accompany this period of transition. Mother needs to help her child in this process, which has been referred to as one of disillusionment. Up until now, mother has given her baby the illusion that the world is his oyster and that all needs will be satisfied immediately. This belief in things and people is necessary in infancy. But gradually, the child must discover that, while the world can provide satisfaction for some needs and wants, it does not do so automatically. A switch must occur from the notion of need to that of wish or desire. This signals an acceptance of external reality, including the awareness of other people and their feelings.

Anger need not be destructive Learning to wait is not easy, and anger is not an uncommon response during this process. Mothers who fear anger and associate it with abandonment, can't tolerate anger in their children. They want to be loved at all times, even idolized. Without realizing it, they prevent their children from learning that anger is not destructive. By tolerating the anger and surviving it, you provide reassuring proof that thoughts and feelings can't destroy. Your baby will eventually come to realize that you are neither a wicked witch nor a good fairy, but a human being. He will then be better able to accept himself as such. This may sound reasonable, and it shouldn't be difficult to pull off. But, from my experience, many mothers have a great deal of trouble during this stage in their child's development. What makes it so rough?

I have found that these women have had a troubled relationship with their own mother that was never resolved, got replayed in marriage and activated again when they themselves became mothers. A large number of them have come from divorced homes. As well as losing their father via divorce, they frequently suffered the loss of their mother through work and/or depression. Their mother may have used them to satisfy her own emotional needs, never giving them the room they needed to develop as individuals. It is no wonder that a similar pattern gets activated when these children become women and have children of their own. They are so afraid of the loss of important relationships, that they cower in the face of confrontation and would rather give in, even to their own child, than face these feelings again.

Separation without trauma The task of the next phase, called 'rapprochement', is for the baby to learn how to separate *without* trauma. Mothers need to be 'emotionally available' during this period, while physically giving the child some breathing room. Donald Winnicott, a paediatrician who is also a psychoanalyst, spoke of the ability to be alone as beginning to develop here, when the child is alone in the presence of his mother. What does that mean? It means being left alone to explore the world and discover one's own inner life, free from intrusions by mother and her needs. The alternative is what Winnicott calls a 'false self'. The 'false self' is built up of reactions to mother's and others' needs and expectations for the child, rather than reflecting the unique individuality of the child.

Troubles later on Each new stage of development brings with it special problems and concerns as well as newfound abilities. The 2-year-old begins to experience fears. He now recognizes the limits of his power, and tends to feel small and helpless in a big and often confusing world. Fears can make going to sleep at night problematic.

Graduating from a cot to a bed can also cause new difficulties with sleep. While understanding and accommodation to your child at these junctures in development are necessary, your firm attitude regarding sleep will carry over to each new stage. If a good, solid sleep habit has been formed in the first year of life, all subsequent trouble spots, like fear of the dark, getting up to go to the potty or needing a drink of water, will die out in a short time. If a sleep problem has existed from infancy, these new difficulties just get added to the existing problem. You then will be faced with a complex and tenacious situation. At this point, unlike the case of a 9-month-old who is having new difficulties falling asleep due to a spurt in motor development, a simple solution is unlikely. This doesn't mean you should throw in the towel and forget about trying to find a cure for the sleep disorder. But it does mean looking at your contribution to the problem, as well as the child's, and instituting a programme of change – as outlined in this book – based on your unique history together.

The fact that you're reading this book signifies a desire to begin the process of change. Understanding your baby's needs is paramount, and this book, along with others cited at the end of this chapter, can broaden that understanding. An understanding of your own reactions and difficulties also may be a necessary step. Further reading in this area can be of great value as well. If you find that you're still struggling with mixed feelings about letting your baby separate, you might consider professional counselling.

10 What a Difference Healthy Sleep Can Make

Healthy sleep appears to come so easily and naturally to our newborn babies. Effortlessly, they fall asleep and stay asleep. Their sleep patterns shift and evolve as the brain matures during the first few weeks and months. 'Day/night confusion' – long sleep periods during the day and long wakeful periods at night – is bothersome, but the problem is only one of timing. The young infant still does not have difficulty falling asleep or staying asleep.

But after several weeks of age, natural sleep rhythms and patterns can be shaped by parents into sleep habits.

As we have seen, the development of healthy sleep habits is *not* automatic. In fact, parents can and do help or hinder the development of healthy sleep habits. Of course, children will spontaneously 'fall asleep' when totally exhausted – 'crashing' is a biological necessity! But this is unhealthy, because the extreme fatigue often identified by 'up-cited' behaviour immediately preceding the crash interferes with normal social interactions and even learning.

During the first 6 weeks, you should adopt a watchful, waiting attitude and try to become sensitive to your child's need to sleep. After about 6 weeks, you should begin trying to synchronize your caretaking activities with her now emerging sleep–wake rhythms and putting her down to sleep on a somewhat predictable schedule for naps and at night. And by age 4 or 5 months, this regular schedule should be part of every healthy baby's routine. Using the never before published data on children's sleep habits presented at the outset of this book, you can then continue to fine-tune your child's sleep habits as he grows from a toddler to a teen.

Important Point

Sleep is a biological function. When it is greatly disturbed early in life, studies show that recovery to healthy patterns is difficult.

When children learn to sleep well, they also learn to maintain 'optimal' wakefulness. This notion of optimal wakefulness or optimal alertness is important, because we often tend to think simplistically of being either awake or asleep. But there are more than two states. There are gradations in sleep and wakefulness. As we have seen, just as there are differing levels of being asleep (from deep sleep to natural arousals), there are differing levels of wakefulness (from being 'wide awake' to being groggy).

The importance of optimal wakefulness – being 'bright eyed and bushy tailed' – was discussed about twenty-five years ago by Dr Barbara Fish, a child psychiatrist:

Disorders in the development of arousal and attention may have repercussions in many areas of the developing personality. An infant must be able to maintain alertness, to inhibit crying and random movement, and to sustain focused visual and auditory attention before he can develop an organized perceptual experience of the world beyond his body boundaries. Underresponsiveness, or an inability to sustain attention, or an inability to screen out irrelevant internal or external stimuli represent primitive disturbances of arousal and attention.

If your child does not get all the sleep he needs, during the day he may seem either drowsy or hyperalert. If either state lasts for a long time, the results are the same: a child with a difficult mood and hard-to-control behaviour, certainly not one who is ready and able to enjoy himself or get the most out of the myriad of learning experiences placed before him.

'With our busy lifestyles, how can we keep track of nap schedules and regular bedtime hours?' 'Is it really true that I can harm my baby by giving him love at night when he cries out for me?' 'How can I be sure that sleep is really that important?'

These are questions that many parents ask me. They will

often refer to something they have read to support different ideas, and will conclude by saying that since this whole issue is 'so controversial', they would rather let matters stay as they are. If you think your child is not sleeping well and if you disagree with the suggestions in this book, ask yourself, how long should you wait for improvement to occur? Three months? Three years? If you are following the opinion of a professional who says you must spend more time with your child at night to make him feel more 'secure', ask that professional, when will I know we are on the right track? Don't wait forever. After all, if you are losing money by consistently following the advice of a stockbroker who says: 'Be patient, things will change', it is reasonable to ask yourself: 'How long should I wait before some improvement should occur before switching financial advisors?' If you are thinking of switching paediatricians, consider what Dr Charles E. Sundell, who was then the doctor in charge of the Children's Department at the Prince of Wales' General Hospital, wrote in 1922, 'Success in the treatment of sleeplessness in infants is a good standard by which to estimate the patience and skill of the practitioner.'

He also wrote, 'A sleepless baby is a reproach to his guardians, and convicts them of some failure in their guardianship.' So don't think that worrying about sleeplessness is just a contemporary issue. In fact, Aulus Cornelius Celsus wrote in AD 130 that 'infants and children who are still of tender age (may be) attacked by . . . wakefulness at night'. Sleeplessness in our children and worrying about sleeplessness have been around for a long time!

The truth is that modern research regarding sleep/wake states only confirms what careful practitioners, such as Dr Sundell, observed over sixty years ago. He wrote:

The temptation to postpone the time for a baby's sleep, so that he may be admired by some relative or friend who is late in arriving, or so that his nurse may finish some work on which she may be engaged, must be strongly resisted. A sleepy child who is kept awake exhausts his nervous energy very quickly in *peevish restlessness*, and when preparations are at last made for his sleep *he may be too weary to settle down*. Physiological proof of this indisposition for slumber is to be found in the *increased reflex-irritability of a sleepy child, an irritability* which is soon soothed into sluggishness should sleep be not too long delayed, but *which persists and increases if the balm of sleep is withheld.*

Regularity of habits is one of the sheet-anchors by which the barque of an infant's health is secured. The re-establishment of a regular routine, after even a short break, frequently calls for *patient perseverance* on the part of the nurse, but though the child may protest vigorously for several nights, *absolute firmness seldom fails to procure the desired result.* (Emphasis added.)

In Chapter 3, we looked at many myths about sleeping that are based only on opinions, traditions, or social customs. Often, popular magazines and books present these myths as facts, simply because they have been repeated so often in other similar publications.

Don't be misled. The actual facts based on many reputable studies do make good biological sense, and more importantly, are confirmed by every mother who has raised more than one child.

Each baby born *is* unique. It's a little like snowflakes, or even roulette . . . except there are no losers, only winners. The obvious ways in which babies are born to be individuals include the amounts of physical activity, durations of sleep, and crying. But babies also differ in more subtle ways – some are much more regular than others. The more regular baby is easier 'to read', she seems to have her own schedule for feeding and sleeping. Also these babies tend to cry less and sleep more. So don't blame yourself if you happen to have an irregular baby who cries a lot – it's only luck . . . but maybe social customs affect how you feel about it.

In societies where the mother holds the baby close all the time, and her breasts are always available for nursing and soothing, there are still great differences among babies in terms of fussiness and crying. But the mothers compensate by naturally increasing the amount of rhythmic, rocking motions or nursing. She may not even expect the baby to sleep by herself, away from her body. As the baby grows up, the child might share the bed with her parents for a long time. This is not necessarily good or bad.

But, it's different from the expectations of most Western, middle-class, white families. So not only do babies sleep differently, every society's expectations condition parents' feelings in differing ways. Please do not assume that less developed societies are more 'natural' and thus 'healthier' in their child-rearing practices. After all, strychnine and cow's milk are equally 'natural', but have altogether different results.

How much we are bothered by infant crying or poor sleep habits might partially reflect what we have absorbed from our society's and our own family's expectations about how to be 'good' parents. Do we want to carry our baby all the time, 24 hours a day, or do we want to put the baby down sometimes to sleep? If we are greatly bothered by his crying or our guilt about not being 'good' parents, this may interfere with our developing a sense of competence as parents; we may feel that we cannot later influence sleep patterns in our child. As we have seen, this sets the stage for future sleep problems.

Remember

Sleep problems not only disrupt a child's nights – they disrupt his *days* too, by: (1) making him less mentally alert, more inattentive, unable to concentrate, or easily distracted and (2) by making him more physically impulsive, hyperactive or alternatively lazy.

But when our children sleep well, they are optimally awake and optimally alert to learn and to grow up with charm, humour, and love. When parents are too irregular, inconsistent or oversolicitous, when mothers or fathers are overly absorbed in their children, when marital problems are left unresolved, the resulting sleep problems converge to the final common pathway: excessive nighttime wakefulness and crying.

Please do not just simply assume that children must pass through different 'stages' at different ages that inevitably create sleep problems . . . just as acne occurs during adolescence.

Parents create sleep problems.

Parents can prevent sleep problems.

Parents can correct sleep problems.

Parents who favour a more gradual approach to correcting unhealthy sleep habits often complain of frequent 'relapses' . . . or worse. By worse, I mean that the initial impression of success and the subsequent relapse occurred only in the minds of the parents. In other words, some parents have described to me definite improvement gradually developing over many days; at follow-up a few months later they say everything is wonderful. But at a follow-up several months after that, they say that there was never any improvement at all. Upon reminding them that they had previously described improvement, they state that maybe things had only seemed to be a little better at that time.

I think that some parents swing back and forth between firmness and permissiveness so often, they cannot make any cure stick. They often confuse their wishful thinking with the child's actual behaviour. This is why a sleep diary is so important to document what you really are doing and how your child is really responding. After all, short-term 'successes' might only reflect brief periods when your child crashes at night from chronic exhaustion! Or the actual improvement in sleep habits may be so marginal, that the normal disruptions of holidays, trips, illnesses, or other irregularities constantly buffet the still-tired child and cause repeated 'relapses' of night waking or fighting sleep.

In contrast, parents who accomplish an abrupt retraining programme – the 'cold turkey' approach – to improve sleep habits see immediate and dramatic improvement *without any lasting ill-effects*. These children have fewer relapses and recover faster and more completely from natural disruptions of sleep routines. Seeing a cure really 'stick' for a while gives you the courage to keep a tighter control over sleep patterns and to repeat the process again, if needed.

The stories about Michelle and David among the many other personal accounts in this book contributed by a variety of caring, thoughtful parents should add extra incentive to make a change to correct your child's sleep problems right now – so you can all get on with the best part of having children . . . *enjoying* them! Some parents may need professional help to establish reasonable, orderly home routines, iron out conflicts between parents, or to help the older child with a well-established sleep problem learn to sleep better by himself. To maintain healthy sleep for your young child, please have the courage to be firm, without guilt or fear that she will resent you or love you less. In fact, the very best prescription I can give to create a loving home is a well-rested child with well-rested parents.

> There never was a
> Child so lovely but his
> Mother was glad to see him asleep.
> *Ralph Waldo Emerson*

REFERENCES

1 Healthy sleep

Sleep duration

Anders, T. F., Carksadon, M. A., and Dement, W. C., 'Sleep and sleepiness in children and adolescents', *Ped. Clin. N. Amer.* 27:29–43, 1980.

Anders, T. F. and Keener, M. A., 'Developmental course of night-time sleep–wake patterns in full-term and premature infants during the first year of life: I', *Sleep* 8:173–92, 1985.

Anders, T. F., Keener, M. A. and Kraemer, H., 'Sleep–wake state organization, neonatal assessment and development in premature infants during the first year of life: II', *Sleep* 8:193–206, 1985.

Parmelee, A. H., Schulz, H. R. and Disbrow, M. A., 'Sleep patterns of the newborn', *J. Pediatr.* 58:241–50, 1961.

Parmelee, A. H., Wenner, W. H. and Schulz, H. R., 'Infant sleep patterns: From birth to 16 weeks of age', *J. Pediatr.* 65:576–82, 1964.

Weissbluth, M., 'Sleep duration and infant temperament', *J. Pediatr.* 99:817–19, 1981.

Weissbluth, M. *et al.*, 'Sleep durations and television viewing', *J. Pediatr.* 99:486–8, 1981.

Weissbluth, M., 'Sleep duration, temperament, and Conner's ratings on three-year-old children', *J. Dev. Behav. Pediatr.* 5:120–3, 1984.

Naps

Coons, S. and Guilleminault, C., 'Development of consolidated sleep and wakeful period in relation to the day/night cycle in infancy', *Dev. Med. Child. Neurol.* 26:169–76, 1984.

Emde, R. N. and Walken, S., 'Longitudinal study of infant sleep: Results of 14 subjects studied at monthly intervals', *Psychophysiology* 13:456–61, 1916.

Folkard, S. *et al.*, 'Independence of the circadian rhythm in alertness from the sleep–wake cycle', *Nature* 313:678–9, 1985.

Minors, D. S. and Waterhouse, J. M., 'The sleep–wakefulness rhythm, exogenous and endogenous factors (in man)', *Experientia* 40:410–16, 1984.

Wladimorva, G., 'Study of cyclic structure of daytime sleep in normal infants aged 2 to 12 months', *Acta physiologica et pharmacologica Bulgarica* 9:62–9, 1983.

Sleep consolidation

Bonnet, M. M., 'Effect of sleep disruption on sleep, performance, and mood', *Sleep* 8:11–19, 1985.

Coons, S. and Guilleminault, C., 'Motility and arousal in near miss sudden infant death syndrome', *J. Pediatr.* 107:728–32, 1985.

Stepanski, E. *et al.*, 'Sleep fragmentation and daytime sleepiness', *Sleep* 7:18–26, 1984.

Weissbluth, M., Davis, A. T. and Poncher, J., 'Night waking in 4-to 8-month-old infants', *J. Pediatr.* 104:477–80, 1984.

Sleep Schedule

Abe, K. *et al.*, 'The development of circadian rhythms of human body temperature', *J. Interdisciplinary Cycle Res.* 9:211–16, 1978.

Czeisler, C. A., Weitzman, E. D. and Moore-Ede, M. C., 'Human sleep: Its duration and organization depend on its circadian phase', *Science* 210:1264–7, 1980.

Dreyfus-Brisac, C. and Monod, N., 'Sleep of premature and full term neonates – a polygraphic study', *Proc. of Royal Soc. of Med.* 58: 6–7, 1965.

Emde, R. N., Swedberg, J. and Suzuki, B., 'Human wakefulness and biological rhythms after birth', *Arch. Gen. Psychiatry* 32:780–3, 1975.

Onishi, S. *et al.*, 'Postnatal development of circadian rhythm in serum cortisol levels in children', *Pediatrics* 72:399–404, 1983.

Weissbluth, M., 'Modification of sleep schedule with reduction of night waking: A case report', *Sleep* 5:262–6, 1982.

2 Disturbed sleep and sleep problems

Mood and performance

Beltramini, A. U. and Hertzog, M. E., 'Sleep and bedtime behavior in preschool-aged children', *Pediatrics* 71:153–8, 1983.

Dement, W. C. and Carksadon, M. A., 'Current perspectives on daytime sleepiness: The issues', *Sleep* 5 (Supplement 2):S56–S66, 1982.

Dixon, K. N., Monroe, L. J. and Jakim, S., 'Insomniac children'. *Sleep* 4:313–18, 1981.

Fibiger, W. *et al.*, 'Cortisol and catecholamines changes as functions of time-of-day and self-reported mood', *Neuroscience Biobehavioral Reviews* 8:523–30, 1984.

Gunner, M. R. *et al.*, 'Coping with aversive stimulation in the neonatal period: Quiet sleep and plasma cortisol levels during recovery from circumcision', *Child Dev.* 56:824–34, 1985.

Harrison, G. A., 'Stress, catecholamines, and sleep', *Aviation, Space and Environmental Medicine* 56:651-3, 1985.

Hauri, P. and Olmstead, E., 'Childhood-onset insomnia', *Sleep* 3:59–65, 1980.

Hicks, R. A. and Pellegrini, R. J., 'Anxiety levels of short and long sleepers', *Psychological Reports* 41:569–70, 1977.

Johs, M. W. *et al.*, 'Relationship between sleep habits, adrenocortical activity and personality', *Psychosomatic Medicine* 33:499–508, 1971.

Kales, A. *et al.*, 'Biopsychobehavioral correlates of insomnia. III: Polygraphic findings of sleep difficulty and their relationship to psychopathology', *Intern. J. Neuroscience* 23:43–56, 1984.

Lucey, D. R., Hauri, P. and Snyder, M. L., 'The wakeful "Type A" student', *Int. J. Psych. Med.* 101:333–7, 1981.

Price, V. A. *et al.*, 'Prevalence and correlates of poor sleep among adolescents', *Am. J. Dis. Child* 132:583–6, 1978.

Simonds, J. F. and Parraga, H., 'Prevalence of sleep disorders and sleep behaviors in children and adolescents', *J. Amer. Acad. Child Psychiatry* 4:383–8, 1982.

Sundell, C. E., 'Sleeplessness in infants', *Practitioner* 109:89–92, 1922.

Tan, T. L. *et al.*, 'Biopsychobehavioral correlates of insomnia. IV: Diagnosis based on DSM III', *Amer. J. Psychiatry* 141:357–62, 1984.

Night waking

Coulter, D. L. and Allen, R. J., 'Benign neonatal sleep myoclonus', *Arch. Neurol.* 39:191–2, 1982.

Earls, F., 'Prevalence of behavior problems in 3-year-old children', *Arch. Gen. Psych.* 37:1153–7, 1980.

Fukumoto, M. *et al.*, 'Studies of body movements during night sleep in infancy', *Brain and Development* (Tokyo) 3:37–43, 1981.

Karacan, I. *et al.*, 'The effects of fever on sleep and dream patterns', *Psychosomatics* 9:331–9, 1968.

Richman, N., 'A community survey of characteristics of one- to two-year-olds with sleep disruption', *Amer. Acad. Child Psychiatry* 20:281–91, 1981.

Weissbluth, M., 'Modification of sleep schedule with reduction of night waking: A case report', *Sleep* 5:262–6, 1982.

Weissbluth, M., Christoffel, K. K. and Davis, A. T., 'Treatment of infantile colic with dicyclomine hydrochloride', *J. Pediatr.* 104:951–5, 1984.

Weissbluth, M., Davis, A. T. and Poncher, J., 'Night waking in 4- to 8-month-old infants', *J. Pediatr.* 104:477–80, 1984.

Excessive daytime sleepiness

Hoddes, E. *et al.*, 'Quantification of sleepiness: A new approach', *Psychophysiology* 10:431–6, 1973.

Stepanski, E. *et al.*, 'Sleep fragmentation and daytime sleepiness', *Sleep* 18–26, 1984.

Sleep walking
Kales, A. *et al.*, 'Somnambulism. Clinical characteristics and personality patterns', *Arch. Gen. Psychiatry* 37:1406–10, 1980.
Klackenberg, G., 'Somnambulism in childhood – Prevalence, course, and behavioral correlations', *Acta Paediatr. Scand.* 71:495–9, 1982.

Sleep talking
Reimao, R. N. A. A. and Lefevre, A. B., 'Prevalence of sleep-talking in childhood', *Brain Dev.* 2:353–7, 1980.

Night terrors
Kales, J. D. *et al.*, 'Sleep walking and night terrors related to febrile illness', *Am. J. Psychiatry* 136:1214–15, 1979.
Weissbluth, M., 'Is drug treatment of night terrors warranted?', *AJDC* 138:1086, 1984.

Nightmares
Cason, H., 'The nightmare dream', *Psychological Monographs* 46(5, whole no. 209), 1935.
Cellucci, A. J. and Lawrence, P. S., 'Individual differences in self-reported sleep-variable correlations among nightmare sufferers', *J. Clin. Psychology* 34:721–5, 1978.

Head banging and body rocking
Abe, K., Oda, N. and Amatomi, M., 'Natural history and predictive significance of head-banging, head-rolling and breath holding spells', *Develop. Med. Child Neurol.* 26.644–8, 1984.

Bruxism
Reding, G. R., Rubright, W. C. and Zimmerman, S. O., 'Incidence of bruxism', *J. of Dental Research* 45:1198–1204, 1966.
Reding, G. R. *et al.*, 'Sleep pattern of bruxism: A revision', *Psychophysiology* 4:396, 1968.
Reding, G. R., Zepelin, H. and Monroe, L. J., 'Personality study of nocturnal teeth grinders', *Perceptual and Motor Skills* 26:523–31, 1968.

Narcolepsy
Yoss, R. E. and Daly, D. D., 'Narcolepsy in children', *Pediatrics* 77:1025–33, 1960.

Family bed
Klackenberg, G., 'Sleep behavior studied longitudinally', *Acta Paediatr. Scand.* 71:501–6, 1982.

Lozoff, B., Wolf, A. W. and Davis, N. S., 'Co-sleeping in urban families with young children in the United States', *Pediatrics* 74:171–82, 1984.

Lozoff, B. L., Wolf, A. W. and Davis, N. S., 'Sleep problems seen in pediatric practice', *Pediatrics* 75:477–83, 1985.

Rosenfeld, A. *et al.*, 'Sleeping patterns in upper-middle class families when the child awakens ill or frightened', *Arch. Gen. Psychiatry* 39:943–7, 1982.

3   Common myths about sleeping

Solid foods and feeding practices affect sleeping

Beal, V. A., 'Termination of night feeding in infancy', *J. Pediatr.* 75:690–2, 1969.

Deisher, R. W. and Goers, S. S., 'A study of early and later introduction of solids into the infant diet', *J. Pediatr.* 45:191–9, 1954.

Grunwaldt, E., Bates, T. and Guthrie, D., 'The onset of sleeping through the night in infancy. Relation to introduction of solid food in the diet, birth weight and position in the family', *Pediatrics* 26:667–8, 1960.

Jones, N. B., Brown, M. F. and MacDonald, L., 'The association between perinatal factors and later night waking', *Develop. Med. Child Neurol.* 20:427–34, 1978.

Lavie, P. *et al.*, 'Gastric rhythms during sleep', *Behavioral Biology* 23:526–630, 1978.

Parmelee, A. H., Wenner, W. H. and Schulz, W. R., 'Infant sleep patterns from birth to 16 weeks of age', *J. Pediatr.* 65:576–82, 1964.

Robertson, R. M., 'Solids and "sleeping through"', *Brit. Med. J.* 1:200, 1974.

Salzarulo, P. *et al.*, 'Alimentation continue et rhythmic veille-sommeil chez l'enfant', *Archives Françaises de Pediat.* (Suppl) 36:26–32, 1979.

Schulz, H. *et al.*, 'REM latency: Development in the first year of life', *Electroencephalogr. Clin. Neurophysiol.* 56:316–22, 1983.

Schulz, H. *et al.*, 'Spontaneous awakenings from sleep in infants', *Electroencephalogr. Clin. Neurophysiol.* 61:267–71, 1985.

Wright, P., MacLeod, M. A. and Cooper, M. J., 'Waking at night: The effect of early feeding experience', *Child Care Health Dev.* 9:309–19, 1983.

Teething causes night waking

Radbill, S. X., 'Teething in fact and fancy', *Bull. of the History of Medicine* 39:339–45, 1965.

Tasanen, A., 'General and local effects of the eruption of deciduous teeth', *Annales de Paediatrac. Fenniae* 14: Supplement 29, 1969.

Growing pains cause night waking
Oster, J. and Nelson, A., 'Growing pains. A clinical investigation of a school problem', *Acta Paediat. Scand.* 61:329–34, 1974.

A long night's sleep will make up for short naps
Weissbluth, M., 'Sleep duration and infant temperament', *J. Pediatr.* 5:817–19, 1981.
Weissbluth, M., 'Sleep duration, temperament, and Conners' ratings of three-year-old children', *J. Pediatr.* 5:120–3, 1984.

Children will sleep as much as they need
Etzel, B. C. and Gewirtz, J. L., 'Experimental modification of caretaker-maintenance high rate operant crying in a 6- and a 20-week-old infant (*Infans tyrannotearus*): Extinction of crying with reinforcement of eye contact and smiling', *J. Exper. Child Psychology* 5:303–17, 1967.

Catering to a children's regular sleep schedule produces inflexible children
Weissbluth, M., 'Sleep duration, temperament, and Conner's ratings of three-year-old children', *J. Dev. Behav. Pediatr.* 5:120–3, 1984.

During sleeptimes, emotional problems develop if parents ignore their child's crying
Thomas, A. and Chess, S., 'Genesis and evolution of behavioral disorders: From infancy to early adult life', *Am. J. Psychiatry* 141:1–9, 1984.

4 How crybabies become crabby kids (or, once a crab always a crab)

Introduction

Breslow, L., 'A clinical approach to infantile colic: A review of 90 cases', *J. Pediatr.* 50:196–206, 1957.
Illingworth, R. S., ' "Three months" colic', *Arch. Dis. Child* 29:167–74, 1954.
Meyer, J. E. and Thaler, M. M., 'Colic in low birth weight infants', *Amer. J. Dis. Child* 122:25–7, 1971.
Pierce, P., 'Delayed onset of "three months" colic in premature infants', *Amer. J. Dis. Child* 75:190–2, 1948.

Wessel, M. A. *et al.*, 'Paroxysmal fussing in infancy, sometimes called "colic" ', *Pediatrics* 14:421–34, 1954.

Some babies cry a little, some cry a lot
Aldrich, C. A., Sung, C. and Knop, C., 'The crying of newly born babies: II. The individual phase', *J. Pediatr.* 27:89–96, 1945.
Boon, W. H., 'The crying baby', *J. Singapore Paediatric Society* 24:145–7, 1982.
Brazelton, T. B., 'Crying in infancy', *Pediatrics* 29:579–88, 1962.
Emde, R. N., Gaensbauer, T. J. and Harman, R. J., 'Emotional expression in infancy. A biobehavioral study', *Psychological Issues* 10:1–200, 1976.
Illingworth, R. S., 'Crying in infants and children', *Brit. Med. J.* 1: 75–8, 1955.
Lester, B. M. and Bookydis, C. F. Z. (eds), *Infant Crying* (New York: Plenum Press) 1985.
Lounsbuery, M. L. and Bates, J. E., 'The cries of infants of differing levels of perceived temperamental difficultness: Acoustic properties and effects on listeners', *Child Development* 53:677–86, 1982.
Rebelsky, F. and Black, R., 'Crying in infancy', *J. Genetic Psych.* 121:49–57, 1972.
Snow, M. E., Jacklin, C. N. and Maccoby, E. E., 'Crying episodes and sleep-wakefulness transitions in the first 26 months of life', *Infant Behavior and Development* 3:387–94, 1980.
Zeskind, P. S. and Huntington, L., 'The effects of within-group and between-group methodologies in the study of perceptions of infant crying', *Child Devel.* 55:1658–65, 1984.

What happens when a baby does not stop crying?
Carey, W. B., 'Clinical application of infant temperament measurements', *J. Pediatr.* 81:823–8, 1972.
Carey, W. B. and McDevitt, S. C., 'Revision of the infant temperament questionnaire', *Pediatrics* 61:735–9, 1978.
Carey, W. B., 'Temperament and increased weight gain in infants', *J. Dev. Behav. Ped.* 3:128–31, 1985.
Crockenberg, S. B. and Smith, P., 'Antecedents of mother–infant interaction and infant-irritability in the first three months of life', *Infant Behavior and Development* 5:105–19, 1982.
Collins, D. D. *et al.*, 'Hereditary aspects of decreased hypoxic response', *J. Clin. Invest.* 62:104–10, 1978.
DeVries, M., 'Temperament and infant mortality among the Masai of East Africa', *Am. J. Psychiatry* 141:1189–94, 1984.
Freedman, D. G., 'Ethnic differences in babies', *Human Nature* 2:36–43, 1979.

Matheny, A. B. *et al.*, 'Behavioral contrasts in twinships. Stability and patterns of differences in childhood', *Child Dev.* 52:579–88, 1985.

Monnier, M. and Gaillard, J. M., 'Biochemical regulation of sleep', *Experientia* 36:21–9, 1980.

O'Connor, L. H. and Feder, H. H., 'Estradiol and progesterone influence: A serotonin mediated behavioral syndrome (myoclonus) in female guinea pigs', *Brain Res.* 293:119–25, 1984.

Schulz, H. *et al.*, 'REM latency: Development in the first year of life', *Electroencephal. Clin. Neurophys.* 56:316–22, 1983.

Shaver, B. A., 'Maternal personality and early adaptation as related to infantile colic', in Shereshefsky, P. M. and Yarrow, L. J. (eds), *Psychological Aspects of a First Pregnancy and Early Postnatal Adaptation* (New York: Raven Press) 1974.

Stenger, K., 'Therapy of spastic bronchitis', *Med. Klin.* 51:1451–5, 1956.

Sullivan, C. E. *et al.*, 'Ventilatory responses to CO_2 and lung inflation in tonic versus phasic REM sleep', *J. Appl. Physiol: Respirat. Environ. Exercise Physiol.* 47:1304–10, 1979.

Tandon, P., Gupta, M. L. and Barthwal, J. P., 'Role of monoamine oxidase-B in medroxyprogesterone acetate (17-acetoxy-6 gamma-methyl-4-pregnene-4-3, 20-dione) induced changes in brain dopamine levels in rats', *Steroids* 42:231–9, 1983.

Thomas, A., Chess, S. and Birch, H. G., *Temperament and Behavior Disorders in Childhood* (New York: New York University Press) 1968.

Watanabe, K., Inokuma, K. and Nogoro, T., 'REM sleep prevents sudden infant death syndrome', *Eur. J. Pediatr.* 140:289–92, 1983.

Webb, W. B. and Campbell, S. S., 'Relationship in sleep characteristics in identical and fraternal twins', *Arch. Gen. Psychiatry* 40:1093–5, 1983.

Weissbluth, M., 'Infantile colic and near-miss sudden infant death syndrome', *Med. Hypoth.* 7:1193–9, 1981.

Weissbluth, M. *et al.*, 'Sleep apnea, sleep duration, and infant temperament', *J. Pediatr.* 101:307–10, 1982.

Weissbluth, M. and Green, O. C., 'Plasma progesterone concentration and infant temperament', *J. Dev. Behav. Ped.* 5:251–3, 1984.

Weissbluth, M., Christoffel, K. K. and Davis A. T., 'Treatment of infantile colic with dicyclomine hydrochloride', *J. Pediatr.* 104:951–5, 1984.

Weissbluth, M. *et al.*,'Respiratory patterns during sleep and temperament ratings in normal infants', *J. Pediatr.* 106:688–90, 1985.

Brief sleep durations and night waking

Dunst, C. J., and Lingerfelt, B., 'Maternal ratings of temperament and operant learning in two- to three-month-old infants', *Child Devel*. 56:555–63, 1985.

Weissbluth, M., 'Sleep duration and infant temperament', *J. Pediatr*. 99:817–19, 1981.

Weissbluth, M. and Liu, K., 'Sleep patterns, attention span, and infant temperament', *J. Dev. Behav. Ped*. 4:34–6, 1983.

Weissbluth, M., Davis, A. T. and Poncher, J., 'Night waking in 4- to 8-month-old infants', *J. Pediatr*. 104:477–80, 1984.

Weissbluth, M., *Crybabies. Coping with Colic: What to Do When Baby Won't Stop Crying*. (New York: Arbor House) 1984.

Weissbluth, M., 'Infant colic', in Gellis, S. S. and Kagan, B. M. (eds) *Current Pediatric Therapy*, 12th edn. (Philadelphia: W. B. Saunders) 1986.

Are poor sleep habits congenital?

Etzel, B. C. and Gewirtz, J. L., 'Experimental modification of caretaker-maintenance high-rate operant crying in a 6- and 20-week-old infant (*Infans tyrannotearus*): Extinction of crying with reinforcement of eye contact and smiling', *J. Exper. Child Psychology* 5:503–17, 1967.

Richman, N. *et al.*, 'Behavioral methods in the treatment of sleep disorders – a pilot study', *J. Child Psychol. Psychiat*. 26:581–90, 1985.

Weissbluth, M., 'Modification of sleep schedule with reduction of night waking: A case report', *Sleep* 5:262–6, 1982.

Williams, C. D., 'The elimination of tantrum behavior by extinction procedures', *J. Abnormal and Social Psychology* 59:269, 1959.

'Crab-ology' and 'Mum-itis'

Karelitz, S. *et al.*, 'Relation of crying activity in early infancy to speech and intellectual development at age three years', *Child Develop*. 35:769–77, 1964.

Ogden, T. H., 'The mother, the infant and the matrix: Interpretations of aspects of the work of Donald Winnicott', *Contemporary Psychoanalysis* 21:346–71, 1985.

5　Sleeping and learning: Rest for success

Sleep patterns, intelligence, learning and school performance

Anders, T. F., Keener, M. A. and Kraemer, H., 'Sleep–wake state organization, neonatal assessment and development in premature infants during the first year of life: II', *Sleep* 8:193–206, 1985.

Bonnet, M. H., 'Effect of sleep disruption in sleep, performance, and mood', *Sleep* 8:11–19, 1985.

Busby, K. and Pikik, R. T., 'Sleep patterns in children of superior intelligence', *J. Child Psychol. Psychiatry* 24:587–600, 1983.

Denenberg, V. H. and Thoman, E. B., 'Evidence for a functional role for active (REM) sleep in infancy', *Sleep* 4:185–91, 1981.

Dunst, C. J. and Lingerfelt, B., 'Maternal ratings of temperament and operant learning in two- to three-month-old infants', *Child Dev.* 56:555–63, 1985.

Fibiger, W. 'Cortisol and catecholamine changes as functions of time-of-day and self-reported mood', *Neurosci. Biobehav. Rev.* 8:523–30, 1984.

Hayaski, Y., 'On the sleeping hours at school, children of 6 to 20 years', *Psychol. Abstracts* 1:439, 1927.

Julius, M. W. *et al.,* 'Relationship between sleep habits, adreno-cortical activity and personality', *Psychosomatic Medicine* 33:499–508, 1971.

Matheny, A. D. and Dolan, A. B., 'Childhood sleep characteristics and reading achievement', *JSAS Catalog of Selected Documents in Psychology* 4:76, 1974.

Terman, L. M., *Genetic Studies of Genius, Vol. 1: Mental and Physical Traits of a Thousand Gifted Children* (Stanford University Press) 1925.

Weissbluth, M., 'Sleep duration and infant temperament', *J. Pediatr.* 99:817–19, 1981.

Weissbluth, M., 'Sleep duration, temperament, and Conners' ratings of three-year-old children', *J. Develop. Behav. Pediatr.* 5:120–23, 1984.

Weissbluth, M., 'How sleep affects school performance', *Gifted Children Monthly* 6:14–15, 1985.

Poor quality breathing (snoring and allergies)

Anderson, O. W., 'The management of "infantile insomnia"', *J. Pediatr.* 38:394–401, 1951.

Ballenger, W. L., *Diseases of the Nose, Throat and Ear* (Philadelphia: Lea & Febiger) 1914, p. 337.

Brouillette, R. *et al.*, 'A diagnostic approach to suspected obstructive sleep apnea in children', *J. Pediatr.* 105:10–14, 1984.

Brown, S.-L. and Stool, S. E., 'Behavioral manifestations of sleep apnea in children', *Sleep* 5:200–1, 1982.

Flemming, B. M., 'A study of the sleep of young children', *J. of the Amer. Assoc. of Univ. Women* 19:25–28, 1925.

Guilleminault, C. *et al.*, 'Sleep apnea in eight children', *Pediatrics* 58:23–31, 1976.

Guilleminault, C. and Dement, W. C., '235 cases of excessive daytime sleepiness', *J. of Neurol. Sciences* 31:13–27, 1977.

Kahn, A., Mozin, J. and Casimir, G., 'Insomnia and cow's milk allergy in infants', *Pediatrics* 76:880–4, 1985.

Klein, G. L. *et al.*, 'The allergic irritability syndrome: Four case reports and a position statement from the Neuroallergy Committee of the American College of Allergy', *Ann. Allergy* 55:22–24, 1985.

Kravath, R. E., Pollack, C. D. and Borowiecki, B., 'Hypoventilation during sleep in children who have lymphoid airway obstruction treated by nasopharyngeal tube and T and A', *Pediatrics* 59:865–71, 1977.

Lind, M. G. and Lundell, B. P. W., 'Tonsillar hyperplasia in children. A cause of obstructive sleep apneas, CO_2 retention, and retarded growth', *Arch. Otolaryngol.* 108:650–4, 1982.

Mangat, D., Orr, W. C. and Smith, R. O., 'Sleep apnea, hypersomnolence, and upper airway obstruction secondary to adenotonsillar enlargement', *Arch. Otolaryngol.* 103:383–6, 1977.

Mauer, K. W., Staats, B. A. and Olsen, K. D., 'Upper airway obstruction and disordered nocturnal breathing in children', *Mayo Clinic Proceedings* 58:349–53, 1983.

Weissbluth, M. *et al.*, 'Signs of airway obstruction during sleep and behavioural, developmental, and academic problems', *J. Devel. Behav. Ped.* 4:119–21, 1983.

Weissbluth, M., Davis, A. T. and Poncher, J., 'Night waking in 4- to 8-month-old infants', *J. Pediatr.* 104:477–80, 1984.

Locating the problem

Brouillette, R. and Thach, B. T., 'A neuromuscular mechanism maintaining extrathoracic airway patency', *J. Appl. Physiol: Respirat. Environ. Exercise Physiol.* 46:772–9, 1979.

Brouillette, R., Fernbach, S. K. and Hunt, C. E., 'Obstructive sleep apnea in infants and children', *J. Pediatr.* 100:31–40, 1982.

Chokroverty, S., 'Phasic tongue movements in human rapid-eye-movement sleep', *Neurology* 30:665–8, 1980.

Felman, A. H. *et al.*, 'Upper airway obstruction during sleep in children', *AJR* 133:213–16, 1979.

Haponik, E. F. *et al.*, 'Computerized tomography in obstructive sleep apnea. Correlation of airway size with physiology during sleep and wakefulness', *Am. Rev. Resp. Dis.* 127:221–6, 1983.

Remmers, J. E. *et al.*, 'Pathogenesis of upper airway occlusive during sleep', *J. Appl. Physiol: Respirat. Environ. Exercise Physiol.* 44:931–8, 1978.

Wilkinson, A. R. *et al.*, 'Electrocardiographic signs of pulmonary hypertension in children who snore', *Brit. Med. J.* 282:1579–81, 1981.

Finding the answers
McGeary, G. D., 'Help a snorer', *JAMA* 245:1729, 1981.
Simmons, F. B., *et al.*, 'Surgical management of airway obstruction during sleep', *Laryngoscope* 87:326–38, 1977.

Enjoying the cure
Guilleminault, C. *et al.*, 'Children and nocturnal snoring: Evaluation of the effects of sleep related respiratory resistive load and daytime functioning', *Eur. J. Pediatr.* 139:165–71, 1982.

Hyperactive children
Busby, K., Firestone, P. and Pivik, R. T. 'Sleep patterns in hyperkinetic and normal children', *Sleep* 4:366–83, 1981.
Greenhill, L. *et al.*, 'Sleep architecture and REM sleep measures in prepubertal children with attention deficit disorder with hyperactivity', *Sleep* 6:91–101, 1983.
Porrino, L. J. *et al.*, 'A naturalistic assessment of the motor activity of hyperactive boys', *Arch. Gen. Psychiatry* 40:681–7, 1983.
Simonds, J. F. and Parraga, H., 'Sleep behaviours and disorders in children and adolescents evaluated at psychiatric clinics', *J. Dev. Behav. Pediatr.* 5:6–10, 1984.
Weissbluth, M. and Lui, K., 'Sleep patterns, attention span, and infant temperament', *J. Dev. Behav. Pediatr.* 4:34–6, 1983.
Weissbluth, M., 'Sleep duration, temperament, and Conners' ratings of three-year-old children', *J. Dev. Behav. Pediatr.* 5:120–3, 1984.

6 How tired children suffer: overweight and overinjured. Will I abuse my child?

Injuries
Carey, W. B., 'Clinical application of infant temperament measurements', *J. Pediatr.* 81:823–8, 1972.
Richman, N. A., 'A community survey of one- to two-year-olds with sleep disruptions', *J. Amer. Acad. Child Psychiatry* 20:281–91, 1981.
Weissbluth, M., 'Sleep duration and infant temperament', *J. Pediatr.* 5:817–19, 1981.
Weissbluth, M., 'Sleep duration, temperament and Conners' ratings of three-year-old children', *J. Dev. Behav. Ped.* 5:120–3, 1984.

Overweight
Carey, W. B., 'Temperament and increased weight gain in infants', *J. Dev. Behav. Ped.* 6:128–31, 1985.
DeVries, M. W., 'Temperament and infant mortality among the Masai of East Africa', *Am. J. Psychiatry* 141:1189–94, 1984.

Child abuse
Piers, M. W., *Infanticide Past and Present* (New York: W. W. Norton) 1978.

7 How to help your family enjoy silent nights: establish healthy sleep habits

Anders, T. F. *et al.*, 'Sleep habits of children and the identification of pathologically sleepy children', *Child Psychiatry and Human Development* 9:56–63, 1978.

Asnes, R. S., Sautulli, R. and Beuporad, J. R., 'Psychogenic chest pain in children', *Clinical Pediatrics* 20:788–92, 1981.

Czeisler, C. A. *et al.*, 'Human sleep: Its duration and organization depend on its circadian phases', *Science* 210:1264–7, 1980.

Howarth, E. and Hoffman, M. S., 'A multidimensional approach to the relationship between mood and weather', *Brit. J. Psych.* 75:15–23, 1984.

Kirmil-Gray, K. *et al.*, 'Sleep disturbances in adolescents: Sleep quality, sleep habits, belief about sleep, and daytime functioning', *J. of Youth and Adolescence* 13:375–84, 1984.

Lozoff, B., Wolf, A. W. and Davis, N. S., 'Sleep problems seen in pediatric practice', *Pediatrics* 75:477–83, 1985.

Price, V. A. *et al.*, 'Prevalence and correlates of poor sleep among adolescents', *Am. J. Dis. Child.* 132:582–6, 1978.

Van Tassel, E. B., 'The relative influence of child and environmental characteristics on sleep disturbances in the first and second years of life', *J. Dev. Behav. Pediatr.* 6:81–6, 1985.

Waller, D. A. *et al.*, 'Recognizing and managing the adolescent with Kleine–Levin syndrome', *J. Adolesc. Health Care* 5:139–41, 1984.

8 Return to peaceful nights: Correcting unhealthy sleep habits

The first 3 to 4 months
Etzel, B. C. and Gewirtz, J. L., 'Experimental modification of caretaker-maintained high-rate operant crying in a 6- and a 20-week-old infant (*Infans tyrannotearus*): Extinction of crying with reinforcement of eye contact and smiling', *J. Exper. Child Psychology* 5:303–17, 1967.

Fagan, J. W. *et al.*, 'The effects of crying on long-term memory in infancy', *Child Develop.* 56:1584–92, 1985.

Four months to the first birthday
Caren, S. and Searleman, A., 'Birth stress and self-reported sleep difficulty', *Sleep* 8:222–6, 1985.

Douglas, J. and Richman, N., *My Child Won't Sleep* (Harmondsworth: Penguin Books) 1984.

Hirschberg, J. C., 'Parental anxieties accompanying sleep disturbance in young children', *Bulletin of the Menninger Clinic* 21:129–39, 1957.

Klastskin, E. H., Jackson, E. B. and Wilkin, L. C., 'The influence of degree of flexibility in maternal child care practices on early child behavior', *Amer. J. Orthopsychiat.* 26:79–93, 1956.

Mahler, M. S., 'On the first three subphases of the separation–individuation process', *Int. J. Psycho-Anal.* 53:333–8, 1972.

Thomas, A. and Chess, S., 'Genesis and evolution of behavioral disorders: from infancy to early adult life', *Am. J. Psychiatry* 141:1–9, 1984.

Webb, W. B. and Agnew, H. W., 'Regularity in the control of the free-running sleep–wakefulness rhythm', *Aerospace Med.* 45:701–4, 1974.

Weissbluth, M., 'Modification of sleep schedule with reduction of night waking: A case report', *Sleep* 5:262–6, 1982.

Winnicott, D. W., 'The capacity to be alone', in Winnicott, D. W., *The Maturational Processes and Facilitating Environment* (New York: International Universities Press) 1965.

The second and third years (12 to 36 months)

Gutelius, M. F. and Kirsch, A. D., 'Controlled study of child health supervision: Behavioral results', *Pediatrics* 60:294–304, 1977.

Largo, R. H. and Honziker, U. A., 'A developmental approach to the management of children with sleep disturbances in the first three years of life', *Eur. J. Pediatr.* 142:170–3, 1984.

Williams, C. D., 'Case report. The elimination of tantrum behavior by extinction procedures', *J. of Abn. and Social Psychology* 59:269, 1959.

Young children: three years old and over

Cullen, K. J., 'A six-year controlled trial of prevention of children's behavior disorders', *J. Pediatr.* 88:662–6, 1976.

Jones, D. P. H. and Verduyn, C. M., 'Behavioral management of sleep problems', *Arch. Dis. Child.* 58:442–4, 1983.

Richman, N. *et al.*, 'Behavioral methods in the treatment of sleep disorders – a pilot study', *J. Child Psychol. Psychiat.* 26:581–90, 1985.

Richman, N., 'A community survey of one- to two-year-olds with sleep disruptions', *J. Amer. Acad. Child Psychiatry* 20:281–91, 1981.

Wright, L., Woodcock, J. and Scott, R., 'Treatment of sleep disturbance in a young child by conditioning', *Southern Med. J.* 63:174–6, 1970.

Other ideas

Cuthbertson, J. and Schevill, S., *Helping Your Child Sleep Through the Night* (New York: Doubleday) 1985.

Douglas, J. and Richman, N., *My Child Won't Sleep* (Harmondsworth: Penguin Books) 1984.

Ferber, R., *Solve Your Child's Sleep Problems* (New York: Simon & Schuster) 1985.

McGarr, R. J. and Hovel, M. F., 'In search of the sandman: Shaping an infant to sleep', *Education and Treatment of Children* 3:173–82, 1980.

9   A sleep disorder – my child?

Annotated bibliography

Bettleheim, B., *The Uses of Enchantment* (New York: Random House) 1975. A wonderful book by a noted child psychiatrist which elaborates a child's need for fantasy in order to work out the many dilemmas they face in growing up, and how fairy tales can aid them in their struggles.

Caplan, L., *Oneness to Separateness* (La Leche) 1978. A detailed look at the process of separation and how the infant emerges from union with mother to become an individual.

Dreikurs, R., *Children: The Challenge* (New York: Hawthorne/Dutton) 1964. A practical guide to child management based on respect for both parent and child which advocates a firm, consistent approach.

Frailberg, S., *The Magic Years* (New York) A marvellous book describing the fascinating inner world of the young child.

Winnicott, D. W., *The Child, the Family and the Outside World* (New York: Penguin) 1964. This book is a compilation of talks Winnicott gave on the BBC and is loaded with insights, as well as suggestions, based upon his many years as a paediatrician and psychoanalyst.

Books for parents to share with children at sleepy times

Bang, M., *Ten, Nine, Eight* (Harmondsworth: Picture Puffins) 1983, ages 6 to 36 months.

Brown, M. W., *Goodnight Moon* (New York: Harper) 1947, ages 1 to 3.

Hoban, R., *Bedtime for Frances* (New York: Harper) 1960, ages 2 to 6 years.

Larrick, N., *When the Dark Comes Dancing.* A bedtime poetry book, ages 1 to 10 years.

Newfeld, M., *Where Is Your Sleep?* (New York: McElderry) 1983, ages 2 to 6.

10   What a difference healthy sleep can make

Bernstein, D., Emde, R. and Campos, J., 'REM sleep in four-month infants under home and laboratory conditions', *Psychosomatic Med.* 35:322–9, 1973.

Coons, S. and Guilleminault, C., 'Development of sleep–wake patterns and non-rapid eye movement sleep stages during the first six months of life in normal infants', *Pediatrics* 69:793–8, 1982.

Emde, R. N. and Metcalf, D. R., 'An electroencephalographic study of behavioral rapid eye movement states in the human newborn', *J. Nervous and Mental Dis.* 150:376–86, 1970.

Fish, B., 'The maturation of arousal and attention in the first months of life: A study of variations in age development', *J. American Acad. Child. Psychiat.* 2:253–70, 1963.

Harper, R. M. *et al.*, 'Temporal sequencing in sleep and waking states during the first 6 months of life', *Experimental Neurology* 72:294–307, 1981.

Jacklin, C. N. *et al.*, 'Sleep pattern development from 6 through 33 months', *J. Ped. Psych.* 5:295–302, 1980.

Klein, K. E. *et al.*, 'Circadian Performance Rhythms: Experimental Studies in Air Operations', in *Vigilance: Theory, Operational Performance and Physiological Correlants*, ed. by Robert R. Mackie. NATO Conference Series III, Human Factors, vol. 3 (New York: Plenum Press) 1977.

Salzarulo, P. and Chevalier, A., 'Sleep problems in children and their relationship with early disturbances of the waking–sleep rhythms', *Sleep* 6:47–51, 1983.

Schulz, H. *et al.*, 'REM latency: Development in the first year of life', *Electroencephalogr. Clin. Neurophysiol.* 56:316–22, 1983.

Still, G. F., *The History of Pediatrics* (London: Oxford University Press) 1931, p. 18.

Sundell, C. E., 'Sleeplessness in infants', *Practitioner* 109:89–92, 1922.

Index